MW00993918

Cloud Nine

Memoirs of a Record Producer

RICHARD PERRY

Redwood Publishing, LLC
Orange County, California

For full song lyric permissions, turn to page 357.

Please turn to page 355 for a list of photo credits.

Book is printed in the United States of America.
First printing, 2020

Published by:
Redwood Publishing, LLC
Orange County, California
www.redwooddigitalpublishing.com

Book Design:
Cover Design By: Graphique Designs, LLC
Cover photo: © Joe Schmelzer (taken for the *Wall Street Journal*)
Interior Design By: Ghislain Viau

ISBN: 978-1-952106-32-3 (hardcover)
ISBN: 978-1-952106-33-0 (paperback)
ISBN: 978-1-952106-34-7 (ebook)

Library of Congress Control Number: 2020923970

10 9 8 7 6 5 4 3 2 1

I dedicate this book to the loving memory of my parents,

Sylvia and Mack Perry

Contents

Preface

Once I embarked upon the writing of this book, I was most concerned about two things: whether I would remember the events of my early years and how I could structure them in a way that would be interesting and entertaining to someone who's never heard my name before. One night as I sat down to write, I saw seven typewritten pages sitting in the center of my desk. They were typed in a very old font and age had yellowed the pages, which my instincts told me had been typed circa 1950s and clearly not by a professional secretary—there were too many mistakes and corrections. They were written in the third person like someone who was reporting from the sidelines. As I read them, I was surprised to discover a detailed and loving account of our family; the pages started with the day my parents met in 1939, calling it "the true beginning in the life of Richard Perry," and ended with my graduation from the University of Michigan in 1964. I had no idea how they got there.

I assumed it must have been my mother—it had her love and insight all over it. To solve the mystery, I sent copies to her and to my three younger brothers hoping they could provide the answer. My mother swore she had never seen the papers before and had no idea who could have written them, nor had my brothers. It never dawned on me that such a document could have come from my father, as its warm and observant style wasn't something I would ever have associated with him. The main thing I did with my father was play ball—I would pitch and he would catch! It's not that he didn't love his children, but his parents were Russian immigrants who didn't know how to communicate love to their children, so he just did what he was taught, *or didn't do what he wasn't taught.*

When he was on his deathbed, my mother called one afternoon and put my father on the phone; this would be the last time I would speak to him. It was then that he told me for the first time that he loved me. Both of us were weeping.

After combing through all family members for clues, I had to deduce that it was indeed my father who wrote those mysterious seven pages. After all, he had been paying closer attention to the events in my early life than I ever realized, to what mattered.

Who knows? Maybe he had an inkling that one day his first-born might have a book to write and would need to know the very beginnings. The question remains: How did those pages appear on my desk from out of nowhere? Till this day it will remain a mystery, but I allow myself the right to believe that someone somewhere wanted them to be there.

Chapter 1

A Kid is Born in Brooklyn

At the age of six, I was about to participate in my first grade "show and tell." My parents and I stuffed as many instruments as we could into my briefcase. I was nervous and excited as I lugged the briefcase into my homeroom at P.S. 197. Quietly, I waited for my turn to be called. Somehow, I sensed that, with my collection of instruments, my "show and tell" was going to be memorable.

When my name was finally called, I walked to the front of the room and began to hand out tambourines, sand blocks, cymbals, bells, maracas, and other instruments. Speaking out clearly and confidently so they could hear me in the back of the room, I asked them to play and sing along with me to the only song I knew: "You Are My Sunshine!"

"OK, everybody, one, two, three," I said, and I launched into it. "You are my sunshine, my only sunshine, you make me happeee when skies are grey." I sang as loud as I could to give the others confidence. Almost immediately, they all joined in, singing at the top of their lungs and banging away on their various instruments, having more fun than they'd ever had in school.

Even at a young age, I recognized that bringing music into people's lives and making them happy was a harbinger of things to come. Little did I know that my life would take me on a journey that led me to the highest echelons of the music industry, working with artists such as Ray Charles, Barbra Streisand, Rod Stewart, The Beatles (contributing on the Ringo Starr albums), Carly Simon, Pointer Sisters, and many others.

* * *

The date was June 18, 1942. The war in Europe was in full swing, but down on Kings Highway and Bedford Avenue in the Flatbush section of Brooklyn, I was about to be born—the first of four boys.

My father, Mack Perry, was a somewhat whimsical, idiosyncratic man with many hobbies: He rode a motorcycle and flew his own plane, once flying it *under* the Bronx-Whitestone Bridge. He figured that *anyone* could fly *over* it!

I was a shy kid, especially in front of girls I didn't know. Yet whenever my father walked me to school, he would say to each girl we came across, "Heelllo, little girl, have you met Richard Perry?" I hated it and wanted to disappear, but he kept on doing it. That was my father.

He also took eight-millimeter home movies for twenty-five years, all meticulously kept in wooden cigar boxes with the date and place on each reel. After high school, the films went missing and when, twenty-two years later, they showed up, I edited them into a documentary: the story of our family.

My mother, Sylvia, was a strong, ambitious woman—somewhat of an anachronism in the '40s when society expected women to be housewives. She was a classically trained pianist who studied at Juilliard and taught piano at Brooklyn College. My father was a chemist by trade when he and my mother decided to join forces in an effort to bring music to children. They researched the public schools and discovered that there were no opportunities for students in the elementary levels to participate in music programs. There are countless numbers of kids who are not especially gifted musically, but who can still derive something therapeutic by hitting a drum or other percussive instruments, particularly in small groups where it becomes a fun social experience.

To fill what my mother viewed as a terrible void, she and my father decided to start the first company ever to manufacture musical instruments

Mack and Sylvia Perry

My father on his 1930 Indian Scout motorcycle.

for young people. They named the company Peripole and began by making rhythm band instruments: drums of all shapes and sizes, xylophones, triangles, tambourines, bells, sand blocks, and cymbals. This included nearly every Latin American instrument, such as congas, bongos, maracas, güiros, and cowbells. Peripole became the main supplier to schools across the country as well as the first company to distribute autoharps, woodwind recorders, and song flutes.

Although my father had natural musical instincts, music was really my mother's passion, and she was the driving force behind the business. I don't know if it was a conscious strategy on her part, but the way she made it all work within the confines that trapped so many women in those conservative times was to make sure my father was seen as the person in charge, the "Commander." I had to laugh when my brother Roger recently reminded me that when the business hit a snag one year, my mother asked the "Commander" to take the reins, and he, instead, went ice-skating.

Roger was born two years after me but has a much clearer memory than I do of the early years in the tiny three-room apartment where we lived. I do remember that we would often watch our parents dance the tango in the living room. I knew that we grew up in a loving environment. Roger validated this when he recalled, "They were totally into each other." Looking at their old photos reveals that they had a powerful chemistry. That must have been the glue that held it all together in spite of Sylvia's overwhelming forcefulness.

Peripole began in October 1945 in my parents' living room, moved from there into a storefront shop, and then later, a factory. Mack and Sylvia Perry became leaders in the field of music education, receiving Lifetime Achievement Awards from the Music Educators National Conference as well as Distinguished Service Awards from the states of California, Texas, Florida, Wisconsin, Oregon, and Tennessee.

In 1992, seven years after my father's death, my mother entered into a partnership with my youngest brother Andrew, who was practicing medicine in Oregon. Sylvia moved to Oregon and became executive director of the new company, while Andrew was designated president. Even at the age of ninety-seven, she continued to help run the business. I will always affectionately remember her as a force of nature. As of this writing, my mother has passed away, but Peripole is still thriving and occupies a 12,000-square-foot building in Salem, Oregon.

* * *

In 1950, I went to camp for the first time. It was called Camp Harmony, and it was located near Plainfield, New Jersey. My mother worked there as the music and dramatics counselor. She put on the Rodgers and Hammerstein musical *Oklahoma!* that summer, with camp counselors cast in most of the lead roles and the chorus composed of campers. Watching my mother rehearse the show and being introduced to all those memorable songs, I gained my first exposure to a musical—and what a musical it was! I was unaware that it was the show that changed the face of musical theater (the first to be based on a play rather than being simply a musical revue). I was enthralled! Even though I was only eight, I felt the special magic that permeates one's whole being when in the presence of a great musical as it's being mounted.

My father never studied a specific instrument but, as I mentioned, his instinct for music was right on. As I got older, he taught me the Mills Brothers theme song, "Goodbye Blues." It had no words, but it was my introduction to vocal harmonies and a moving vocal bass line. The song had a big influence on me, particularly when, years later, I discovered the joy of doo-wop. My father is also the reason I became familiar with the timeless melodies and sounds of Glenn Miller, Artie Shaw, The Andrews Sisters, and many others. He introduced me to the neighborhood record shop, Victor's, near Kings Highway and East 18th Street, where I would spend many thrilling hours in the years to come, perusing and buying records.

Around this time, I began to suffer from symptoms of what today would be called Obsessive-Compulsive Disorder (OCD): excessive eye-blinking, rubbing my fingers along the sides of my mouth, and feeling compelled to step on every line while walking on the sidewalk.

As though that wasn't enough, I was faced with several other challenges. For one, I stuttered. Eventually, I was able to reduce it considerably, but there are times, even now, when the stutter comes back. On top of that, I had unusually big ears. Unfortunately for me, those were the days when all boys had Marine-like buzz cuts—no way to hide those ears beneath a hippie "fro" as I did a decade or so later. In addition to my large ears, I was severely bucktoothed, and I had to endure ten grueling years of orthodontia that included metal braces, rubber bands, the works. My nicknames were Bugs and Dumbo.

It isn't surprising that I developed a serious inferiority complex regarding my appearance, which became greatly exacerbated when I started to play kissing games like Post Office, Truth or Consequences (also known as Truth or Dare), and Spin the Bottle with the kids who lived on my block. When it was a girl's turn to pick someone to kiss, I was always the last to be chosen. I believe one big reason that I've grown up to be relatively strong and confident is due to the unconditional love and support I got from home. But another major factor would soon appear on my horizon.

The year 1952 proved to be a turning point for me. My family moved into a spacious, three-floor house in a nearby residential area of Brooklyn. More importantly, I was admitted to an exceptional, competitive all-boys prep school in Brooklyn, Poly Prep, which I attended from fifth grade through high school.

Poly Prep's campus was every bit as beautiful as any Ivy League college, and the educational opportunities were top notch. However, it was the extracurricular activities that were life-changing for me.

It was at the age of ten that I embarked on what would become my life's passion: music. I took drum lessons at Poly Prep with "Uncle Frank" Hancock and soon was playing in the high school band. Another event around this time would have an impact on my sense of self: the school's annual speech contest. Every student had to memorize and then recite a major poem or declamation in front of all of his classmates. A winner would be declared from each grade, and then each winner would deliver their declamation in front of the entire student body. The champion of the lower school (grades 5, 6, and 7), middle school (grades 8 and 9), and upper school (grades 10, 11, and 12), would be honored. My choice for my first year at the age of ten was *O Captain! My Captain!* by Walt Whitman.

Poly Prep entrance

Poly Prep Campus

I won the grand prize that year (grade 5) and again the next two years—grades 6 and 7. This was not only an unprecedented feat in the history of the school but was particularly satisfying for me as a stutterer. Ironically, whenever I spoke in front of an audience, my unexpected confidence would make my stuttering disappear. It was these speaking contests that instilled in me a love for theatrical and public performance. In the ensuing years, I earned the lead roles in all the school plays. There were times in class when I couldn't put two words together, but the minute I got on stage, I was free.

During these formative years, my interest in sports also began to flourish. I became quite good at swimming and softball and developed a special love for track and field, especially the high jump, for which I had a natural affinity. Together with music and drama, athletics became a very important part of my young life.

It was at this time, the early '50s, that I discovered pop music. The first radio DJ I listened to was Martin Block who had a show on ABC called *Make Believe Ballroom*. This was years before the birth of rock 'n' roll, and to say that the music of the day was white-bread Pop would be a huge

Poly Prep football field

understatement. Artists such as Patti Page, Teresa Brewer, and Perry Como dominated the charts.

One of the records that particularly caught my attention was "How High the Moon" by Les Paul and Mary Ford. Because Les Paul invented multi-tracking, this was the first record on which an artist was able to overdub his or her own voice and sing harmony with their lead vocal. Les Paul was one of the truly brilliant recording pioneers, discovering not only multi-track recording but also inventing the first solid body electric guitar, which was named after him. The Gibson Les Paul is still one of the most sought-after guitars by everyone from Eric Clapton to Jeff Beck. Les Paul is considered one of the architects of rock 'n' roll. At the time of this writing, three original Les Paul guitars had just been auctioned for five million dollars.

I would listen to the radio every night while going to sleep, and one night, I stumbled on a station all the way at the left end of the dial, around 1600 AM. The call letters were WPLJ and it broadcast from Newark, New Jersey. The nighttime DJ was Raymon Bruce, and he would introduce himself by bellowing out: "IYY AM THE BRUCE—CALLED RAYMON!" This was my introduction to rhythm-and-blues, and I was spellbound. R&B, known at the time as "race music," was slowly emerging from the shadows of musical culture.

A few months later, a group called the Four Deuces made a record that became the theme song for the station. They called it "WPLJ," which stood for White Port & Lemon Juice. In the following years, I noticed that all the pop stations were located near the middle of the radio dial while all the R&B stations were relegated to the "back of the bus"—way at the end of the dial—making it more difficult for white listeners to come across them. As many of the songs were about sex, R&B also got a bad rap as "nasty" music.

Three seminal, groundbreaking records evocative of the period were "Work with Me, Annie" by Hank Ballard & the Midnighters; the answer record, "Roll with Me, Henry," by Etta James; and "Sixty Minute Man" by Billy Ward & the Dominoes. The music was starting to change, and the radio had become my best friend. And I needed all the friends I could get because I was soon to face yet another, even more horrific, physical challenge.

* * *

By the first half of the twentieth century, Polio had spread all over the world, reaching epidemic proportions in the United States, even afflicting our beloved president, Franklin Delano Roosevelt. It was a baffling disease because no one knew how it was contracted or how it spread, and it affected everybody differently.

One afternoon in late August 1955, I went swimming at the Hotel St. George in downtown Brooklyn. At the time, it was the largest indoor pool in the world. When I got home, I had a splitting headache. An hour later, I could only prop myself up on my elbows—a sure sign of polio, the doctor informed us. A short while later, I was completely paralyzed. We went right to the hospital where I was given a spinal tap, with no anesthesia—that confirmed the diagnosis.

I was taken to the Kingston Avenue Hospital. It was a very exclusive hospital—you had to have polio to get in. The doctors told my parents I would never walk again, but guess what? No one told me! As long as I had my radio, I was fine. I looked upon what should have been a nightmare as just a temporary bump in the road.

Only two other students from Poly Prep contracted the disease. The first, Russell Trauerts, was immediately placed in an iron lung: a cylindrical metal tube that enclosed your entire body with only your head protruding. A small mirror stationed above your head made it possible for you to see a visitor's face. It was used for the most dire polio cases—designed to press down on your chest to keep you breathing when your lungs were paralyzed.

Russell was also in Kingston Avenue Hospital, and his mother had become a full-time nurse there. She went out of her way to make sure I was well taken care of and would frequently wheel Russell in his iron lung over to my room so we could visit. We became friends, but sadly, in less than a year, he died.

The other polio case from the school was Andy Gurley. He'd been one of the most accomplished athletes in the history of Poly Prep, excelling in football, basketball, and baseball. After his illness, he had to wear braces for the rest of his life—fixed crutches that fit around his forearms instead of resting under his arms. A very handsome young man, he completed his education, went to Gettysburg College, eventually became chairman of a major investment banking firm, had a large family, and lived in the very exclusive community of Scarsdale, New York. I was always inspired by how his life turned out despite his polio.

I was lucky. I was in the hospital for only three months. When I got home, I had to learn how to walk again—a physical therapist came to our home three times a week for a year. Working my way up from having my right leg completely paralyzed, I eventually gained full mobility in my toes, but my right calf remained atrophied. I was left with just fifteen percent of my muscle capacity, leaving my knee and ankle connected mainly by the calf bone. Fortunately, my right thigh regained full strength and allowed me to walk without a very noticeable limp. My left leg, amazingly, emerged unscathed and has carried more than its normal share of weight and responsibility throughout my life.

I was even able to continue my career as a medal-winning high jumper during high school. I was determined. I figured I really only needed one leg to jump over the bar and that happened to be my good leg! Before polio, I dreamt of being a decathlete. Although that would no longer be possible, it didn't diminish my love of competing in as many events as I could. Consequently, I also participated in the 120-yard high hurdles, shot put, discus, and javelin. I also loved to swim and, to this day, I am able to do laps in all four strokes: butterfly, backstroke, breaststroke, and freestyle.

As I progressed through my life, there were two sports I was determined not only to learn but to become fairly adept at—tennis and skiing. I can say in all honesty that despite the physical limitations polio placed on me, I have accomplished both my goals. Skiing and tennis have given me more pride and pleasure than anything I've ever experienced. Even though I didn't embark on either sport until my mid-thirties, I have skied from the top of Aspen Mountain to the bottom without stopping, and I once aced John McEnroe and Guillermo Vilas with my serve—for real.

* * *

During my teenage years, I voraciously consumed all kinds of music. I started taking drum lessons at age ten and received my first drum kit at age thirteen. With that, I was able to form a band with my friends. We called ourselves The Legends. My parents let me use the living room for our rehearsals and my drums were set up there. They also got me a unique record player with a large, industrial-looking speaker that plugged into the turntable and put out more sound than anything I had ever heard before. I would place the speaker right behind the drums and turn the volume all the way up while playing along to Chuck Berry's "Maybellene," Little Richard's "Long Tall Sally," and other favorites of mine.

By the time I turned sixteen, we had become a very popular band and were much in demand for dances all over Brooklyn. As a bonus, it proved to be a great way to meet girls—which was helpful, since Poly Prep was an all-boys school at the time. It was primarily through this experience that I came to know all the songs in the Great American Songbook repertoire, i.e., Cole Porter, George Gershwin, Johnny Mercer, Rodgers and Hart, and countless other songwriting geniuses. Even though my heart and soul were immersed in rock 'n' roll, this gave me an entirely different musical education, and I learned the most magnificent songs ever written by craftsmen who were at the top of their game.

After a few years of playing drums, I got tired of being in the back of the bandstand at our gigs. It was also starting to become a royal pain in the ass to set up my drums, take them down, and pack them up at the end of the gig. (There were no such things as roadies in those days.) So, I proceeded to teach myself the saxophone and took to it like a fish to water. That summer I went to a two-week intensive music camp at the University of New Hampshire where I played three saxes (alto, tenor, and baritone) in the dance band.

While I was in high school, my parents got permission for me to audition and subsequently play oboe in the Brooklyn College Symphony Orchestra. Somehow my mother had convinced me to study the oboe, probably because there weren't many oboe players since it was the most difficult instrument to play. You had to press your lips tightly together against a very small double reed, not an easy task with my buckteeth.

I was one of the youngest musicians in the group. Being surrounded by an entire orchestra of about fifty musicians with everyone playing their individual parts in these great symphonic works, and listening to it come together into a glorious musical whole, was a major high. I also liked the fact that the oboe was also the one instrument that the entire orchestra tuned to.

Playing the oboe was a challenge, but for nine years, I diligently stuck with it until I became quite good. Years later, I was proud to be an oboist when I discovered that George Martin (the Beatles producer) and Mitch Miller were accomplished oboists. The last piece I mastered on the instrument was entitled "Six Metamorphoses After Ovid." It consisted of six individual pieces inspired by the six gods of Greek mythology. There were no time signatures; it was just free form, with more notes than I'd ever seen on a page before.

* * *

Poly Prep had a tradition of producing a well-known Gilbert and Sullivan operetta every other year. In my junior year, they did *The Mikado*, the most famous one of all. I was cast as Pooh-Bah, one of the lead roles. This was truly my first experience performing in musical theater, and for those who are familiar with the works of Gilbert and Sullivan, it was a daunting experience for a fifteen-year-old stutterer. One of the songs I had to sing went, in part:

To sit in solemn silence in a dull, dark dock,
In a pestilential prison with a life-long lock,
Awaiting the sensation of a short, sharp shock,
From a cheap and chippy chopper on a big black block.

A dull, dark dock, a life-long lock, a short, sharp shock, a big, black block

To sit in solemn silence in a pestilential prison,
And awaiting the sensation from a cheap and chippy chopper
On a BIG....BLACK....BLOCK!

I subsequently played the leads in all the school plays of my final two years. The eight years at Poly Prep left me with some of the happiest moments of my life. The beautiful campus, the personal warmth between faculty and students, and its many enjoyable activities gave me a variety of experiences I will never forget. In my senior year, I climaxed my career there by being inducted into the school's honor society, the Oasis, for those who had attained exceptional achievement in every aspect of school life.

Chapter 2

The Birth of Rock 'n' Roll

In the fall of 1954, something happened that would change the face of Pop music forever. A Cleveland DJ, Alan Freed, had developed a rabid following. Calling himself "Moondog," he played R&B music as much as Raymon Bruce did—the first black DJ I'd discovered on the AM radio during my pre-teen years. The only difference was that Freed was white. He was also very passionate about the integrity of the music. Since no pop stations would touch R&B, it became a common practice for certain white pop artists to cover very bland and uninspired versions of these classic songs, but Freed was steadfastly loyal to the originals and wouldn't touch the cover versions. He also pioneered shows at the Cleveland Arena that he called "Moondog Balls." These events attracted thousands of teenagers, both black and white, unheard of at the time.

Meanwhile, a 50,000-watt station in New York, WINS, was dying in the ratings, even though its powerful signal could reach across New England and even to parts of the Midwest. Morris Levy was known as the "Godfather of the record industry" because of his long-term and well-documented relationships with members of the Genovese crime family, as well as his striking, gruff-sounding voice and physical resemblance to the Marlon Brando character in the first *Godfather* film. Morris, known by his friends as "Moishe," always had his ear to the ground. When he became aware of Freed's rising popularity in Cleveland, he quickly became his manager. He then convinced the program director of WINS to take a chance by going against the moral code of society and the industry and put Alan Freed and his "race music" on the air in the prime 7-10 p.m. slot, where he would be heard by hundreds of thousands. It was a balls-out, risky move, but the minute Freed hit the airwaves, he created spontaneous combustion the likes of which no one had ever experienced.

Freed exuded a kind of manic energy combined with a personality that made people trust him as he led them down the yellow brick road. A veritable Pied Piper of teenagers, black and white, he introduced them to an entirely new musical experience. Suddenly they were all listening to the same music played by this wild man, who would hoot and holler and pound on a phone book while the up-tempo records played, giving the whole thing the feeling of a live performance. Even though Freed was held accountable in some circles for inciting juvenile delinquency, he was actually a very decent man who tried to be a positive role model as he broadcast every night on the Moondog Show.

There was a street character who hung out in front of the Brill Building nearly every day. He looked homeless, had a long, white beard, and wore robes that were torn and tattered. Coincidently, he was also known as Moondog and somehow, many years earlier, he had appeared on some obscure radio broadcast under his name: Moondog. He sued Alan Freed in court over the use of the name, and he won the case! Suddenly Freed's identity had been taken away.

Freed had started his broadcast each night with the sound of wolves howling. Then he would play some big-band stripper music and say:

"Come on everybody out there in the Moondog kingdom, let's jump and shout and Rock 'n' Roll all night long, cause it's time for THE MOONDOG SHOW!"

The afternoon after the judge's decision, Freed's inner circle gathered in Morris Levy's office to commiserate. It was time to come up with another name for the show. This was a huge decision. They came up with "The Jump

Show" and "The Big Beat," but those didn't feel right. So, after a process of elimination, Freed eventually decided to go with a name that has come to represent an entire genre: "ROCK 'n' ROLL." He felt that it best described how the music moved you, and if he couldn't use his name, then he'd put the emphasis on the music. He then refined it by calling it his Rock 'n' Roll Dance Party. When he went on the air with it that night, rock 'n' roll was born. So, thank you, *Moondog*!

In September 1956, Freed held the first of many historic live shows at the Brooklyn Paramount Theater. This first anniversary show featured about ten different acts and they usually did eight shows a day, alternating with a movie. The Paramount Theater bosses were afraid that attendance would be weak, so Morris Levy, ever the shrewd negotiator, struck a brilliant deal with the theater: He would put up all the money for the shows, and in return he would receive ninety percent of the box office and the theater would receive ten percent. Thus, they were guaranteed at least a small profit, and to ease their fears, Tony Bennett was added to the weekend shows to give them some box office punch—it wasn't necessary. The shows went on to break all box office records in the history of the Paramount theaters, the previous one having been held by Dean Martin and Jerry Lewis.

I was determined to see the show, but all my friends were afraid to go since it meant riding the BMT Subway all the way to DeKalb Avenue in downtown Brooklyn. None of us had ever ventured that deeply into this strange, unknown neighborhood, but at the ripe old age of thirteen, I HAD to go, even if I went alone.

As I emerged from the subway station, with each step, more and more of the theater would be revealed across the street—it was an awesome sight! My heart was pounding! The Brooklyn Paramount occupied an entire city block with lines around the corner, four-deep, and policemen on horseback to keep the crowds from getting out of control.

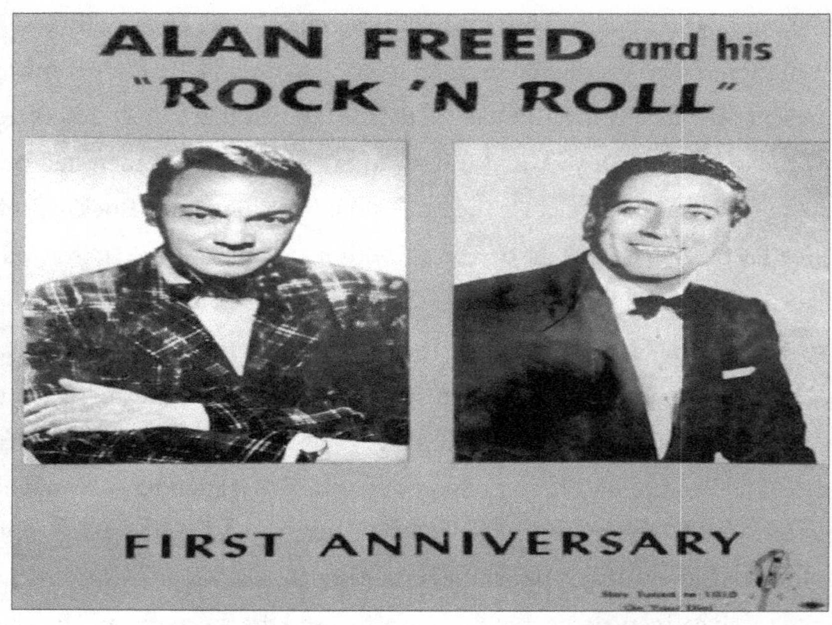

Program booklet for First Anniversary show.

The Brooklyn Paramount

The Brooklyn Paramount

When I finally got inside the theater, a show was in progress, and I was told that the only seating left was in the balcony. I ran up the stairs and could hear Chuck Berry on stage. I felt like I was about to faint as I flung the door open and was greeted by a wall of people crammed in as if they were in a subway car at the peak of rush hour! There wasn't an inch of space to get in, BUT I HAD TO SEE CHUCK! He was playing "Maybellene," my favorite of his songs at the time. I'd memorized the lyrics when I was thirteen and still know them to this day! I managed to squirm in a few feet and stood on my tiptoes; it was just enough that I could barely see him doing the duck walk across the stage!

This was the first time I had ever seen a live show. It was an amazing feeling—like having sex for the first time! After Chuck's set, I immediately went down to the orchestra and grabbed a seat in the third row for the next show.

After the movie, you could hear the musicians talking behind the curtain, getting ready to come on. The feeling was intense as Alan's voice bellowed out, "This is Alan Freed saying welcome to the first anniversary *Rock 'n' Roll Dance Party*!" As the curtain opened, Alan ran out wearing a red and green plaid razzle-dazzle sport jacket, which became sort of his trademark. There on stage was a fourteen-piece big band lineup featuring King Curtis, Sam "The Man" Taylor, and "Big Al" Sears. Tenor sax was THE instrument of the decade. Almost all the hits of the day had sax solos, and this was one

This was Chuck Berry in his prime,
something very few people got to see.

the finest examples of the unique style of rock 'n' roll sax playing—sort of a growling sound coming from the throat, with some barking thrown in.

Alan then introduced the first act: "So, here to start our first anniversary show is Red Prysock on Mercury Records, grabbin' that horn and blowin' strong, with 'HAND CLAPPIN!'" What followed next was quite simply the best rock 'n' roll sax jam I'd ever heard. What a launching pad for the show! Souvenir programs were sold in the lobby; they had a glossy paper front and back cover with pictures of the artists inside. Naturally, I bought one. As the years went by, I acquired a program booklet for every show I attended: The First, Second, and Third Anniversary Shows, along with the Christmas and Easter Jubilee of Stars. When I could, I would go around the block to the stage door for autographs—ANY autograph. I remember how thrilled I was to get Eddie of the Royaltones! With the help of some divine intervention, I miraculously have managed to hold on to these program booklets for *over fifty years*!

What really impressed me was the picture on the Third Anniversary cover—Alan, his second wife Jackie, and all his children. The man really promoted family values. Jackie was also involved in Alan's rock 'n' roll life. She was in charge of the numerous dedications that poured into the Rock 'n' Roll *Dance Party* every night. It was the first time the listeners could connect their feelings to a specific song. If they were too shy to speak directly, they could use the words to express their emotions to their loved ones. Here is a sample:

> *To Adrienne, it's me, Vito...Please listen to the words of this song, they will tell you how I really feel about you, baby. I want you to be my girl, forever.*

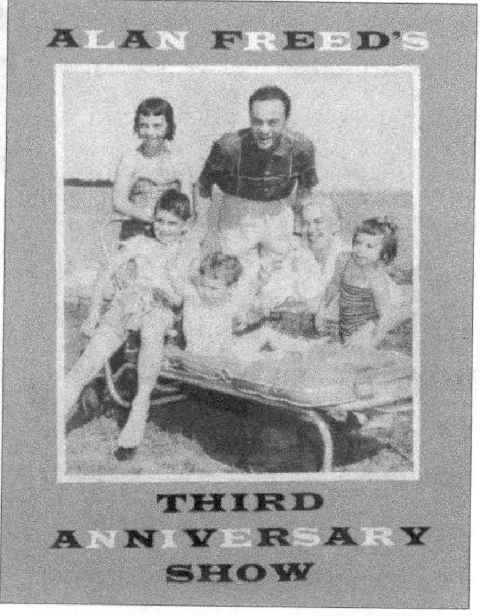

Original program booklets for the Second and Third Anniversary shows.

These dedications were highlighted by the tenderness and sincerity of Alan's delivery and became a big part of his magic, some of them would be several minutes long. He would also routinely give the label and the record number of each song he played. At the end of every Brooklyn Paramount show, Alan would call Jackie out to share the stage with him amidst a thunderous ovation.

I was very blessed to be able to see all my rock 'n' roll heroes in these shows: Fats Domino, Jerry Lee Lewis, Buddy Holly, and "Big Joe" Turner. But the two acts that were really life-changing for me were Little Richard and Bo Diddley—the two greatest live artists I'd seen for the first twenty-five years of my life that truly embodied the spirit and essence of rock 'n' roll.

I'd always thought that Little Richard had never made a live recording, nor were any of the rock 'n' roll shows recorded live. But I was wrong! Alan *did* take them on the road to a few select New England venues, and I have to thank my old pal Peter Wolf, of the J. Geils Band, who gave me four well-recorded bootleg LPs of the Freed shows, probably recorded in Boston, Pete's hometown. I was very fortunate to have a great friend in Wolf who somehow found these bootlegs and knew how much they would mean to me.

Alan and Jackie

The highlight of these recordings was one of Little Richard performing "Lucille." It captured all the brilliance of his live performance and is one of the greatest recordings I've ever heard, with Chuck Berry's "Roll

Over Beethoven" close behind. Listening to them now, with Alan Freed's introductions, fills me with vivid memories of being there to witness the rock 'n' roll child being born.

Little Richard performing on stage.

In my opinion, the birth of rock 'n' roll was the most significant musical and cultural development of the twentieth century. The Hit Parade, featuring songs like "How Much Is That Doggie in the Window?," "The Naughty Lady of Shady Lane," and "Oh! My Pa-Pa," were replaced with the anthem of the era, "Shake, Rattle, and Roll," along with "Good Golly, Miss Molly," "Ain't That a Shame," and "Great Balls of Fire." This monumental change created the foundation of a whole new way for people to relate to music. The real beauty of it was that, while rock 'n' roll really began with the birth of R&B, it also brilliantly incorporated different styles of music from all over the country.

Rockabilly, a synthesis of country and R&B, became a very important part of the movement. This was spearheaded by Sam Phillips' historic Sun Records in Memphis, the label that gave us Jerry Lee Lewis, Johnny Cash,

Bo Diddley performing.

Roy Orbison, Carl Perkins, and of course, Elvis Presley. Buddy Holly hailed from Lubbock, Texas, under the guidance of Norman Petty and Ritchie Valens from Pacoima, California.

Then there were the countless black vocal groups, mostly from Harlem, who had no instruments—only their voices. They would rehearse on the street corners in their neighborhood, under the lampposts, singing a cappella. This soon became the real heart and soul of the movement, as it gave countless young kids a chance to get out of poverty. When they felt they had something special, they would take the subway to midtown Manhattan and go straight to the Brill Building at 1619 Broadway, or two blocks away to the more modern version of it at 1650 Broadway. In these two buildings, you could find about eighty percent of the independent record labels. The groups would make the rounds of all the companies, auditioning right on the spot, hoping to attract someone's ear and catch a break. Some of the outstanding acts who broke through were The Five Satins, Frankie Lymon and the Teenagers, The Flamingos, The Cadillacs, The Heartbeats, Little

Partying at the Brooklyn Paramount during one of the shows.

Anthony and the Imperials, and countless others. This music has endured for over sixty years and still has a huge fan base all across the country. Many years ago, it officially became known as doo-wop. Twice a year, PBS, the public broadcasting station, has fundraising specials hosted by Jerry Butler. They feature about twelve of the best-known doo-wop groups, who still sound and look great performing their hits flawlessly complete with dance moves. These specials have been the biggest fundraisers in PBS history—a tribute to the enduring love people have for doo-wop.

I became completely addicted to this new music, and as I approached my sixteenth year, I discovered that I had quite a good bass voice. I was determined to sing every bass part of every record, black or white. The bass part was different from the other background parts. It required a special talent and was one of the primary signatures of the doo-wop style. You had to sound a little moronic to give it the authenticity that was essential for true doo-wop. There wasn't a record that Alan Freed played that I couldn't cop the bass part. I was passionate about this music (and still am). As a result, I quickly turned The Legends (the dance band which I had formed a few years prior) into a singing group. We still called ourselves The Legends, and every morning for two years, just before classes, we would huddle in the back of our homeroom, singing all of our favorite songs. At lunch break, we would do the same in the third-floor bathroom because it had a great echo. In time, we were invited to perform at all the school dances.

Upon graduation, The Legends pulled together what little money we had and at last we achieved our most sought-after goal: to make a real demo recording. In 1960, there was only one demo studio in all of Brooklyn—it was in the basement of a house. But we made it happen, and we were all really proud that we had done it, especially since we had to record STRAIGHT TO DISC! The song we chose was a cover of an R&B oldie, "Zoom, Zoom, Zoom," by The Collegians. Now I had something legitimate to play for record companies in my supreme quest—to get a record deal!

After a year of making the rounds at the various recording companies, we finally got a break. In 1961, Dick Jacobs, who produced Jackie Wilson's records, signed The Legends to Coral Records (Buddy Holly's label and a subsidiary of Decca). But it wasn't an easy start. First, as there was a previous group known as The Legends, we had to change our name. Then, our lead singer went off to study medicine and wanted out, so we had to find a replacement. I discovered an R&B singer who worked in the factory at Peripole spraying lacquer on tambourines. His name was Rodney Garrison. Since the other three members had the same first name as I did, Richard, my father came up with an inspired name for the group—THREE DICKS AND A ROD! We settled on The Escorts.

One notable record we did on that first session was called "Gaudeamus." At our commencement ceremony from Poly Prep, the graduating senior class all sang the classical Latin hymn "Gaudeamus Igitur." Two years later, I thought it would be fun to try a doo-wop version sung completely in Latin. It began with the strings and organ playing the traditional melody. Then I launched into a crazy-sounding baseline:

"YEAH PIPPA TOOMBAH, HICK, HIKE, HOKE, PIPPA TOOMBAH HULIUS, OOBY DOOBY DOOM WAH."

We segued into our satirical doo-wop version with a very funky rhythm. The record became a mini-classic and, years later, found its way onto a few R&B compilations. We recorded twelve singles over a three-year period. It was a real learning experience for me as we had to come prepared to do four songs in a three-hour session and that was it—no editing, no double tracking vocals, no overdubbing, no nothing! The only good thing was that the musicians were first-rate, including Mickey "Guitar" Baker of Mickey & Sylvia fame (who can forget "Love Is Strange"?), Leroy Glover on keyboards (he played that haunting organ on Ruby & The Romantics' "Our Day Will Come"), and Bernard "Pretty" Purdie on drums. He would display a sign that read: "*'Pretty' Purdie, The Hit Maker.*" This was my first professional experience in a recording session.

Chapter 3

Michigan and Beyond

In 1960, I began the next phase of my life as a student at the University of Michigan. A week after I arrived on campus in Ann Arbor, in the thick of the presidential campaign, John F. Kennedy spoke on the steps of the Michigan Union. I was standing about twenty yards away from him.

Kennedy on the steps of Michigan Union.

No one had ever seen a candidate who looked or talked like that before. Someone in the crowd bellowed out, "What a president!"

Everyone was spellbound by Kennedy's ideas and charisma. It was the first time I knew of that students were actively interested in presidential politics. During the eight years that preceded JFK, all we had was Eisenhower—not much for a teenager to get excited about. That was the night that Kennedy unveiled his plan for the Peace Corps.

In 1984, I was at a dinner party hosted by my friend Bobby Shriver, whose mother, Eunice Kennedy Shriver, was JFK's sister. His father, Sargent Shriver, was also there. President Kennedy had appointed him to head up the new venture, and when I mentioned that I was in the crowd during that amazing speech, he told me that if the response from the students hadn't been so overwhelmingly enthusiastic, there might never have been a Peace Corps.

While at Michigan, my musical tastes expanded considerably. I started to cultivate a love for jazz. It was during this period—1959 to 1964—that modern jazz was exploding. Leading the charge were artists like The Dave Brubeck Quartet (featuring the brilliant alto saxophonist Paul Desmond) with their classic album *Time Out*, a groundbreaking LP in the evolution of jazz and one of the best-selling jazz recordings of all time, reaching number two on the Billboard Pop Chart. It featured two stellar cuts, "Blue Rondo à la Turk" and "Take Five." The latter became a Top 40 single, a rarity for jazz recordings.

Lambert, Hendricks, and Ross, the greatest vocal group in jazz, were the first artists to put the lyrics of their songs on the back of the album cover, and with songs like "Twisted," "Moanin,'" "Charleston Alley," and "Cloudburst," (Jon Hendrick's masterpiece that could be considered the forerunner of rap), made you realize what great songwriters they were, not to mention their vocal prowess.

The Four Freshmen blew me away in concert at Hill Auditorium, on the Michigan campus! They were equally proficient at singing and playing their own instruments. Brian Wilson, the genius behind the Beach Boys, has long acknowledged The Four Freshmen as one of his primary influences and idolized them for their vocal arrangements and harmonies.

Then of course, there was Stan Getz, the king of romantic jazz tenor saxophonists, who, together with Antônio Carlos Jobim, co-founded the

Dave Lambert, Jon Hendricks, & Annie Ross

bossa nova movement in 1961, spearheaded by one of the greatest records ever made, "The Girl from Ipanema," which was a huge global hit. To this day, I listen to Brazilian music as much as any other genre of music, particularly Jobim's, whom I consider to be one of the greatest songwriters of all time.

Another one of my favorites was Chet Baker, the best white trumpet player who ever lived. He was not only a great musician, but he was also a pop culture figure respected by the likes of James Dean and Sinatra and became a staple of cool jazz with his penetrating tone and unique choirboy voice.

Then, there was the ultimate, most magnificent Miles Davis. I consider his *Sketches of Spain* and *Kind of Blue* two of the most cherished albums of my life. The evolution of Miles' sound can be documented by his use of the

The Four Freshmen

Antônio Carlos Jobim

Chet Baker

Harmon mute, which he held close to the microphone in a way that grew to be his signature. He was known for his phrasing, especially in ballads, which was spacious, melodic, and relaxed. The nocturnal quality of Davis' playing and his somber reputation, along with his whispering voice, earned him the lasting moniker of "Prince of Darkness," adding a patina of mystery to his public persona.

It was also around this time that I began to discover the most important female jazz singers, Billie Holiday and Ella Fitzgerald. To this day, I make it a point to listen to Billie and Ella for at least a few hours a week. Little did I know then that in just six years, I would be producing an album with Ella. But more about that later...

* * *

Miles Davis

Perhaps the biggest influence that University of Michigan had on me was that it introduced me to the world of musical theater. The school had an organization on campus known as MUSKET. Every year, Musket would put on a major musical, which, I believe, was the most professional college production of a musical in the country. From the day of my first rehearsal, I thought to myself, "Holy shit! This is the real deal." Every person in the cast had an excellent voice.

In my freshman year, the show was *Kismet,* a highly underrated musical. It's an Arabian Night fantasy, with music adapted from melodies by the famed Russian composer, Alexander Borodin. Just a few gems that came from the show are "And This Is My Beloved," "Baubles, Bangles, and Beads," and "Stranger In Paradise."

The lead role of Hajj the Beggar was played by Jack O' Brien. It was very inspiring for me to be in this show and watch Jack work. He had theater in his blood and went on to become one of the most admired, versatile, and Tony

Ella Fitzgerald

Billie Holiday

Award-winning directors in Broadway history. He has directed everything from the Houston Grand Opera's revival of *Porgy and Bess* to *The Full Monty, Hairspray, Dirty Rotten Scoundrels,* and Tom Stoppard's trilogy of plays, *The Coast of Utopia*. He is considered one of the best directors of all time, equally adept in dramas and musicals, Shakespeare, and opera. Jack directed a revival of Rodgers and Hammerstein's *Carousel* for Broadway in 2018.

When you are in a show, it is normal to devour the original cast album. It was while doing so in this case I discovered Alfred Drake, the greatest singer-actor in the history of American musical theater, with a rich baritone voice and a striking physical presence. In addition to creating the original male lead of Curly in *Oklahoma!,* Drake played the lead role of Fred in the Cole Porter classic, *Kiss Me Kate* (based on Shakespeare's *The Taming of The Shrew*), and, of course, there was *Kismet*. In 1965, when Richard Burton assembled what he felt were the finest actors on the planet to

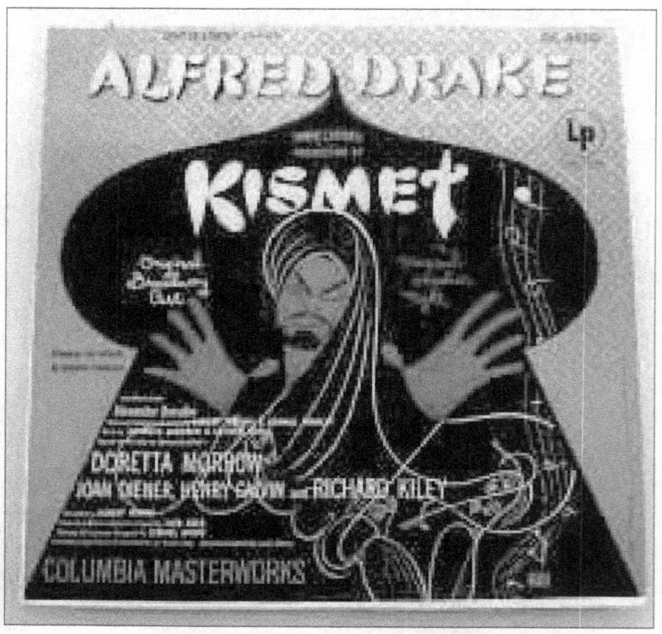

Kismet Original Cast LP

perform *Hamlet* on Broadway for a limited six-week run, he cast Alfred Drake in the role of Claudius. I used to fantasize that I could go back in time and see Drake in *Kismet.*

For my remaining three years at Michigan, I was cast as the male lead in all of the MUSKET productions. I was blessed with the gift of having a resonant, bass-baritone voice that could be heard over the orchestra in the last row of the balcony. I couldn't get enough theater and started taking as many acting courses as possible along with private voice training. Having truly fallen in love with the smell of the greasepaint and the roar of the crowd, I began thinking seriously about a career in musical theater.

There was a cantankerous old Austrian professor on the music school faculty by the name of Josef Blatt. He was the director of the University Opera Society and conductor of the University Symphony Orchestra. When it came to compliments, he didn't give ice away in winter, and was known for being a sheer perfectionist, impossible to please. When I sang for him, he gave me a unique compliment, telling me in his crusty, Austrian accent,

"You would be a sure success in opera."

"Thank you, Professor Blatt," I responded, "but why do you think so?" (I expected him to say something flattering about my voice.)

"Because there is a shortage of tall, lean basses!" he replied.

* * *

During this time, American folk music took major steps forward, particularly with the emergence of one Bobby Zimmerman, better known as Bob Dylan, who was a life-changer for nearly all of us. With the songs of Peter, Paul and Mary, who had major hits with Dylan's "Blowing In The Wind" and "Don't Think Twice, It's All Right"; the queens of folk, Joan Baez and Judy Collins; and The Band, which performed and recorded with Dylan on numerous occasions, this music began to spread its wings and appeal to a much wider audience. It also had a strong influence on the music of the late sixties and seventies.

I didn't care much about folk music prior to the sixties. But, as luck would have it, my parents developed a friendship with Pete Seeger. Pete had spent a good deal of his time in the West Indies during the '50s, where he became very interested in steel drums. Since it was difficult and costly to ship them to the US, Pete wanted to create a company with my parents that would manufacture steel drums in America, and in the process, they became friends. I remember one day, we visited him and his family in Beacon, New York, where we watched him chop down a tree; and once, he came to our house in Brooklyn and played banjo in our living room for an hour.

I learned that Pete had a group called The Weavers and we had an album of theirs, *The Weavers, Live at Carnegie Hall.* I later discovered that The Weavers were considered one of the primary inspirations of the American folk music revival of the '50s and '60s, which led to what became known as folk rock. But at the time, it wasn't a big deal to me. After all, it wasn't rock 'n' roll. All I knew was that they looked old to me. They did have one song that I was familiar with—"Goodnight Irene"—but I saw it as just a song to be sung around the campfire. I later found out that this "campfire" song was a massive hit and had reached number one on the *Billboard* chart where it remained for thirteen weeks!

As I continued at Michigan, it gradually became clear that this "family friend" was a folk music icon, highly revered by most of my friends, as well as by people throughout America. I came to discover that Pete was not only a huge figure of historical importance in the development of folk music over the previous twenty years, but that his music had its roots in political activism, civil rights, environmental issues, and protests against the increasingly unpopular Vietnam War. He had also formed an alliance with

Woody Guthrie, and the groups with which they performed during the '40s and '50s had had a huge influence on the emergence of topical songwriting during the turbulent 1960s.

So, when it was announced that Pete Seeger was coming to Ann Arbor to give a concert in February of the following year, it became a must-see event for everyone I knew. When I came home for the Christmas holiday, I told my mother that this guy, Pete Seeger, who we'd visited a few years earlier, was considered some kind of God—and asked her if there was any way that her "old friend" Pete could give me a call when he came to Michigan to perform, because I'd love to have him over for dinner. I figured it didn't hurt to ask. My mother called Pete's wife, a beautiful Japanese woman named Toshi. She said that she would give him my number and he would call me if he could, but it was not certain that he'd be able to come at all, since he would likely be called to appear in front of the House Un-American Activities Committee. He was suspected of being a Communist sympathizer.

As the time drew closer to the date of the concert, it seemed doubtful that Pete would show up. My three roommates were all Folk music addicts, and they became totally despondent when it looked less and less likely that Pete would get permission to perform. It would have been the closest that any of them would ever come to one of their heroes.

One roommate with whom I had become particularly close was the biggest folk music junkie of all, and he turned me on to many other folk artists. His name is Sam Zell (yes, *that* Sam Zell, the future billionaire investment magnate from Chicago). We were also fraternity brothers and would tool around campus on our Vespa motor scooters, usually with a girl on the back, going to football games at Michigan Stadium. One time, we drove to Detroit for a double date forty miles away. We wanted to make a good impression, so we dressed in sport jackets, ties, and topcoats. The only problem was that this was in the dead of winter, so we had to stop at every Howard Johnson's along the way and put our hands under the hot air blowing machine to prevent from getting frostbite.

You might be interested to know that Sam is the former owner of the *Los Angeles Times*, the *Chicago Tribune*, and five other major newspapers and their affiliated TV stations, which he bought ten years ago for seven and a half billion. When Sam was in Los Angeles to negotiate the deal, he became close to a long-time friend of mine, David Geffen. David called and shocked the hell out of me when he told me that Sam had asked David if he knew me. Geffen then put together a dinner party so Sam and I could renew old memories. It had been *forty-five years*. Just to add a little extra spice to the evening, David had a surprise guest, Mike Nichols.

As Pete Seeger's concert date grew nearer, at last, it was announced that he had received the necessary clearances and was definitely coming to Ann Arbor—though I still had no idea whether or not he would contact me. That Friday afternoon, the day before the concert, the phone rang around 3:00 p.m. I was at a class, so Sam answered the phone.

"Is Richard Perry there, please?"

"He'll be home soon. Can I tell him who's calling?"

"It's Peter Seeger."

At that point, Zell almost passed out. I returned Pete's call as soon as I got home, and he graciously accepted my invitation to come to dinner. We put our little kitchen table in the middle of the living room. In order to keep some sense of dignity, we established that each of us could invite no more than four friends, and they would arrive in stages after we'd eaten so it wouldn't get too crowded all at once. I went to pick up Pete at his hotel on my motor scooter. He hopped on the back, and I proceeded to give him a tour of the campus. At that point, I felt like hot shit. I mean how would a freshman kid come to know a legend like Seeger, much less be driving him around on the back of a Vespa!? Let me tell you, it was a fucking thrill!

When we got back to the apartment and sat down for dinner, some of our friends arrived during the salad course, even though we'd made it clear that no one was to show up until after dinner. Since we had a very limited sitting area, it was decided that our friends would sit on the floor. Everyone was so eager to meet Pete, that by the time we started our main course, every inch of floor space was occupied, which was a little strange. Just imagine: There we were, sitting at the table in the living room, surrounded by all our friends sitting on the floor. After dinner, Pete, ever the gracious man, grabbed my Martin guitar and sang a few songs, leaving everyone in a state of awe!

The concert was the following night, and I've never experienced anything quite like it. On several songs, such as "Oh, Mary Don't You Weep," he would divide the audience into three sections and then give each group a different part to sing. The highlight of the concert was an inspirational song that almost everyone was hearing for the first time. With hundreds of people singing in three parts, it moved me deeply. The song was "We Shall Overcome."

The music of Pete Seeger and the spirit he conveyed has touched our souls for over half a century, especially such eternal standards as "If I Had A Hammer" and "Turn, Turn, Turn," both of which he wrote. On May 3, 2012, there was a one-night only, star-studded concert event at Madison Square Garden that was a tribute to Seeger, celebrating his ninetieth birthday. It featured more than forty artists and was headlined by Bruce Springsteen, who had already paid homage to Pete with his 2006 album, *We Shall Overcome: The Seeger Sessions.* The album won the Grammy Award for Best Traditional Folk Album and sold more than 700,000 copies. Regrettably, our paths never crossed again. Seeger passed away on January 27, 2014, at the age of ninety-four.

(Top and bottom) Pete Seeger in concert.

Chapter 4

1962—A Year to Remember

One of the main things I had on my bucket list as I entered my twenties was to put The Escorts together with some musician friends of mine and play New York clubs. It was the summer of '62, the year of the Twist, and the mecca of all clubs was the Peppermint Lounge, located on West 45th between Sixth and Seventh Avenues. The club attracted a high-society crowd, including Jackie Kennedy, and became so big that it even had a hit record named after it: "Peppermint Twist" by Joey Dee and the Starliters.

Every Friday, *The Daily Mirror*, a local newspaper, would run ads on the back three pages for the local clubs in Brooklyn, Queens, and Long Island. I had to start somewhere, and as luck would have it, I came across a club right in the neighborhood on Coney Island Avenue and Avenue J. The name was the Lollypop Lounge and it featured live music. That afternoon, we auditioned and got the gig starting the following night—we were buzzed! The Escorts featured Rodney Garrison on most lead vocals, Richie Rosenberg on background vocals and percussion, myself on vocals and percussion, and Richie Berg—known as "The Count" on clavinet. He specialized in Little Richard, Fats Domino, and Jerry Lee Lewis numbers.

Playing all oldies, we rocked the house and the dance floor was packed. About two hours into the gig, a girl walked up to the bandstand and pulled on my sleeve while we were in the middle of a song. I figured she was drunk, so I ignored her at first, but after we finished the number, she yanked on my sleeve again. I had never seen a girl like her before—very raw. She wore hip-hugger pants, high spiked heels, and a halter-top, leaving her midriff bare.

"Can I sing with you guys?" she asked me. I asked her what she wanted to sing.

"Do you know 'Lonely Nights' by The Hearts?"

This request kind of blew me away. "Lonely Nights" was a little known early R&B classic and happened to be the first record I'd ever bought. Years later, when I told this to Paul Simon, he found me a 78-rpm copy—a true, rare jewel. It was (and still is) one of the most soulful recordings I'd ever heard.

"What's your key?" I asked her.

"What do my keys have to do with this?" she replied. "Why do you want my keys?"

"Never mind. Just start singing and we'll follow you."

I was immediately intrigued with the sound of her voice. She had a nasal yet soulful quality, a little like Rosie of Rosie and the Originals (of "Angel Baby" fame). As the song went on, I couldn't help but think, "This is fucking good."

On stage with The Escorts at The Lollypop Lounge.

When we finished, the crowd went nuts. The girl was in shock. It was the first time she had sung with a band in public, and with a real microphone. More importantly, there was a little bit of magic happening between us. She reluctantly gave me her phone number, figuring that all I wanted was to get into her pants. I later confessed that I was still a virgin so she had nothing to fear. I called her the next day to ask if she would consider rehearsing with the group and proposed she come on board as our lead singer. I was searching for a different sound and was already planning to replace Rodney, our former lead singer. When I told her that we had a record deal and had already released two singles, any doubts she may have had quickly evaporated.

We rehearsed in the basement of my family home, which had an upright piano, knotty pine wood paneling, cream linoleum floors, and two salmon-colored faux-leather couches. This room held a special place in my development during the formative years and beyond. The rehearsals got off to a flying start, and within a few days, this girl—Goldie Zelkowitz was her name—became a permanent member of The Escorts. She was totally from the street, but I found her to be a breath of fresh air. We started to hang together almost twenty-four/seven and, inevitably, fell for each other. After a week together, I'm happy to say that finally, at the ripe old age of twenty, I was no longer a virgin! I guess you could say I was a late bloomer.

Since I had my parent's house in Brooklyn to myself for most of the summer, Goldie often spent the night, also a first for me. One Saturday afternoon, we were lying in the sun on a couple of lounge chairs in our small backyard. We were both wearing bathing suits, although Goldie's was a bikini—the first time I had ever seen a bathing suit like that. My grandmother, who'd moved into the apartment that we'd lived in for the first ten years of my life, had developed a terrible habit of occasionally dropping by without calling first, especially when she knew I was there alone. So, imagine my surprise—or should I say shock—when my grandmother suddenly appeared in the backyard! Not that Goldie and I were doing anything, but still…that bikini! My grandmother's jaw dropped. I introduced her to Goldie but didn't take the interaction further than that. Goldie and I continued to lay in the sun until my grandmother left. I felt bad about ignoring her, but what else could I do? I certainly didn't want to encourage her to stay.

My grandmother was originally from Russia and was very old-fashioned, so it's safe to say that meeting Goldie in that tiny bikini didn't make the greatest first impression. From that day on, my grandmother ragged on Goldie, to the point where the family couldn't take it anymore. In her thick Russian accent, she would say to me, "Vat do you see in that girl? She's not for you. She's trash."

I knew that Goldie was a total street chick, but she was different from anyone I'd ever known before, much less dated. I was twenty years old and felt completely capable of making my own decisions. Most important, when it came to girls—it was none of my grandmother's goddamn business! Hey, I was getting laid for the first time!

With Goldie now a part of our group, we were a lot more appealing to the night clubs. Our next gig was at Trude Heller's Versailles, located on the corner of Sixth Avenue and West Ninth Street in the West Village. It was a well-known hot spot that featured live music. After a couple of performances, we sort of became the house band and ended up playing there for a solid month. I remember that one night, as we were about to go on, the news broke that Marilyn Monroe had died. Nobody in the crowd knew about it yet, and while it was shocking to hear, we knew the show had to go on.

Playing at Trude's was a cool gig throughout the summer. We often opened for Candido, the famous conga player. The only drag was dealing with the owner, Trude Heller, who had all the warmth and charm of a Nazi drill sergeant.

One day, on a whim, Goldie decided to dye her hair from blonde to jet-black. It gave her a very different look. Suddenly, I had an idea. My grandmother's nagging about Goldie had gone from bad to worse, so I decided to invent a new persona for Goldie to go with her different hair—I named her Diane Lloyd. I told my grandmother that I had broken up with Goldie and wasn't going to have anything to do with her anymore. Then, about a week later, I told her that I had a new girlfriend and wanted them to meet. We planned on stopping at the house that night on our way to the gig, and I had prepared her for the audition with my grandmother: "Now, just remember these three things: Leonard Bernstein, Lincoln Center, and the Guggenheim Museum. Just casually work those into your conversation."

Goldie joins the band.

My father, who was in on the ruse, answered the door, "Hello, Diane. I'm Richard's father, come right in. This is his grandmother." They exchanged pleasantries and then my grandmother asked about her interests. In her Brooklyn accent, "Diane" replied, "Oh, I just love Lenny Bernstein, and I've seen him at Lincoln Center as often as possible. I also love da Guggenheim Museum. Geez, it's my favorite of all da museums." We left shortly afterward, and as soon as we were gone, my grandmother exclaimed, "Anyone can see that this is a girl with CLASS—SHE'S GOT CULTURE!" For the rest of her years, my grandmother never knew the truth.

As the summer of '62 neared its end, The Escorts reached their pinnacle: They managed to get booked at The Peppermint Lounge for the last week in August. It gave me a real sense of accomplishment to have scaled the mountain in just a little over two months. My brother Roger, whose hobby was photography, took pictures of the group at all of our gigs. I will always be deeply indebted to him for giving me permanent memories of this unforgettable experience.

Just before going back for my junior year at Michigan, Dick Jacobs, our A&R man at Coral Records, wanted The Escorts to come with our new lead

The Escorts on stage at Trude Heller's.
Left to right: Me, Goldie, Richie Rosenberg, and The Count.

On stage at the Peppermint Lounge.

singer into the studio and record four new sides. Dick did Jackie Wilson's records. Naturally, we were all excited. Goldie and I wrote a song called "Submarine Race Watching," which was about parking your car and making out. Then I came up with the idea of doing pop arrangements of two of my favorite songs from *West Side Story*: "Somewhere" and "One Hand, One Heart." We all thought that "Somewhere" should be the next single.

At first, the record didn't go anywhere, but since Ann Arbor was just forty miles from Detroit, I started a regular communication with Gerry Lacoursiere, the local Decca promotion man, to see if we could get the record started somehow. Finally, he got one of the larger stations in Detroit, WJBK, to test the record. The reaction was mixed: Most people liked it, but some were adamantly against it, thinking that Goldie had the worst voice they had ever heard.

As Thanksgiving break was rapidly approaching, WJBK opted to go balls out and play the record every hour for the weekend before Thanksgiving, and let the listeners decide if the record was a hit or not. Did the fans love or hate Goldie's voice? The switchboard immediately lit up because we all know that everyone always roots for the underdog. So, by Monday, not only was the vote overwhelmingly positive, but the other two Top 40 stations—CKLW, and the ABC affiliate, WXYZ—added the record.

Jumping to "Peppermint Twist."

All three stations wanted The Escorts to appear live at their record hops for the upcoming Thanksgiving holiday weekend. A record hop was a dance that each DJ would sponsor at different locations all over the city. They usually took place in roller rinks, high school gyms, armory halls, and the like. The kids would dance throughout the evening, and several acts would stop by to perform their hits. They entered through the back door, got up on a makeshift stage with a speaker behind them, and would then lip sync to the record and do their choreographed moves. After their performance, they'd immediately leave by the same back door, would jump into their manager or promotion man's car, and hurry to the next record hop. They would do about five each night. This is how every artist promoted their records back then. It was a nice way for the artist to pay back the DJs for helping to break their records and make them into hits.

On Tuesday mornings, the new radio station charts would come out and the DJs would be plugging their record hops taking place that weekend, saying that the group with the number-one record would appear. As I did every Tuesday, I tuned in the week of Thanksgiving. I knew that campus would be shut down for the holiday, so I wanted to hear where the record hops would be happening that week. Frankie Valli and the Four Seasons had the current number one record, "Big Girls Don't Cry," so I figured I would put my time off from school to good use and try to meet Frankie at a nearby hop. I turned the volume up on the radio, but instead of Frankie Valli, the DJ was announcing that the group with the NEW number one record was THE ESCORTS with "SOMEWHERE." This had become a really big deal—the listeners had voted and spoken. It was the talk of the town! In her book, *Lollipop Lounge*, Goldie said the following about the announcement:

> *Coral Records made all the arrangements for me. They picked me up and took me to the airport where I boarded a plane to Detroit. When I landed, I took a cab to meet Richie at his apartment on the University of Michigan campus in Ann Arbor, and the wildest thing happened during the cab ride. The radio was on and suddenly I heard my voice. I was singing "Somewhere." I started whooping at the driver. "Hey! That's me! That's me!"*
>
> *It was the first time I'd ever heard myself on the radio. Then it hit me—I DID have a number-one record! The DJ was yelling about a record hop that night. MY record hop! Wow, what a feeling! I will never forget it. It didn't seem real. The DJ kept going on and on about the hop. And of course, the number one group—The Escorts with Goldie Zelkowitz—will be there.*

I couldn't believe the DJ was actually saying my name, Zelkowitz! How did that happen? "That's me, that's me! I'm Goldie!," I cried to the driver.

"Oh yeah?" he said, giving me a withering, just another loony look in the rearview mirror, "Lady, if that's you on the radio, then I'm Frankie Valli."[1]

It was our turn to perform at the record hops now! We did our first slew of performances the Wednesday night before Thanksgiving. (Because of the holiday, record hops were happening earlier that week.) What a thrill! On Thursday morning, Goldie and I woke up to the sounds of marching bands and big crowd noises. We opened our window and were treated to the sight of a huge Thanksgiving Day parade in the street below. Here we were in Detroit, appearing all over the city with the number-one record, and to top it off, we got a Thanksgiving parade!

No. 1 in Detroit!

Friday night was the highlight of the weekend. The biggest R&B DJ in Detroit was "Frantic" Ernie Durham, who had a big Friday show starting at midnight at the 20 Grand Bowling Lanes, with about ten acts. Chuck Jackson was the headliner. There was a theater adjoining the bowling alleys that held about five hundred people. We had to go in the front entrance but before entering, we got up on a wooden box while a big fat cop frisked us. We were then hurried into the theater and told to stay as close along the back wall as possible. The room was packed and everyone was standing since there were no seats. It was a strange feeling when I realized that we were the only white people in the place. We finally got to the dressing room, which was the size of a large closet and shared by all ten acts performing that night. It was pretty claustrophobic, but very exciting, as the girls were putting on their makeup at the same time the guys were checking themselves out in the mirror and going over their dance moves.

This was the early days of Motown, and Detroit was a private testing ground for new artists of that genre. That night they had two new groups on the bill that they were looking to break: The Supremes and The Temptations! The Supremes were promoting their new single, "Let Me Go the Right Way" and the Temps had "The Way You Do the Things You Do." Who knew that at some point in my future, I would produce memorable albums with both of these artists: Diana Ross' *Baby It's Me* in 1977, and *For Lovers Only* by the Temptations in 1995. I still derive a great deal of pleasure from these albums.

I'll never forget our performance that night; the crowd of people was bigger than we had ever performed for before. I had accomplished beyond what I had set out to do with the group, and I finished out my degree at Michigan feeling very fulfilled.

Unfortunately, we all agreed that The Escorts didn't have much of a future, so we retired the group. With that, Goldie and I also parted ways. Perplexed about what she would do with her life going forward, she teamed up with a female drummer, Ginger Panebianco, and they started the first all-girl rock band, called Goldie and the Gingerbreads. They were pretty well known, even more so in Europe, where they opened several shows for The Rolling Stones. The band broke up in 1968, and she then created, together with Michael Zager and Aram Schefrin, an American jazz fusion band known as Ten Wheel Drive. They played all the rock and pop festivals, the Fillmore East, and in 1973, in Carnegie Hall. During that time, she was frequently compared to Janis Joplin. In fact, at the Atlanta Pop Festival, Janis sat in with the band. Goldie was known as Genya Ravan for the rest of her career.

* * *

During my final two years at Michigan, I took as many acting courses as I could and played the role of Nathan Detroit in *Guys and Dolls* and the male lead in the Leonard Bernstein musical *Wonderful Town*, and the then-popular Broadway show, *The Boy Friend.*

After two years of trying, I gained admittance to the prestigious thirty-three voice Michigan Men's Glee Club, chosen from thousands of students in all areas of study. The group would participate in several international festivals, where they usually took home a first-place trophy, competing against the finest glee clubs in the world. Whenever they performed, they wore white tie and tails.

By December of 1964 I had earned my degree in music and theater, so I packed up my trusted car, a Sunbeam Rapier, and left Ann Arbor at 6 p.m. I drove nonstop to Brooklyn and arrived at our family home at 8 a.m. As much as I'd cherished my years at Michigan, I was more than ready to move on to the next phase of my life. Broadway—here I come!

As I settled into living at home after being away for four years, I began to pursue my career in musical theater in earnest. I was accepted into a music theater class at the very prestigious Herbert Berghof Studio on 120

Me and Linda Herrick in "The Boy Friend."
(December 1963, Ann Arbor, Michigan)

Bank Street in the West Village. I also began to take private voice lessons with Rawn Spearman, a music professor from Columbia University, went to every chorus call and audition that I could find, and voraciously read *Backstage* and *Variety* from cover to cover the minute the new weekly issues hit the newsstand. I was optimistic that sooner or later I would get a job in the chorus of a new musical, at the very least. I was confident that something would eventually break my way.

Chapter 5

Finding My Way to Cloud Nine

It was certainly quite a shift in my career to go from aspiring Broadway star to record producer. People frequently ask me how I became a producer. I think it's a fascinating story punctuated by several strokes of good luck.

My brother Roger had a hobby of buying beat-up BMW motorcycles. He would fix them up and sell them for a handsome profit. He was so obsessed with this hobby that a year after he began, he drove one by himself across the country, from Brooklyn to San Francisco—a daunting journey, to say the least.

One afternoon, he had just put the finishing touches on a real beauty, and I asked him if I could take it for a spin. My father decided to come along for the ride, so he hopped on the back and off we went, father and son, just cruising the neighborhood.

As I approached a red light, something—or someone—caught my eye. In the first stopped car, I immediately noticed the back of a girl's head. She had great-looking, long, bright-red hair. Gradually creeping the bike past the other cars, I pulled alongside the car and casually turned my head to the right to look at the girl. Lo and behold, it was Marilyn Kupersmith (later to be known as Marilyn Vance). I hadn't seen her in nearly five years—since high school. Marilyn was the best dancer in our crowd, and we would dance to Little Richard all the time.

We both pulled over to the side of the road to catch up, and she told me that she was engaged to Kenny Vance. He was a member of Jay and the

Americans, a very popular group in the early to mid-'60s who had several major pop hits, and in 1964, they opened for The Beatles in Washington, DC. I had heard about Kenny for many years and was excited to meet him, so I invited the two of them over to my house, and Marilyn accepted.

I had an intuitive feeling that Kenny Vance and I would be great friends. He and Marilyn came over the following night, and he told me that Leiber and Stoller had produced the first hit by Jay and the Americans, "She Cried." He then proposed the idea that he and I might try and write some songs together and said he could get us a meeting with Leiber and Stoller! That would be the equivalent of someone who wanted to become a priest being told that he could have an audience with the Pope.

Leiber and Stoller were the most successful songwriting-producing team prior to The Beatles. Their BMI and ASCAP awards lined the walls of their office floor to ceiling for about thirty yards. Some of their most memorable songs were "Hound Dog," "Kansas City," "Stand By Me," "Jailhouse Rock," "On Broadway," and "Is That All There Is?" (made famous by Peggy Lee). They also wrote classics performed by The Coasters, most notably "Yakety Yak" and "Charlie Brown."

Several years ago, there was a musical revue on Broadway, "Smokey Joe's Café," comprised entirely of Leiber-Stoller songs. It was the longest-running revue in Broadway history, and ultimately, several companies were performing it all over the world. Every writer in the Brill Building and 1650 Broadway revered Leiber and Stoller and sought to attain their level of creativity and prominence. I had admired their talent for years.

Kenny and I got together almost every night, me on the Baldwin grand piano in my living room and Kenny leaning on it working on the lyrics. After a few weeks, we'd written three songs that we felt were worthy of playing for Leiber and Stoller. Kenny set up the meeting with Jerry Leiber, whom he said was much more laidback and forgiving than Mike Stoller. Jerry had a great sense of humor, and Kenny wisely thought that we would be considerably more at ease with him than with Mike, a no-nonsense kind of guy.

The day of our big meeting, Kenny hopped on the back of the Heinkel motor scooter that Roger had found for me—a rare German brand that had extra horsepower, so you were allowed to drive it on highways, through tunnels, and across bridges. As we emerged from the Brooklyn Battery Tunnel (now known as the Hugh L. Carey Tunnel) and onto the West Side Highway, we got off at the Forty-ninth Street exit and we pulled over for lunch at a hot dog stand. We then cruised up Fiftieth to Broadway, pulled over and parked close to 1619 Broadway—the Brill Building!

Jerry and Mike had recently created a new label, Red Bird Records, in partnership with George Goldner, a smooth, charismatic, yet complex man with a teenager's ear for music. I was not yet familiar with his name, in spite of his legendary reputation. Red Bird was the hottest new label at the time, producing such classic hits as "Chapel of Love" by The Dixie Cups, "I Wanna Love Him So Bad" by The Jelly Beans, "Leader of the Pack" and "Remember (Walking in the Sand)" by The Shangri-Las (brilliantly produced by the late "Shadow" Morton), and "The Boy from New York City" by the Ad Libs.

As we entered the famous Brill Building, the mecca of the record business, I had high hopes yet a certain apprehension about the meeting. After all, it's not every day that you get to meet Leiber and Stoller! As we entered the reception area of the Red Bird offices, there was an electric feeling in the air. A striking couple entered just after us. George Goldner bolted from his office and warmly greeted Ike and Tina Turner, then escorted them into his office.

Leiber's secretary then came out to greet Kenny.

"Oh, Kenny," she said, "I've been trying to reach you. Jerry got called away to a meeting, but Mike will see you."

The Brill Building

Kenny turned white as a sheet as we entered Stoller's office. We weren't prepared to play these songs for Mike Stoller! Leiber was like a buddy, but Stoller was your toughest college professor.

The first song was called "I Found My Boy." We had rehearsed with both of us singing together, but halfway through playing it for Stoller, Kenny stopped singing, leaving me hung out to dry. Looking back, I can't say that I blamed him. I felt like dropping out myself. Upon concluding the song, I looked at Mike for a response. He didn't say a word, just shrugged his shoulders, with this baffled look on his face as if to say, "I can't find words to describe how mediocre that was. Therefore, no comment."

We moved on to the second song, "Memories," and Kenny dropped out again. It elicited the same response from Stoller. We wisely decided to eliminate the third song and thanked the man for his time.

Though I was crestfallen, I was determined to learn from the experience. I clung to one of the main credos in my life, "If at first you don't succeed, try, try again." Kenny and I went back to the drawing board that very night. Ironically, over the years, I became close friends with both Jerry and Mike, and we'd get a good laugh when I repeated the story every now and then, especially when I mimicked that look on Mike's face.

* * *

A few days after our meeting with Stoller, on a crisp March Sunday morning, I reached for the Arts and Leisure section of the *New York Times*. As I opened to the first inside page, I almost freaked out at what I saw, a DOUBLE PAGE ad that read:

> *RICHARD RODGERS is proud to announce the opening of THE NEW YORK STATE THEATER at LINCOLN CENTER debuting with a limited six-week production:*
>
> *KISMET starring ALFRED DRAKE and nearly all of the original cast*
>
> *Produced by RICHARD RODGERS*

I could not believe it! Not only was I going to realize my longtime fantasy of seeing my idol, Alfred Drake, perform in this musical, but I would have a very real opportunity to actually be in the show! What could be more perfect!! I waited to hear more about the auditions, and when they were announced a few months later, I was ready. I felt confident in my performance skills and thought I would absolutely be selected for the show—there was no doubt in my mind that this would be my first Broadway break. I felt that this was blessed with divine intervention. It was meant to be!

During this time, Kenny and I continued writing, and one day he asked me if a friend of his could come over and hang out while we worked. His friend's name was Gary Katz, and he introduced himself as an insurance salesman with a dream to be in the record business. He ended up coming over every night after that and sitting on my living room couch reading *Billboard* and *Cashbox*. After about ten days of watching us work, he approached me. "I want to start an independent production company, and I want you to be my partner."

I was flattered to be his choice of business partner, but I didn't feel prepared to start a company. On top of that, I was not ready to give up on my dream to be on Broadway just yet. I tried to let him down easy and blamed my financial situation. "I'd love to, but I don't have any money," I told him.

He persisted. "That's OK—I have the money, but I don't have any talent." He was confident that we would be successful.

Shortly after that conversation, Gary raised $10,000, which in those days was quite substantial. Gary seemed determined to show me that this was a real business opportunity. The money he'd raised would give us the backing to set up a first-class recording session with the best of everything: arranger, engineer, studio, and musicians. Gary's approach to the business was very unusual. He wanted to open up an office in the 1650 Broadway Building right away. Normally, you would work "off the street" for years, or until you had an armful of hits under your belt. Then and only then would you make the bold move of opening an office. His strategy was completely the opposite! But it was his money, and I would have an office with *my name* and the name of *my company* on the door—among the same doors that I had spent years pounding on, making the rounds, looking for my big break. Now I would be sitting behind one of those doors, building my own company. People would be knocking on *my* door! This was just too good to be true—it was a totally intoxicating feeling! Other tenants in the building would walk by our office and say, "Who the fuck are these guys?"

In the midst of my nirvana, I suddenly realized that I was going to have to make a life-changing decision: roll the dice with this risky business opportunity, or continue to try and make it as a musical theater star. It didn't take long to make my decision—the risky one! I felt genuinely confident that I could be successful on whichever path I chose. However, were it not for this unique opportunity, I seriously doubt that I would have thought of embarking on a career as a record producer. Back in 1965, it was much more difficult to put the necessary elements together to actually make a record, much less have it become a hit.

About two weeks later, after Gary and I signed the papers that officially made us business partners, we headed straight to 1650 Broadway and selected a four-room suite of offices—one for each of us, a rehearsal room with a rented upright piano and a tape recorder that I brought from home, and a reception area that we hoped would soon hold many up-and-coming singer/songwriter stars. Our doors opened on June 21, 1965; I had just turned twenty-three. We called the company CLOUD NINE PRODUCTIONS, which certainly evoked the blissful state I was in.

This was a surreal experience. I could not believe what was happening to me. Cloud Nine quickly became a beehive of activity. In those days, there was a stream of talent making the rounds of the record and publishing companies, just as I had done for years not too long before this. Our publishing company was Youngblood Music, Inc. I immediately began to prepare for my first real session.

I knew who I wanted on my creative team: arranger Artie Butler, who did the charts for many of the hits on Red Bird, and engineer Brooks Arthur, the most in-demand engineer in New York. I knew which musicians I wanted as well. We'd hold the session at Mirasound Studios, the hottest studio in New York. It was located in the back of a "hooker hotel," called the Hotel America, on West 47th between 6th and 7th.

The only thing I was lacking was a great song. The search was proving difficult since the best publishers weren't eager to give their best material to an unknown producer. I had to prove myself first. My only option was to find a collaborator so we could write the songs ourselves.

One day, a writer from Harlem named Melvin Edwards walked into my office and asked if we needed a collaborator. It was as if the stars aligned. We immediately started working together. After a week of writing every day, we came up with a gem! It was called "I Feel in My Heart (That I'm Falling in Love)." The artists I chose were a sultry female lead singer and four guys singing background. I called them The Cherries.

At long last, the day of the session arrived, and I was beyond excited. Kenny was a silent partner in Cloud Nine—after all, he'd put me together with Gary. He was in our office every day when he wasn't on the road with Jay and the Americans, and the only person I wanted by my side. He was 'my man.' As Kenny walked with me to the studio that day, I turned to him and said, "Now, Ken, tell me one more time, what exactly does this 'four track' mean? Do you actually have FOUR separate tracks?"

My musical background made up for my lack of technical knowledge. It gave me the confidence to communicate with this all-star group of musicians, and I was able to tell them quite specifically what and how I wanted them to play. My many years of drumming paid off, too—much of my musical direction was focused on the drummer, Gary Chester, and making sure his sound was just right.

The session was a triumph! The song started out like classic R&B then went into a Latin jam. I felt I had done something special.

The Cloud Nine office happened to be located right next door to one of the hottest production companies at the time, Kama Sutra Productions, which had just started its own label, debuting with the highly respected band, The Lovin' Spoonful. They brilliantly delved into R&B, country, folk, and pop, led by the exceptional songwriting and musicianship of John Sebastian. Kama Sutra had three partners, but the one who ran the company was a colorful, Damon Runyon-esque Broadway character. His name was Artie Ripp. Even though I had not quite finished the record, my partner Gary, played it for Artie without telling me. Artie flipped! After he played it for his partners, the three of them marched into my office. I was surprised to see them all standing in front of me and immediately assumed something was wrong. I asked them if everything was OK.

Artie was full of energy—he couldn't stand still and practically shouted at me, "We just heard your record, and we think it's a hit!! We want to buy it! From now on, anytime you want to go in the studio again, it doesn't matter who the artist is, or what song it is, you're covered!"

I could not have asked for a better response. Just a few weeks after starting our own business, we had been given carte blanche to make any record we wanted. If I needed any further confirmation that I had made the right decision, this was it! Looking back, if I hadn't taken that motorcycle ride four months earlier and had the confidence to approach a woman just based on an attraction to the back of her head, my life would have probably turned out very differently. This was just the beginning of my career as a record producer.

About a week later, I was in my office when suddenly a woman barged in. She was a striking dark-haired beauty who pointed a finger at me and spoke in a very precise, authoritative manner.

"You are a smash!" That was all she said. I was caught off guard but quickly realized her reaction was not meant to be startling. It was her way of congratulating me on the record I had just produced, which gave me a total rush. There's nothing quite like getting complimented on your work, especially when the compliment comes from a beautiful girl you don't even know. She exuded an air of confidence that I found instantly attractive.

She went on to tell me that she ran the Kama Sutra office next door and had just come back from doing some PR in Los Angeles. While there,

Linda Goldner

she had heard my record for the first time and apparently had decided she needed to meet me as soon as she was back in New York. She couldn't believe that the new kid in the office next door had not only produced this record but co-written the song as well! Her name was Linda Goldner, and she was the daughter of George Goldner. Naturally, my first thought was to ask her for a date, as she was the most attractive girl I had ever seen. I was mesmerized! She had beauty, brains, knew the business inside out, and had a great ear for music. There was just one problem: Word on the street was that if anyone in the business tried to ask her out, her father would make sure they never got to a second date! I decided that I wouldn't let that little threat stand in my way, so we made plans to have dinner and see *The Sound of Music* the following night.

We went to Jack Dempsey's restaurant, a popular industry hangout located on the ground floor of the Brill Building. I've always been attracted to a girl with an appetite, so when Linda proceeded to order five courses—shrimp cocktail, Caesar salad, roast prime rib with creamed spinach, baked potato, and apple tart—it blew my mind. By the time we finished dinner, I was totally smitten! Soon we became inseparable, and it was clear that she had to arrange a dinner for her father, George, and me to meet. I felt very confident about meeting him. How could he object to a nice Jewish boy with a college degree? What's more, I was sure that when he heard my record, he would see that I had talent!

As expected, George immediately gave his approval and a great friendship was born. It didn't take long for me to learn every detail of his history in the record business as both a producer and promoter without peer. He'd begun by bringing Latin music, later to be known as salsa, into the popular culture of America, by founding a label solely for these artists: Tico Records. Formed in 1948, Tico quickly became home to the biggest Latin bands of the day—Tito Puente, Joe Loco, Tito Rodriguez, Machito, among many others. Four years later, he presented the Tico All-Stars at Carnegie Hall.

He later became one of the true pioneers in the birth of rock 'n' roll with "Gee" by The Crows, widely regarded as the first R&B record to cross over to the pop charts; The Cleftones then had a major hit with "Little Girl of Mine"; and most importantly, George produced Frankie Lymon and the Teenagers' international mega-hit, "Why Do Fools Fall in Love?" Only thirteen at the time, Frankie must have been an inspiration to Michael Jackson, for they both had prodigious talent at a very young age.

George's next labels were called Gone and End Records. Some of the classic hits from these labels were "I Only Have Eyes for You" and "Lovers Never Say Goodbye" by The Flamingos; "Tears on My Pillow" by Little Anthony and the Imperials; "Maybe" by The Chantels, featuring the towering female voice of the '50s, Arlene Smith; and, perhaps my favorite doo-wop oldie of all time, "Could This Be Magic?" by The Dubs.

It seemed that everything George touched turned to gold, but he did have one problem, or should I say addiction—he was a compulsive gambler. After a down period, he would turn to Morris Levy to raise the money to pay off his gambling debts in return for the assets of his hugely successful companies. The acquisition of these assets formed the foundation of Morris' recording and publishing empire in the years to come. George always seemed to bounce back, start another label, and come up with a slew of new hits. Except his luck took a downturn once again, and in 1962, he had to join forces with Morris at Roulette Records, a label they had formed together several years earlier. While at Roulette, George did produce a No. 1 record with "Easier Said Than Done" by The Essex, but he had always been his own boss and really couldn't stomach working for Morris.

Jerry Leiber and Mike Stoller, who, in spite of their legendary success, had never been able to get their own label off the ground, offered George a partnership in a new company they were about to launch: Red Bird Records. The first release, which was handpicked by George, was titled "Chapel of Love," and went straight to No. 1. George was back on top of the world again! Meanwhile, Linda was so proud of her father, and she and I were falling in love.

I proceeded to make several records for Kama Sutra. By now, I had formed great relationships with many of the top publishers, so I was able to hear many songs first. One in particular was brought to me by my good friend of twenty years, Ed Silvers. It was called "I Want a Guarantee" and was the first recorded song written by the legendary team of Nick Ashford and Valerie Simpson. I thought it was a home run, and the artist I chose for it was a little dynamo of a singer named Sandy Jackson. But problems began to develop with Kama Sutra. They were such a hot company that they started to become greedy.

One day I got a call from Ahmet Ertegun who wanted me to meet with him and Jerry Wexler at their Atlantic Records office at West 58th Street.

They told me they loved "I Want a Guarantee," and wanted to buy it, but Kama Sutra insisted on not a penny less than twice the recording costs, and as a consequence, the record never came out! It was hard to believe that Ahmet Ertegun and Jerry Wexler, two of the most revered names in the music industry, wanted MY record, and Kama Sutra wouldn't make the deal! My first record, "I Feel in My Heart," never got released either. (That was the one Artie Ripp and his partners had flipped over in the first place.) This was the worst thing that could happen to a young, emerging record producer—the first of many disappointments that I encountered as I navigated my way through the business in the years to come. At least I was developing a reputation on the street for making good records!

* * *

One day, Kenny Vance came into the office with the strangest person I had ever seen—TINY TIM. He had long, unkempt, curly hair that looked bizarre even in the era of long hair. He wore white clown makeup on his face, with a slight touch of rouge on his cheeks. Reaching into his shopping bag to pull out a ukulele, he proceeded to sing songs from the '20s through the '60s in a variety of voices, ranging from what would become his trademark falsetto, to Bing Crosby, Cab Calloway, Al Jolson, country-western, Bob Dylan, and numerous others. He blew me away, and I immediately lunged for the tape recorder to capture some of his unique sound. I soon found out that he had been thrown out of virtually every record company. Little did I know that in two years, I would make music history with this strange person.

Chapter 6

A Sharp Left Turn

A few months later, as my relationship with Kama Sutra continued to deteriorate, George Goldner called me and said that we needed to have a very important conversation. George informed me that Sonny Franzese, a well-known Mafia boss in the Colombo crime family, owned a piece of Kama Sutra. Apparently, at some time prior, Kama Sutra had been in desperate need of a financial infusion so they'd borrowed money from the people you never want to go to for this kind of help. Now Franzese was flexing his Mafia muscle.

George let me know that Sonny was about to step in and take over Kama Sutra and advised that I remove myself from Cloud Nine in order to eliminate any Mafia association. Even before I had heard this news from George, I had been getting increasingly irritated with the failure of Kama Sutra to release what I felt were very strong records. The carte blanche they'd so generously offered just months before had come back to haunt me. Instead of an exclusive relationship, I wanted to be free to do business with any company that was willing and eager to release my records. The meeting with Ahmet and Jerry Wexler had definitely taught me a lesson.

When I shared my feelings with Gary, we had a marked difference of opinion. He liked the exclusive relationship with Kama Sutra, primarily because his wife had just had a baby, and he welcomed the security that Kama Sutra offered—regardless of its source. In the end, I decided to leave

Cloud Nine and all its assets to Gary and start a new company with Linda. We called it Dynamite Productions.

* * *

With that, I was back at square one. Now that things looked differently, I wondered whether I had chosen the right road after all. I did, however, make a few production deals—one with the legendary songwriter-producer, Bert Berns. "Piece of My Heart," "Twist and Shout," "Cry Baby," "Hang on Sloopy," and "Here Comes the Night" were just a few songs that Bert co-wrote. He had recently started a new label, Bang Records, and the first artists he signed were Van Morrison ("Brown Eyed Girl") and Neil Diamond ("Solitary Man"). I produced The Harptones for Bang, a well-known group from the doo-wop era.

Later on, I found a young girl group, Young Generation, and put out a single, "The Hideaway," on Red Bird. One of the background singers was a cute little twelve-year-old named Janis Siegel. Janis grew up to be a very talented singer. One night many years later, I found myself at the Roxy, a popular Los Angeles club. I was there to see The Manhattan Transfer make their West Coast debut—I had heard from several friends that this group was right up my alley, so I was looking forward to the show.

I was truly impressed with the group, particularly with the primary female singer, who possessed one of the most soulful voices I'd heard in a long time. She brought the house down with a gospel classic, "Operator." I had purchased their album earlier that day but hadn't had a chance to look at it before going to their show. After the performance, as soon as I arrived home, I opened up the album, wanting to play it right away. On the front cover was a pen-and-ink drawing of the group, in a style similar to Al Hirschfeld's, the artist who did a lot of the *Playbill* booklets for Broadway shows. When I turned the album over, there was a funky sepia photo of the group in front of a thrift shop. I looked at that picture very carefully, and suddenly it hit me—the girl in the picture, who I had just seen perform an entire show, was none other than…Janis fucking Siegel!

I couldn't believe her growth, and above all, the transformation of her voice. In 1976, I wound up producing Manhattan Transfer's second album, *Coming Out*. My two favorite tracks are "Chanson D'Amour," where Janis channels Édith Piaf, and "Speak Up Mambo," sung entirely in Spanish and originally made famous by Al Castellanos and His Orchestra.

Linda and I grew Dynamite Productions as best we could, but it was off to a slow start. I continued to meet with Tiny Tim, and we went over his encyclopedic knowledge of songs. I got to know him quite well and decided to do three tracks with him, just for fun. With a small loan from my parents, I cut the tracks, and to keep my budget down, I played all the instruments, as Linda provided A&R support in the control room. To help us out, her father, George, put out a single, "April Showers," on Red Bird. It wasn't the time for Tiny Tim's star to appear in the firmament, but these little records I made with him would play an unexpectedly vital role in my future.

After a while, it became increasingly difficult to keep afloat financially, so I began to look for a job. Very few record companies at the time were looking for staff producers, but fortunately, Artie Ripp always knew how great my potential was. It's just a shame that we couldn't get on the same page, because we could have made hits together from day one. Artie's heart was in the right place, but he would sometimes pile a little too much on his plate and his priorities would get screwed up. However, after all was said and done, he came through for me—big time! So, it was with mixed emotions that I accepted his offer as a staff producer-writer for Kama Sutra. The truth is, I didn't have a lot of options, and it was the first paycheck I'd ever receive.

The company was collecting writer-producers and had a staff of about ten. They were all very talented, and while there was a strong sense of camaraderie among us, in the end, we were all competing against one another for a chance to get our product heard.

I had become a huge fan of Johnny Cash and found that I could sound a bit like him on such classics as "I Walk the Line," "Ring of Fire," and "Folsom Prison Blues." Since quality artists were hard to find, one of the records I produced during that time featured me doing my "Jewish Johnny Cash" on a song I'd written with my writing partner at the time, Thomas Jefferson Kaye. It was called "Have You Seen My Little Sue?"

During this period, I got my first apartment in Manhattan, on West 56th Street between Eighth and Ninth Avenue. This was a significant event in my life. Linda moved in with me, and George gave us a black fur couch from his Red Bird office since the company had recently folded. We hung out most of the time with another Kama Sutra writer-producer, Tony Bruno, and his girlfriend Helena, who had an apartment in the same building. Tony was famous for his gravelly, soulful voice. He had a special talent for sitting down at a piano and making up a song right on the spot, captivating the publisher with his voice and performance, and walking out with a quick hundred bucks. One of the songs that Tony and I collaborated on was entitled, "I Gave You Head in Bed." It had a very soulful feel in the verses and built up to a powerful chorus. Tony's interpretation was priceless.

Linda and I began to have our ups and downs and, while we loved each other, the negatives started to outweigh the positives. She temporarily moved to LA, which left me in a state of total depression for one of the few times in my life. I tried to concentrate on work, but that, too, was going nowhere. It was at this time that I was introduced to marijuana, which I found to be stimulating yet very comforting. Pot is not a drug for everyone, but it fit me like a glove. Some people, myself included, find that it gives them an expanded creative headspace. Music and marijuana just seem to be homogeneous. I once had a palm-reading by a French psychic who said my palm was like that of an old Native American man who smoked the pipe every day.

Although Linda had an impressive job wxorking for Bob Rafelson and Bert Schneider, the producers of *The Monkees* TV show, she was missing me too, and as we talked on the phone one Saturday afternoon, on the spur of the moment, she decided to take the next plane to New York.

It certainly helped to have Linda by my side, but New York was starting to feel very claustrophobic to me. I yearned to experience the magic of LA, and my instincts told me that my career would flourish in that environment.

When it was announced that Kama Sutra was opening a West Coast office and needed an A&R presence there, the timing could not have been more perfect for me. Of course, all of the other writer-producers wanted to be the chosen one.

We soon found out that Bob Krasnow was going to head up the LA office for Kama Sutra. Krasnow was a legendary record man through and through, with an extensive history in all facets of the business, including a long relationship with George Goldner, and subsequently, with Linda. While they were finding the right location for the office in LA, Krasnow made several visits to New York, and we would all get high and listen to music together. He and I soon developed a close friendship and this, incidentally, put me in the driver's seat for the LA position. However, because I wanted it so much, I was wracked with anxiety and doubted that it would ever happen. Finally, one night, the phone rang, and Artie Ripp's deep voice resonated as he said the words I'd been longing to hear: "Be at JFK tomorrow morning at ten. We're going to LA."

It was the happiest moment of my life!

To go to LA with a job, a cool office, and Bob Krasnow, the best luminary to guide me, was all I could have asked for. Could this be Cloud Nine a second time around?

Chapter 7

The Summer of Love

As it turned out, my life took a major step forward with the move to Los Angeles in March 1967. I couldn't have asked for a better time to be there. Three months later it became known as the "Summer of Love." The Age of Aquarius was truly dawning, and psychedelia was in full Technicolor-lava-lamp bloom. Nearly every weekend there were love-ins held at Griffith Park, Elysian Park, and similar venues throughout the city where hundreds of hippies would gather to indulge in a variety of drugs and free love. Billboards advertising various albums lined the Sunset Strip, and the Whisky a Go Go would feature The Doors, Smokey and the Miracles, Led Zeppelin, and Martha and the Vandellas. Rock and R&B acts co-existed

in the same clubs on successive nights and the streets were alive, vibrating with the sound of music.

One of the things that really struck me was how the city was laid out. Compared to the flat roads of New York City, the streets of Los Angeles took you up into the Hollywood Hills above Sunset Boulevard. It was like driving into the clouds! I'd never seen anything like it before, but that was nothing compared to the views from those hillside houses that looked down at the vast expanse of Los Angeles. I got lucky and found a cozy guesthouse off of Sunset Plaza Drive, about a mile above Sunset, with my own private view of the city below.

Driving down Sunset to the office each morning was a phenomenal high. I kept thinking I was in a dream. Kama Sutra had secured offices on the ground floor of the Original Sound Records building on Sunset and La Brea, right around the block from the A&M Records complex on the original Charlie

Whisky a Go Go (Sunset Boulevard)

Chaplin Studios lot. At the time, it was one of the hottest locations in the city. The office was cool, complete with 1967 shag carpeting and wood paneling.

I started hanging out with a guy named Jim DeMarco, who was well-connected and knew what was happening around town. He told me about a club called the Hullabaloo. It was located on Sunset, across from the Hollywood Palladium, and held about five hundred people. The place had headline acts Thursday through Saturday, ranging from Wilson Pickett to Eric Burdon and The Animals appearing. But the real treat was Friday night—about ten groups would appear from midnight 'til dawn! The club had a revolving stage, so while one band was on, another would be setting up backstage, behind the curtain. When the first group finished, the stage would swivel around and the next group was ready to play. Each act would play a thirty-minute set, and the transitions between bands only took a few minutes. In the course of six hours, I saw Buffalo Springfield with Neil Young performing "Mr. Soul"; Stephen Stills doing "Bluebird"; and Love, a popular LA band led by Arthur Lee who'd had a big hit with a great but little-known Burt Bacharach song, "My Little Red Book." I also saw The Doors, The Byrds and many others.

After a few hours, DeMarco suggested that we go out to his car and smoke a joint. As we were walking to the car, he introduced me to Humble Harve, who happened to be the hottest DJ on KHJ, the number one Top 40 LA station. Soon, there I was, getting high with Humble Harve in the back seat of DeMarco's car while we were at this outrageous concert until the early hours of the morning! All I could think was, *What a great fucking city! How did I get so lucky to wind up here?*

We stumbled out at 6:00 a.m. The sun was just coming up, my whole body and mind were humming, and I felt as if I'd just been on the world's best acid trip. A few years later, Humble Harve went from the king of radio to a life sentence in prison for murdering his wife—the darkness beneath the rainbow.

The next day, Krasnow informed me that A&M Records had just let go of one of their artists he thought might be an interesting first act for us: Captain Beefheart and His Magic Band. I told DeMarco that I was interested in meeting Beefheart. One night, while we were walking into Canter's—the best deli in the city and a popular late-night hangout frequented by Phil Spector—DeMarco whispered to me that the guy who was coming toward us was none other than Beefheart. I approached him.

"Captain Beefheart, I presume? My name is Richard Perry, and I've been looking for you."

He surprised me by responding, "Richard Perry! I've been looking for you too."

How the hell had he heard of me? I had only been in LA for a couple of months. No matter, the important thing was that we crossed paths in the most literal sense, and the next day, I arranged for him to come to the office with the band to meet Bob Krasnow.

Captain Beefheart, a.k.a Don Van Vliet, hailed from Lancaster, in the California desert. The three band members were like family to Don. They dressed for dinner every night as if they were going to church. They had all recently moved into a funky house in Laurel Canyon. Everyone, from Joni Mitchell to Frank Zappa, to the future governor of California, Jerry Brown, lived in Laurel Canyon at some point during the '60s and early '70s. It just seemed like the place to be. In fact, in 1969, I found a little dream cottage on Wonderland Park Avenue, in the heart of Laurel Canyon. As I got to know the band, they shared some secrets about Beefheart. An odd one was that he apparently had the ability to change channels on the TV without the aid of a remote control. They swore it was true!

We took the band into the studio to do some demos and were blown away by their potential. Don had a little surprise for us that took the band to another level. He had just welcomed another guitar player into the group, a seventeen-year-old prodigy who was one of the most gifted musicians I'd ever heard—a true genius. His name was Ry Cooder. He went on to have a spectacular career that has spanned decades.

After a few weeks of rehearsals, we started recording what was going to be my first album as well as Beefheart's. He came up with an inspired title: *Safe as Milk*. His voice was uniquely expressive, heavily influenced by the blues greats, particularly Howlin' Wolf. There was a great deal of variety in the material, incorporating rock, R&B, jazz, African rhythms, and funky blues, usually with Ry Cooder playing the best bottleneck guitar you've ever heard. Every track had its own personality. Some guest musicians were Taj Mahal on washboard, Milt Holland, a world-renowned percussionist, and Dr. Samuel Hoffman on theremin. (This is a long, phallic-looking electronic instrument that is controlled without any physical contact from the player, most popularly used by The Beach Boys in their masterwork, "Good Vibrations." It changes sounds as the player's hands move around it, and at the time, there were very few on the planet.) We were all infused by the magic of the "magic band."

About one month later, we were deep into the recording when Krasnow walked into the studio with an album under his arm—*Sgt. Pepper's Lonely Hearts Club Band*. It had just come out. After the session, we all crammed into a mixing room the size of a closet with two large studio monitors and listened to the album. My life changed that day. Literally, every radio station was playing the record, all different tracks. Each one was a life-altering experience! I must have listened to that album a few hundred times during the first month of its release.

Safe as Milk was well-liked by the critics and got some meaningful airplay but failed to capture a wide enough audience to be a major hit. Nevertheless, some fifty years later, I get as much positive feedback on that record as anything I've ever done. Langdon Winner, a contributing editor of *Rolling Stone*, called it a "rock masterpiece" and each track "a finely polished gem." I think it's important to mention that this album is a world apart from anything that Beefheart became known for in the ensuing years.

* * *

After I had been in LA for about two months, Linda came out to visit me. Our relationship had been characterized by its many ups and downs, but this visit was nothing but up. The idea of living together in LA held a great deal of excitement and appeal. Since I had to go to New York the following week for the bar mitzvah of my youngest brother Andrew, Linda and I figured, why not just stay an extra week and get married? I thought it highly unlikely that I would meet someone who was beautiful, knew the business, was a great helpmate, and supportive of my work. Always the optimist, I felt I could handle Linda's down times. So, on June 15, 1967, Linda Goldner became Linda Perry.

We spent our honeymoon at the Monterey International Pop Festival. What a honeymoon! Krasnow made sure that we had good seats for every afternoon and evening performance. The whole city had been buzzing about Monterey Pop for months—a giant billboard on Sunset broadcast all the acts that were set to appear. There had never been an assemblage of artists like it before. In addition, the Monterey fairgrounds were the most idyllic setting for a music festival, having been the home of the Monterey Jazz Festival for years, with a seating capacity of only seven thousand.

The festival has come to be remembered mainly as the first time anyone had ever seen Janis Joplin, Jimi Hendrix, and The Who, but every other major band was also on the bill, including Simon & Garfunkel, The Mamas and the Papas, and the artist that, in my opinion, was the highlight of the entire festival: Otis Redding!

At the Saturday night concert, the reigning rock band, Jefferson Airplane, presented a moving set, ending with their major No. 1 hit, "Somebody to

Love." They were also basking in their current No. 1, a song that had become the anthem of the psychedelic revolution, the acid-laced, "White Rabbit." Both songs featured the voice of the rock goddess, Grace Slick. After the Airplane's performance, the evening was over for many in the audience. Since Otis Redding was largely unknown to this mainly psychedelic, hippie crowd, people began streaming for the exit, much to my disbelief and delight.

As Linda and I immediately moved up and got seats in the third row, a four-piece band was introduced. They were Booker T. & The M.G.'s—half black, half white, and very straight looking. The members of this band were the architects of the world famous Stax/Volt Memphis sound, featuring four legendary musicians: Booker T. Jones (organ), Steve Cropper (guitar), Al

Monterey Pop.

Monterey Pop ticket stub.

Jackson Jr. (drums), and Donald "Duck" Dunn (bass). The band performed two of their instrumental hits, "Green Onions" and "Hang 'Em High," played with precision funk. Two horn players then joined the group, and without any great fanfare, one of the band members announced, "Now we'd like to introduce our good friend, Otis Redding."

The six musicians comprising Booker T. & The M.G.'s and The Memphis Horns became Otis Redding's band—that was it. This was dramatically different from the usual fourteen-piece, big band aggregations used by most black singers at the time.

Wearing an emerald-green suit, Otis hit the stage as if he'd been shot from a cannon! He started off with Sam Cooke's "Shake" followed by "Respect." Aretha Franklin had recently done a brilliant cover of this Otis classic, but her version was very different and happened to be the No. 1 record that week. I'll always remember the way Otis introduced it: "And now I'd like to do a song I wrote, that a girl just took away from me."

Otis Redding on stage.

It was thrilling to hear him launch into his version with the horns powering through the arrangement, whereas Aretha's version is best remembered for its creative, acrobatic background vocal licks. Otis' next number was perhaps his greatest, most heart-rending song, the immortal, "I've Been Loving You Too Long."

One of the most noteworthy aspects of Otis' artistry was that even though he was recognized as a brilliant songwriter, he also had an extraordinary ability to interpret other well-known songs. No matter how closely associated they might be to the original artists, Otis would always bring a breath of fresh air to the work, a gift that Aretha also possessed. In point of fact, his next song that night was a mind-blowing version of The Stones' "Satisfaction" that, truth be told, I like even more than the original. He concluded his set with a cover from the Great American Songbook that is probably most famously associated with him, his stirringly unique interpretation of "Try a Little Tenderness."

Many people in the audience had never heard of Otis when he appeared that night. He was not part of the psychedelic movement or the counter-culture revolution, and his huge pop breakout, "(Sittin' On) The Dock of the Bay," which would become a massive No. 1 record all over the world, hadn't been heard yet. The song was based on his experience at Monterey Pop and the Bay area.

Otis Redding was the greatest soul singer of our generation, and he could lift your spirit and exude joyfulness even as he was making your heart break. He was at his peak of popularity when he tragically died in the crash of a private plane six months after Monterey Pop. One can only imagine how bright his star might have shone had he lived. His performance at Monterey Pop was widely considered to be the high point of his career, and in my opinion, one of the greatest live performances I have ever seen.

I bet not many people can say they spent their honeymoon at one of the largest music festivals to happen in the '60s. Linda and I basked in the glory of it for a while, but eventually, it was time to get back to work.

Chapter 8

The Warner Years

After our honeymoon, Linda got a job in A&R with Liberty Records and I was in the RCA recording studios finishing the Beefheart album, *Safe as Milk*. Kama Sutra started a second label, Buddah Records, and this album was meant to be its premier release at the end of July '67. Shortly after the record came out, they decided to move the combined labels back to New York. With this move, they unexpectedly closed the LA office, and I was suddenly out of a job.

The next two-and-a-half months went down as the most depressing time of my life. The only "job" I had was to drive Linda to work every morning. Beyond that, I had no idea how to spend the hours of each day. I was out of work and out of ideas. I did get one break when Linda's father, George, introduced me to his friend, Russ Regan, president of Uni Records (a subsidiary of MCA Music) at the time. After meeting with Russ, he agreed to let me produce a couple of singles with an artist I'd found in San Francisco. Unfortunately though, the artist was on acid almost all day and night, which made making a good record very difficult. To add to this, Linda and I were running out of money, so we had to give up our house and move into a depressing little rundown apartment. It had cottage-cheese ceilings, muted gray floors and furniture, and the view looked right into other buildings. It was a total disaster. I continued to look for new artists to sign, but they weren't exactly falling from the trees, and even if I found one, it was a challenge to get him or her to believe in me—I had no money or company support. Believe me, times were tough.

One day, Bob Krasnow suggested that we take a ride out to Warner Brothers in Burbank and say hello to Lenny Waronker. He was a prominent staff producer with the company. This meeting would prove to be a fortuitous event in my career. At the time, Lenny was producing Randy Newman, Ry Cooder, Van Dyke Parks, and Harper's Bazaar's very successful cover of the Simon & Garfunkel classic, "Feelin' Groovy." Under Mo Ostin's and Joe Smith's leadership, Warner Brothers was the only company that gave their staff producers creative freedom. Lenny was a fine producer, an excellent craftsman, and a genuinely nice guy.

I was desperate to catch a break. I knew I needed to call on somebody for a favor, but that wasn't an easy decision to make; I've always had an aversion to asking for something, especially from someone I hardly know. But if I was going to survive in Los Angeles, I had to do it. So, I swallowed my pride and called Lenny.

This was my last resort and I hoped that our mutual connection to Bob Krasnow would make my request easier to consider. I came out with it as quickly as possible and asked if he would arrange an appointment for me to see Joe Smith or Mo Ostin, heads of Warner Brothers and Reprise Records, respectively. It took a lot of *chutzpah* to ask such a favor; Lenny knew that I had produced the Beefheart album, but he'd never heard anything else I'd done. Warner Brothers and Reprise Records were sister labels under the same corporate umbrella, and it was one of the very few companies with a small, elite group of staff producers. Working there was the "dream job" for someone in my position, and when Lenny called me back to say that I had an appointment with Joe Smith, I was ecstatic! Needless to say, I am forever grateful to Lenny for this ultimate "solid."

I arrived at Joe Smith's office a week later with a stack of records I had produced over the past two-and-a-half years, including the three tracks with Tiny Tim. As soon as he heard them, Joe said that Warner Brothers had just signed Tiny Tim!

It turned out that Mo Ostin had been in New York to sign Jimi Hendrix, who was playing at a hot club called The Scene, and Tiny Tim happened to be the opening act that night. Bathing in his euphoria over Hendrix, and in an act of gut instinct, Mo had thrown caution to the wind and signed Tiny Tim! I had heard that Peter Yarrow of Peter, Paul and Mary—one of Warner Brother's flagship artists—was a big fan and supporter of Tiny, so I asked Joe if Peter was going to produce him. Joe then uttered the words that marked the true beginning of my career:

"No, Peter is not producing Tiny Tim. As a matter of fact, we're looking for the right person to produce him."

At that moment, I knew that even if the Warner Brothers position somehow didn't materialize, I would have the opportunity to make the album I'd wanted to make for years—with Tiny Tim! Moreover, I knew that I had the support from one of the upper-echelon companies, and that meant I would have a real budget!

Two days later, I got the call from Warner Brothers asking me if I could start the following Monday. That had to go down as the new happiest moment of my life. I knew that having an office and a staff producer position at Warner Brothers would finally allow me to fulfill my real potential.

As soon as I arrived on Monday morning, the vice president of business affairs asked me into his office to work out my salary. He offered me $300 per week for the first year, with an increase of $100 per week for the second and third year. I suggested that we just go with the first year and evaluate any raises based on my performance—I was that confident in my ability!

Once I started at Warner Brothers, I couldn't wait to go to work each day! Now, every publisher in town would call to try to make an appointment to bring me their best songs. I had the power to sign new artists, such as Seals & Crofts in a band called Uncle Sound, and Paul Williams, who had a group known as The Holy Mackerel. Mo Ostin and Joe Smith literally became like family to me, and Mo's wife, Evelyn, was a second mother to all of us. Lenny Waronker and I continued a lasting friendship, along with my newfound British friend, Andy Wickham, who had the most progressive A&R ear and was never afraid to express his opinion. Being at Warner Brothers was a joy, and the previous two months of depression faded away like a distant memory. First up on my "to do" list with Warner Brothers: produce the album of my dreams with Tiny Tim.

Chapter 9

God Bless Tiny Tim

The Tiny Tim album was progressing beautifully. Warner Brothers put him up in the Sunset Marquis Hotel, and he lived there while we created the album. We were both excited to be on the precipice together. Two years had passed since we'd first met when Kenny Vance had walked him into my office at Cloud Nine in New York City. From then on, I had nurtured a dream to create a one-man show on record that would utilize all his different voices and bring them to life.

At first, Tiny only wanted to do songs that he embraced from the past, but I convinced him to mix some contemporary songs with the old chestnuts of which he had such a vast knowledge. His multitude of voices and styles included Cab Calloway, Al Jolson, Nelson Eddy/Jeanette MacDonald, Bing Crosby, and a surprisingly authentic country voice, allowing me to be more creative than I have been on any record I've ever produced.

I also supplemented the theatricality of the album by adding sound effects where appropriate. We started off by recording an old, little-known Bing Crosby song, "Welcome to My Dream." Tiny sings a cappella as he invites the listener to his dream, "Will you be here long? Or just passing through?" It's a lovely ballad, and there was no better way to begin the album.

I wanted listeners to close their eyes and feel as if they were floating in the clouds while Tiny serenaded them. His ukulele can be heard faintly in the distance and as the sound gets closer and closer, the Moog synthesizer I was using for the first time bathes Tiny's voice in an echo for the last few notes of his Crosby rendition, to create a dream-like sequence as he sings. His voice gets closer and closer, until he finally starts singing "Tiptoe Through the Tulips."

Up until this point, Tiny had been thrown out of almost every record company. He was certainly unconventional, but that's where I saw his potential. We took great liberties with this album, and Tiny even went so far as to record a personalized message to his listeners at the end of "Tiptoe

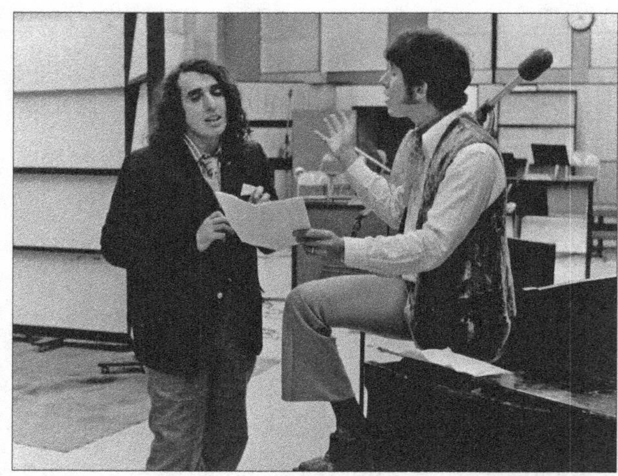

Tiny Tim and me in the studio.

Through the Tulips." This was something that wasn't really done at that time—a record was for songs and songs only! Yet, here Tiny was, speaking directly to his audience.

To see Tiny's album come to fruition was a beautiful thing, and I could tell that Tiny was immensely proud of and grateful for this experience. I was particularly proud of the comments made about the album by respected music critic, Alfred G. Aronowitz, in *Life* magazine:

> *God Bless Tiny Tim is one of the most dazzling albums of programmed entertainment to come along since the Beatles introduced the new genre into pop with Sgt. Pepper's Lonely Hearts Club Band. If Sgt. Pepper's was a wide- screen epic, then God Bless Tiny Tim is a full-length animated feature, with Tiny doing all the voices.*[1]

After two months of hard work, I felt as if I had given birth. Almost immediately, the record created quite a stir. Many people told me how much they enjoyed immersing themselves in the album while on LSD.

One Sunday, I drove Tiny out to a commune known as the Hog Farm, which was run by a pudgy, bushy-haired, clownish character known as Wavy Gravy. Tiny stood at the base of this very large rock and performed with his trusted ukulele for over an hour. About two hundred people, from Hell's Angels to hippies, sat in a circle, holding hands, heads slightly bowed as if in fervent prayer as Tiny cast his spell over them. Most people only knew him from his falsetto "Tiptoe" voice and had no idea that he had several serious sides.

More and more people were discovering the magic of *God Bless Tiny Tim*, including The Beatles, who were turned on to the album by Derek Taylor, their press officer and a trusted member of their inner circle. He was a supporter of Tiny Tim from the beginning and became a dear friend of mine for many years.

The album cover of God Bless Tiny Tim.

Meanwhile, Tiny was basking in his first taste of acceptance, and he held court nightly at the Sunset Marquis for his adoring female fans. One time, he insisted that I come right over to meet The GTOs, which stood for Girls Together Outrageously. It was a sight I'll never forget! The GTOs were a bizarre group of twelve girls assembled by Frank Zappa. Tiny took great pride in introducing me to each one of them. One thing to note: He NEVER called anyone by his or her first name. I was always Mr. Perry, and females were always Miss So-and-So. So, in presenting me to The GTOs, he introduced me as Mr. Perry and then offered the name of each girl, starting each introduction "Miss." This was the first time in his life that he was completely on his own, and he was thrilled and amazed to receive so many admiring female visitors.

One day soon after, Mo Ostin called to tell me that George Schlatter, a highly prominent and successful TV producer, was putting the final touches on an exciting new NBC comedy show that was about to debut in a matter of weeks. George had heard the album and asked to meet Tiny as soon as possible. He wanted to size him up and see if he would be a good fit as a featured guest for the show, which was to be called *Laugh-In*. As I walked with Tiny into the office, the entire production team greeted us, including the hosts—the well-known comedy team of Rowan and Martin. When Tiny took the ukulele out of his shopping bag and started singing, I watched a room full of grown men on their knees, laughing so hard, they were crying. Even though I had seen him do this countless times, the reaction of the room was so infectious, I started crying, too.

When Tiny Tim made his first appearance on *Laugh-In*, the audience took to him right away; he soon became a regular guest, appearing almost every week. It was the perfect showcase for him to be introduced to the American public without them thinking he was a bizarre freak. *Laugh-In* became one of the most groundbreaking shows in the history of television and enjoyed a lengthy run. It helped launch the careers of Goldie Hawn and Lily Tomlin, and even included an appearance by former president Richard Nixon bellowing out the show's thematic slogan, "Sock it to me!"

Once the buzz on Tiny had reached considerable proportions, Johnny Carson became intrigued and decided to give him a shot on *The Tonight Show*. Carson treated Tiny differently—he took him seriously and let him sing "As Time Goes By" in the romantic voice of Bing Crosby along with his familiar falsetto of "Tiptoe." This was the ultimate coup—going from being spat on and laughed at in the streets of New York to becoming a favorite guest of Johnny Carson!

After a few months of working together, Tiny made plans to travel back to New York to visit his parents, and he asked me to come along. They lived in the same apartment he had shared with them for over forty years. Frayed and slightly musty, it sort of reminded me of my grandmother's apartment. His father was Lebanese and a very quiet man, while his mother was like a typical Jewish grandmother. She kept asking him, "Herbert, do you want some more chicken soup?"

As he continued to rise to stardom, he knew that he was probably looking at this apartment for the very last time. His room was the size of a closet, with just a bed, a radio, and a record player. From what I understood, he rarely left it. There was one close friend he had there—the son of the superintendent of the building. He was the only kid besides Tiny who'd stuck around the neighborhood to play ball with each new generation of kids.

Tiny couldn't leave that night without seeing his old friend. When we left his parents' apartment, he darted into a tunnel along the side of the building that led to a concrete backyard where his friend had an apartment. Tunnels like this one were about sixty yards long and very common in these old buildings. They scared the hell out of me, especially at night when it was pitch black. Tiny knocked loudly on his friend's door, but there was no answer. He couldn't accept the fact that no one was home and kept knocking.

Finally, he stopped and reluctantly headed back through that hideous tunnel. I opened the door to the limousine and turned to let him into the car, but he had disappeared. Then I saw him running down the block at full speed, his long, curly hair blowing in the wind. He proceeded to run into the middle of the intersection where he jumped up and down and bellowed out, "This was our ball field!"

He ran to where home plate would have been, took an imaginary swing of the bat and headed to first base. As soon as I realized what was happening, I ran to the pitcher's mound and started to shout out, "Come On Herbie… you're clear at second…now third base Herbie…you're good…all the way home Herbie…Yaaaaay! Herbie hit a home run!"

He crossed home plate, breathing heavily as we jumped up and down together, cheering his imaginary home run. This satisfied him, and he quietly got into the limousine.

*   *   *

"Tiptoe" had become a solid Top 20 hit and *God Bless Tiny Tim* reached No. 7 on the *Billboard* Top 200 album chart. Now it was time to show the world what Tiny was like in concert. We decided to have the first show at the Santa Monica Civic Auditorium in June 1968. At the time, Santa Monica Civic was the most sought-after venue with a 3,500-seat capacity. Tiny was so hot at this time that both of the biggest Top 40 stations, KHJ and KRLA, wanted to promote the concert. We settled that problem by letting them promote it together.

As we prepared for the concert, Roy Silver, Tiny's manager, and I decided that we would make the performance as faithful and theatrical a recreation of the album as possible. For the "Welcome to My Dream" opening, we used a smoke machine that Tiny walked through to make his first appearance. On another number, he started off by quickly repeating, "The birds are coming, the birds are coming," so we brought in live doves and released them over the crowd.

Dressed in white tie and tails, I conducted a twenty-five-piece orchestra and created a Broadway-like overture composed of segments of various songs that had become closely associated with Tiny.

The theater had a rising orchestra pit, and as I waited in the basement of Santa Monica Civic for the concert to begin, Murray Roman, a well-known comedian at the time and one of the opening acts, urged me to get high before going up in the orchestra pit. I debated that decision very carefully and ultimately decided to go for it—and I'm glad I did. As the overture began, the pit slowly rose and dramatically revealed the musicians and me in my white tie and tails…it was a mind-blowing experience for me.

I had a hunch that studying conducting for two years at Michigan would come in handy one day.

Two months later, in August 1968, Tiny Tim headlined at Caesar's Palace in Las Vegas for ten days. It had only been built a few years earlier, so it was the most desirable place to play on the strip. His name appeared on the marquee in bigger letters than anyone who had ever played there. The Caesar's gig was a huge accomplishment; the shows completely sold out and once again, I conducted the orchestra.

When we arrived at Caesar's, Tiny was placed in Frank Sinatra's suite, which was probably the nicest place he'd ever been put up. As he was the headliner, he was treated like royalty; I can only imagine how he must have felt!

Even though he was receiving the star treatment, Tiny still needed to experience in his body and soul that he was actually headlining at Caesar's and that it wasn't a dream. In order to achieve this, he felt compelled to order everything on the menu, and I mean everything! The room service menu at

Caesar's was probably the largest on the planet, so imagine the other hotel guests' surprise upon seeing the room service carts lined up down the hall as far as the eye could see!

In all our time working together, I never saw Tiny eat a bite of food or drink a sip of any liquid. Even that day at Caesar's, I didn't actually see him eat anything. But perhaps his special form of gluttony was a substitute for sex, which seemed all too rare in Tiny's life. (He believed in waiting until marriage.)

Each night after the show, one of Tiny's managers would walk him to his suite to make sure that there were no groupies hanging around. This usually worked out, except once, when his manager neglected to look in the shower of the master bedroom. An hour later, I got a call from Tiny.

Going over the set list at Caesar's.

I answered the phone in my hotel room and right away, Tiny started talking. It seemed he couldn't wait to tell me all about this encounter. "Oh Mr. Perry," he said, "I found a girl hiding in my shower tonight."

"Yes, Tiny. You can speak freely and tell me what happened."

"Well, I'll tell you, Mr. Perry. She asked me to do something I've never heard of."

"Please continue, Tiny."

"Well, Mr. Perry, she asked me to spread honey all over her body."

"Oh my God, Tiny. What did you do then?"

"Then she told me to lick it all off."

"Tiny, that's brilliant! Did you comply?"

"Well yes. I felt it was the proper thing to do."

"You were absolutely right. Congratulations!"

"Oh Mr. Perry, thank you so much for listening!"

"Anytime, Tiny, anytime."

* * *

After the ten-day engagement at Caesar's, we prepared for the crown jewel of in-concert appearances—one night only, October 30, 1968, at Royal Albert Hall.

Royal Albert Hall.

Interior of Royal Albert Hall.

The opening acts were Joe Cocker and the Bonzo Dog Doo-Dah Band. This time we had the fifty-piece London Festival Orchestra, and once again I conducted, wearing my familiar white tie and tails. The show ran two hours, and I had only one three-hour rehearsal the day of the show. Nevertheless, the concert was a triumph, with a sold-out, star-studded house and was considered by many critics to be one of the great events in the history of British pop. One of the many highlights was Tiny's soul-stirring rendition of the Depression-era anthem, "Brother, Can You Spare a Dime?"

Unfortunately, we were not able to film the concert ourselves. It was recorded, although not released until many years later, in a limited edition. It is the only audio document in existence that truly captures the talent, humor, spirit, and soul of Herbert Khaury, who came to be known on three continents as Tiny Tim.

On stage at Royal Albert Hall.

Chapter 10

Fats Is Back

As if the success of Tiny Tim wasn't enough to keep me afloat on cloud nine, Mo Ostin called me into his office one day and told me he was thinking of signing Fats Domino. He asked me if I would be interested in producing him as my next artist for the company. The opportunity to work on an album with one of my teenage heroes had me salivating.

The following night, Mo and I flew to Las Vegas to meet with Fats and see his show at the Flamingo. It was everything we'd hoped for. He rocked the house and had the crowd full of energy; we decided right then that he would be the next artist we signed to Warner Brothers. We went backstage after the show where we had the opportunity to see his valet slowly roll his socks off his feet. Fats then showed us his jewelry collection—diamond and colorful jewel-encrusted rings in various shapes and sizes, colorful brooches and tie clips, and thick bracelets—which made him very proud. Our meeting together went well, and within a few days, I was collecting material for the album, which I called *Fats Is Back.*

The title of the album was easy to figure out: Fats hadn't released a record in eight years, and he'd never had an album in the modern sense—just a collection of single tracks. It was time to give him a real album.

I'd long felt that Paul McCartney had written "Lady Madonna" with a bit of a Fats Domino feel, so I thought it would be cool to have Fats do a rendition of the song on his album. Fats let me know early on that he was not going to play piano on most of the tracks, so the first challenge was finding the right person to play piano on "Lady Madonna." I brought in Larry Knechtel, one of the most brilliant musicians I've ever worked with, and it was the right decision. His performance on this track made it a reality and gave it a life, bringing a Beatles vibe to the track as well as giving it a Fats Domino authenticity.

The second challenge was the song itself: I was struggling to get Fats to connect to the lyrics. He always said, "Just give me something simple and catchy," and this was one of the more complex Beatles songs. Fats was a little confused when we started to rehearse "Lady Madonna" and I thought that I might have pushed him too far. After a few tries, he finally figured out his connection to the song—he had a daughter named Donna! With these kinks ironed out, we were on our way.

I added another Beatles-Domino alliance: "Lovely Rita" from *Sgt. Pepper*. These two Beatles songs were the only tracks I cut in LA, and they really were the "frosting on the cake." I wanted the rest of the album—the "meat"—to be a totally authentic, New Orleans rock 'n' roll.

Quite simply put, New Orleans music is music that makes you feel joyful. This style began with Professor Longhair, long considered the godfather of New Orleans rock 'n' roll. He developed a unique piano style that was part honky-tonk, part barrelhouse, and part his own brand of early R&B. Professor Longhair only taught his special brand of piano to a select few disciples. The first two to learn from him were Antoine "Fats" Domino and Allen Toussaint, the brilliant songwriter-producer who is responsible for such outstanding Lee Dorsey records such as "Ya-Ya," "Working in the Coalmine," and "Ride Your Pony," as well as many hit songs for various other artists, such as, "Yes We Can Can" for The Pointer Sisters, and "Southern Nights" for Glen Campbell. The Professor's third disciple was Mac Rebennack, also known as Dr. John, who had a historic recording career that spanned fifty years, both as a solo artist as well as a featured musician on numerous albums. Last, but not least, and perhaps the most gifted of them all, was the incomparable, the legendary, James Booker. He was the closest thing to Professor Longhair himself.

Fats and me.

Fats wanted to get back to New York so we held the rest of the sessions at the Hit Factory, which had just opened its first location with Gary Kellgren as the engineer. The studio was a small room with great acoustics. The musicians could feel one another's presence as they were placed closely together. I could not have asked for a better group of musicians—all team players. I would unhesitatingly consider them world-class. The lineup was as follows: Chuck Rainey on bass (nineteen years old at the time), Herbie Lovelle (the top R&B drummer in NY), and Eric Gale on guitar (the classiest, most tasteful player on this instrument, further evidenced by the fact that he was Paul Simon's guitarist for years).

As Larry Knechtel was more of a contemporary pianist, and the rest of the album needed the New Orleans sound, Fats hand-picked a new piano player—none other than Professor Longhair's fourth disciple, James Booker.

James was a brilliant musician and really gave the album a completely unique sound of honky-tonk, rock 'n' roll, and jazz. Other than one minor hiccup—he once got too high and had to be helped over to the piano to play—James added some serious clout to the album. I also had Trevor Lawrence on baritone sax as part of the rhythm section.

Fats Is Back *album cover.*

Lastly, three songs called for sax solos, and I was thrilled beyond belief that another one of my heroes from the Alan Freed shows was available—the best tenor sax player on the planet: King Curtis. He had recently played the memorable solo on Aretha Franklin's "Respect." Randy Newman, who had become a friend, asked me if he could do the horn arrangements on three of the most important songs because of his great love of New Orleans music and Fats Domino in particular. They are some of the finest examples of New Orleans horn writing I have ever heard.

This album holds up for me even today, fifty years later, and I never get tired of listening to it. Two extraordinary compliments I received for this record were, first, from my friend of twenty-one years, Leo DiCaprio, who recently asked me for a second copy of *Fats Is Back* because he wore out the first one I gave him years ago by playing it incessantly in his truck. The other great compliment that I'll never forget was the glowing review in *Rolling Stone* from Jann Wenner himself, when the album was originally released in 1968 (article reprinted with permission from Jann Wenner and *Rolling Stone*):

Fats Is Back, Fats Domino (Reprise RS 6304)

Just out of the back of the left speaker comes this scratchy, but very hip, piano then at the right speaker it's an old Fats Domino hit, "Ain't That a Shame" (You made.. Me cry.. When you said.. Goodbye), and back and forth between the speakers run the opening riffs of songs—not just "Blueberry Hill"—nearly forgotten.

A voice then announces that Fats is Back, and he is up full, with a song called "My Old Friends." From the very beginning, put perfectly in the mood, the album is just fantastic: the production is modern, the mixing superb, and Fats is Fats, better than ever, a remembered, beautifully deep and mellow voice.

The segue into the next second track, a perfect set of drum triplets, illustrates how precisely, how masterfully, and how tastefully, the past and present have been combined into this amazing album. The horn arrangements are contemporary, sometimes a little thick, but good; and the King Curtis solos are superb (King Curtis, after all, being a man who was very much there in the beginning and is still a superb session man, as he is here, as well as a soloist in his own right).

The musicians on the session – and this includes the Blossoms who did the vocal back-ups, including a total job on "Lovely Rita"—have done their parts perfectly.

Fats is Back is unequivocally a fine record in all respects. The closing track on side one is "Lady Madonna," surely as good a cover of a Beatles' song as ever has been done. His vocal brings a new depth to the song. It is a rendition which must be heard to be believed!

"Honest Papas Love Their Mamas Better," like nearly everything on this album, has a great rocking shuffle, with a very strong and understated horn section. The record is not a collection of oldies but a tastefully programmed set.

"One For the Highway (Two for the Road)" recalls the great instrumental figures and techniques of early rock and roll, strong, immediate, swinging music. And, at the same time, it is terribly modern.

If "One For The Highway" does not illustrate this, then take Fats' version of "Lovely Rita, Meter Maid," a totally surprising song to include in this production. But the thing that must be realized, and that is realized here, is that it is not surprising at all: the same things that made rock and roll great then, still make great rock and roll today.

"Lovely Rita" begins with a full soprano chorus, picks up Fats' perfectly suited vocal, a chorded piano melodically equal to the Paul McCartney bass line and a set of maracas doing the double-time. Fats does this song like it should be done;—that is the very simple proof of the viability of it all. And it's just too fucking much when Fats cries out "Nobody but you, Rita."

Everyone involved with this album, not least of all Antoine 'Fats' Domino, has done an excellent job. But Richard Perry, the producer, who one assumes to be responsible for the segues, the repertoire, the perfect final fade, the selection of arrangers and so many other aspects, deserves especial credit, for Perry, second only to the man himself, has brought Fats back. **JANN WENNER**

Chapter 11

Five Days in London with Ella Fitzgerald

The third project I did for Warner Brothers was with an iconic artist whom I had idolized for many years. Since the late '30s, when she released her first major hit, "A-Tisket, A-Tasket," Ella Fitzgerald had been widely regarded at the time as one of the all-time greatest singers. When Mo Ostin told me that he was going to sign her, I became obsessed. There was nothing that was going to keep me from working with her.

However, there were two problems from the start. The first was with her longtime manager—and an icon in the industry himself—Norman Granz. He was the owner of Verve Records, her recording home for years until Warner Brothers got into the mix, and he wielded a heavy influence on Ella. After years of being in the driver's seat at Verve, Granz wasn't used to someone else choosing the material, the musicians, and overseeing the arrangements. He especially wasn't too thrilled with the idea of some young producer (me!) calling the shots for his "queen"—even more so since I was pushing to do an album of contemporary material. But Mo had a long relationship with Norman Granz and he put himself on the line, assuring Norman that I was the right person for the job.

The second issue, which complicated matters further, was this: Ella was in the middle of a two-month tour of one-night shows throughout Europe, and she had only five days off in which to record the album. If we didn't record then, we would have to wait six months. To make things even more interesting, the album would have to be recorded in London. I never met a challenge I didn't like, so, naturally, I opted for the five-day program and booked a flight to the U.K. I couldn't have asked for anything more.

On May 21, 1969, we began recording at Olympic Studios in Hammersmith, a suburb of London. Long regarded as a legendary studio complex, it was primarily known as the studio where The Rolling Stones did most of their best work. (For a while, they'd recorded at RCA Studios in Hollywood, but when they'd gone back to Olympic, the sound of their records took a quantum leap forward with tracks such as "Jumping Jack Flash," "Honky Tonk Women," and "Gimme Shelter.")

I booked Studio A, which would accommodate a large rhythm section including strings. I wanted to make Ella as comfortable as possible. Each morning we met in her suite at the Dorchester Hotel, where we reviewed the three songs that we would be recording that night. She was an impressive artist—with just one day to prepare three songs for that night's session, she always showed up ready to sing. In addition to having very little prep-time, never throughout her illustrious career had she tackled material like this: contemporary pop/R&B. To give you an example of what a daunting challenge she was willing to undertake, here's a list of the songs that made up the album:

"Get Ready," "The Hunter Gets Captured by the Game," "Ooo Baby Baby" (all written by Smokey Robinson).

"Got to Get You Into My Life" (from The Beatles' *Revolver* album, written by Paul McCartney).

"Yellow Man" and "I Wonder Why" (both little-known Randy Newman gems, the latter is a gospel/pop song featuring Nicky Hopkins on piano).

"Savoy Truffle" (from The Beatles' *White Album*, written by George Harrison, again featuring Nicky Hopkins on Wurlitzer Electric Piano).

"I'll Never Fall in Love Again" (written by Burt Bacharach and Hal David, recorded by Ella before Dionne Warwick's version was released. Hal said this was his favorite version).

"Open Your Window" (written by Harry Nilsson—the only song that sounds like it was written for her). She scat sings throughout the instrumental on this one, and it really comes across like vintage Ella. Here is the first verse of that song:

Open your window and take a deep sigh,
Think about lettin' the rest of the world go fly a kite,
Takin' it easy, is easy as pie,
And holding your hand is such a natural high.

We spent hours, I sent flowers.
We could be happy alone in a tent
Think of the money we'd save on rent.

As we were recording, you'll never believe which rock 'n' roll band was mixing their new album down the hall. The album was *Let It Bleed*, and the group was The Rolling Stones!

On our first day of recording, Mick and Keith demonstrated what a class act they were. While the band was on a break, they came into the studio to shake hands, introduce themselves to Ella, and welcome her to Olympic Studios. The following night, Mick invited me to stop by their mixing session in Studio C after I finished with Ella.

Studio C at Olympic was probably the most perfect and famous mixing room in the world—it was as intimate as a mixing room should be, and had giant Tannoy studio monitors. As I entered, Glyn Johns was engineering brilliantly. The Stones' producer, Jimmy Miller, sat next to Glyn, while Mick and Keith, a.k.a The Glimmer Twins, stood behind them, overseeing the proceedings. I was thrilled to be there and felt frozen in time as I absorbed this moment.

The song that was playing at full-throttle volume was "You Can't Always Get What You Want." It was clear to everyone in the room that this track was destined to be a Stones classic. It was historically unlike any other Stones songs, especially with the church-like choir singing in the intro, followed by a French horn solo with only acoustic guitar accompaniment before Mick finally starts to sing the first verse: "I saw her today at the reception..." The contrast is stunning; as Mick's voice sounds like a bolt out of the blue. Most importantly, the lyric of the chorus has a relevance that is almost biblical. Along with the choir, the guitar solo plays a big part in the dramatic finale. The choir lifts their voices one inversion every two bars as the song builds to a glorious climax.

About an hour later, they moved on to another tune, the Robert Johnson classic, "Love in Vain," a rare Stones song not written by Mick and Keith. During the playback of this tune, Mick and I were sitting on a small couch in front of the console. I remember he was drinking Coke from the bottle and without looking at me, he just swung his arm around and handed me the Coke to offer me a sip. I thought it was a very welcoming gesture, as if to say, "Here, take a hit from my bottle."

I stopped by The Stones' sessions a few more times that week, and, needless to say, it was an eye-opening opportunity. I kept thinking, *Here I am, watching The Stones mixing* Let It Bleed*! What a stroke of fucking luck!*

Let It Bleed became my favorite Stones album.

* * *

After a whirlwind five days in London I was back in LA, but my work on the Ella record was just beginning. I knew that I would be doing an extensive amount of overdubbing. No matter how good the London tracks sounded, there was no doubt in my mind that they could be taken to another level. For one thing, the technology available at that point made it possible to transfer the recordings from eight tracks to sixteen, which opened the doors of creativity in so many ways.

Having twice as many tracks to work with enabled me to overdub an entire new drum kit, something that had previously been a difficult task. This could be done by moving my master reel onto a new "slave" reel (that's what it was called), then open new tracks to be used for additional recorded information. With all of these tools, I was able to bring new life into every track by adding background singers, strings, horns, drums, percussion, bass, and guitar—whatever seemed necessary. None of this would have been possible without the ability to create more room on the slave reel.

I also did some judicious vocal "comping," which is a vitally important step in assembling the master vocal. This is a process where you meticulously listen to every line of every vocal, picking and choosing the best parts of each one. Ella had cataract problems with her eyes, so every now and then she would miss a word. This made it necessary for me to edit and "bounce" all the best parts onto a final vocal compilation track.

Nicky Hopkins on piano became the "glue" connecting the basic tracks with the overdubs I did in LA. I'd become aware of his artistry through his work with The Rolling Stones, particularly on "Sympathy for The Devil," and I'd booked him for the full week of sessions. He was a joy to work with and always made a creative contribution. This marked the beginning of a long, creative relationship I enjoyed with Nicky for many years. After two months of work on the album, I had added an incalculable number of new elements and the finished product bore almost no resemblance to what the London five-day session sounded like.

After Norman Granz heard the final mixed record, he came to my office and gave it his blessing, but the greatest thrill of all was Ella's reaction. She couldn't believe all the massive changes and improvements, particularly on her vocals after "comping," as well as the magnificent background vocals for which I'd brought in Clydie King, Merry Clayton, and Patrice Holloway to the LA studio. I don't believe Ella had ever had background singers on a record before. When she heard the entire album, she was so blown away that she called me and said, "You're a genius!"

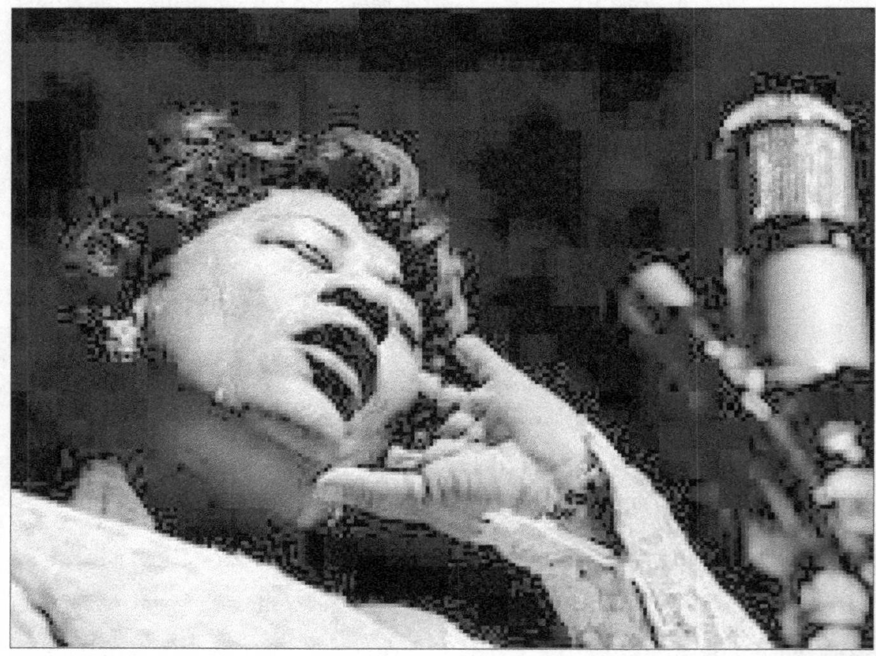

Ella Fitzgerald

Chapter 12

Going Independent

In 1968, while I was working on the Tiny Tim album for Warner Brothers, Linda invited Abe Somer to come to the studio with her and some friends to see me in action. Linda had first met him through a project she'd worked on, and they'd become friends. It was a huge honor to have Abe there.

In the late '60s, Abe had held a weekly seminar at USC in record business law, and it had been attended by most of the future CEOs and VPs of business affairs at top record companies. As the music industry surged through the '60s, it became clear that any record producer who was serious about building (and protecting) a career in music needed the right representation. One of Abe's exceptional qualities—in addition to the fact that he was a brilliant attorney—was his passion for music. At the time, it was a rare combination.

By 1970, with Tiny, Fats, and Ella under my belt, I felt confident enough to leave my job at Warner Brothers and go out on my own, as an independent, producer. Having met Abe two years earlier, it was a natural progression that he would become my attorney. Once Abe and I began to work together, a lifetime friendship was born. He has guided my career ever since, for most of forty-five years.

Abe was also very good friends with the president of Columbia Records, Clive Davis. Abe loved mixing business with pleasure, so he often held parties at his home where he would invite friends and clients of his. Linda and I met Clive and his wife Janet at one of those parties, but we didn't know them well beyond that brief interaction.

As luck would have it, Linda was able to make dinner plans with Janet and Clive. The four of us met at the hottest restaurant in LA at the time—the Black Rabbit Inn—and had a fabulous dinner. Since we were all having such a great time, we invited Clive and Janet to our house to keep things going. I played them almost every record that I had ever produced, and Clive was impressed. I don't think he had heard any of my work, except for maybe Tiny Tim. This would be a turning point for my career, as this dinner cemented a relationship with Clive, and in turn, Columbia Records.

After learning about our dinner, Abe set up an informal brunch a few days later at his house with Clive and me, to discuss the details of my production deal with Columbia Records. That deal would open a big door for me and would help me emerge as a successful independent record producer, turning my music-world dreams into a reality. This was just one of the many deals Abe would negotiate over the years. My friendship with Abe continued to grow, and he began to invite me over for weekend lunches that he regularly hosted. There, I met Lou Adler, Jerry Moss, Chris Blackwell, and David Anderle among many others. We would all get high together and enjoy listening to the records we were each involved with. Those were amazing times; it felt great to accomplish business while having fun.

As I got busier in the studio, my personal life took a different direction and later that year, Linda and I decided to live apart. We loved each other, but we just couldn't figure out how to live together. We remained very deeply connected and continued to hang out and travel together, all the way through the early '70s. The support for each other's success was always there, but ultimately, we made the difficult decision to get a divorce. Linda kept 'Perry,' a name she still carries to this day, and even though the marriage only lasted a few years, we have maintained a solid, loving friendship that has endured for decades. And, as my career began to take off, Linda's own career blossomed—I watched her garner Grammy recognition and go on to become Vice President, Creative Development for Warner/Chappell Music, one of the largest music publishing companies.

Linda and me dining out.

Chapter 13

Barbra

I knew what I wanted to do next as an independent producer. I've always had great admiration for Barbra Streisand's talent. She has, I believe, one of the greatest vocal instruments of all time. Yet she had such an "older" image. I wanted to introduce her to contemporary popular music. I was intrigued with the idea of doing something younger and different with her, taking her in a direction she'd never gone before. I couldn't help but hope that my newborn friendship with Clive Davis would open the doors to working with Barbra, as she was one of the artists that Columbia represented.

Clive had been impressed with the work I'd done with Ella Fitzgerald, and things had certainly worked out the way I'd hoped: He intended to bring me on to work with Barbra.

In 1969, she had released an album with Columbia called *What About Today?* Its very title, along with most of the song choices, showed me that she was looking for a more current sound. But, when I listened to the album I knew she hadn't yet scratched the surface, and I was sure I could help her get there. I felt comfortable enough to give Clive an honest review of the album and discuss my ideas with him: It was time to take Barbra contemporary. He responded by asking me to bring him the songs I had in mind for her! Finally, the moment I had been eagerly anticipating had arrived.

I felt that perhaps my greatest strength as a record producer was to find the right material that would allow the artist to own the songs and make the music their own. I took a lot of time to select the songs that I felt would best launch Barbra into contemporary pop. I brought Clive seven songs to begin with, including three by Laura Nyro: "Stoney End," "Time and Love," and "Flim Flam Man." Laura was the hottest songwriter in the business at the time, and Barbra had a great affinity for her music. There were two Randy Newman compositions: "I'll Be Home" and "Let Me Go," a personal favorite of mine. I also included Gordon Lightfoot's "If You Could Read My Mind," a gem of a song that Warner Brothers hadn't thought of releasing as a single by Lightfoot until Barbra recorded it. After that, that song quickly became the most important one of his career. Then there was the song that became the catalyst for the project—Harry Nilsson's "Maybe," which Clive instantly recognized as a potential piece of classic Streisand material. Clive was excited and immediately set up a meeting with Barbra and me.

Twenty-one years later, Barbra released a four-CD career-retrospective box set called *Just for the Record*. In her detailed liner notes that accompanied the package, she describes what happened:

> *In 1970, I was working on an album called* The Singer *when Clive Davis asked me if I would consider putting the project aside to work with a new producer, Richard Perry, on what Clive called, "a more contemporary album." After meeting Richard and hearing the new songs, I said yes. Our venture was to become* Stoney End.

Barbra was known to be a fierce perfectionist who would always speak her mind, and that made some people uncomfortable. Several friends asked me, "How are you going to work with her?"

My response was always the same. "No problem," I'd say. "Two Jews from Brooklyn can't go that far wrong."

From the first time we met, there was never a doubt in my mind that we would not only have success, but become close friends as well. I was

Stoney End *album cover*

respectful, but not intimidated. Barbra appreciated someone who stood his ground, while at the same time having something creative to offer.

When we first started working together, it was clear to me that she was unfamiliar with most of the contemporary artists on the musical landscape. In a matter of a few weeks, that all changed. I remember one of the calls I got from her late at night: "Get me the new Van Morrison, Marvin Gaye, Randy Newman, Johnny Cash, and the new Joni Mitchell—and by the way, I think she's a gas!" Barbra had totally immersed herself in the pop culture!

As we began spending a considerable amount of time together, we developed a relationship—unfortunately of the brother/sister variety. This didn't exactly thrill me because anyone who has had the opportunity to work with Barbra and get close to her develops a crush. I was not immune.

I found her to be extremely beautiful, with a pervasive sensuality and, at the same time, highly intelligent, sensitive, and yet strong. This, for me, is a perfect combination. I've always found strong women exciting!

We would get together several times a week as I turned her on (musically) and got high on a new world of sounds. Inevitably, the night would end in her kitchen, as we sat at an ice cream parlor table for two and gorged on vanilla Häagen-Dazs, sharing intimate conversation.

Being in her home was a unique experience. It was an exquisite blend of the finest art nouveau and American Arts and Crafts furniture, fabrics, and objets d'art. There were brave color combinations in every room—everything right down to the smallest of details had been personally selected by Barbra. What struck me the most when I first came over was the lighting. It was hard to put my finger on why it felt different, softer than in anyone else's home I'd ever been in—comforting and flattering, coming from everywhere and yet, aside from the strategically placed Tiffany and Dirk van Erp lamps, I could not clearly identify its source. Maybe this was a trick she'd learned from her movie days, but I have since noticed this same luminous aura in every subsequent house of hers I have visited.

After a few weeks together, it was time for Barbra to rehearse each song before we went into the studio. I had already had several meetings with specific arrangers who I felt would be best for each song. They understood the arrangements I was looking for—in other words, what I wanted each instrument to play—particularly the strings, horns, and woodwinds. Everything was taking shape beautifully. This was going to be a real departure for her and a huge moment for me!

On the night before the first session, I met with Barbra alone to go over everything one last time with just me at the piano. After we finished, she suddenly had an eleventh hour attack of massive insecurity about the whole record.

"I can't do this," she exclaimed. "This isn't me...I just don't feel it!"

I responded, "Look, maybe it's my piano playing. I'll cancel the session right now if you want, but you've come this far, so trust me, once we get into it, it will blow your mind. There isn't a song here you can't sing, and sing well, and I promise you, this will be one of the most important and memorable recording sessions of your career. More important, I can't believe that Barbra Streisand would back down from any challenge."

My dash of producer psychology worked (it's a big part of what we do). Barbra's fears began to recede, and she agreed to soldier on. The session the following night became the longest in the history of the LA Musicians Union. As per Barbra's wish, we recorded the entire session live, which was an acoustical challenge of the first order given the scope of the arrangements: a seven-piece rhythm section, twenty-one strings, two horns, two woodwinds, a harp, and four background singers. The rhythm section was composed of some funky musicians with whom she usually didn't work: younger, hipper black musicians; guitar players with long hair; and we even had a female bass player, Carol Kaye, who could play better than any dude. Then there were the string players, who were very conservative types. Normally, when you book string players, the session runs from seven to ten in the evening. For special occasions, they might work an hour of overtime, but that's as late as they would ever stay. They really didn't give a damn—they would just want to get home to their wives in the Valley. (String players always seem to be married and live in the Valley.)

The session took place at the Columbia Records Recording Studios located on Sunset Boulevard right next door to the Hollywood Palladium. It was a huge room, almost as big as an airplane hangar. The session began at 7:00 p.m. and Barbra was scheduled to arrive at 8:00. For the first hour I did what one would never expect the producer of a Streisand recording session to do: I sat on the floor and tuned the drums! On most of her previous records, you'd never even hear the drums. First, I checked the microphone placement, a critical step in getting a good sound on the snare (that's the drum you hit with a stick, the one that provides the backbeat). It's imperative that the rim of the snare head be tightened just right, giving it a crisp pop as opposed to a tubby quality. Then I did the same on each tom-tom—usually there are two side toms and a floor tom. Finally, I got to the most important drum of all—the kick drum, the one you hit with a foot pedal with a beater attached. Getting the kick to cut through the track is the key to a great drum sound, and if you have a great drum sound, you have a track! Everything else can be replaced, if necessary. As I had been playing drums since the age of ten, I was intimately familiar with them and felt comfortable getting them ready for the session.

On most tracks, you would record the rhythm section separately, with the drums in their own isolation booth. That separation gives the track a much more modern sound—or it did in 1970. I implored Barbra to let me do it that way, but she was used to recording everything live and liked hearing the whole track all at once. I could understand and appreciate that, as it really is ultimately the most exciting way to make a record. As producer, I was faced with a formidable challenge: I had to create a contemporary sound for Barbra—the whole *raison d'être* for the album—while adhering to traditional, old-school techniques.

Barbra hadn't arrived yet, which was a good thing, because I was still figuring out how best to set up the drums for the live session. Earl Palmer, a legendary drummer who'd played on most of Little Richard's records, sat behind the drum kit. It was positioned in the middle of the huge recording room, so there were hardly any sound baffles to contain the loudness of the instrument. I had him tighten the kick drum as much as possible, but it was boomy and still didn't have enough attack in the sound to cut through the thirty-eight musicians and background singers.

When you have so many open mics in the room, it wreaks havoc with the drum sound, but I knew it was crucial that the drums, especially the kick, sounded absolutely right in order to give "Stoney End" a contemporary validity. This was a necessary element not only on this track, but to help carve an identity for the entire album.

I pulled out all the tricks I had up my sleeve. First, I asked Earl to remove the outer head of the kick drum and we stuffed a pillow inside the shell, then placed a big weight on it to keep it from moving. Then, I covered the whole kick drum with a thick blanket, for that was ultimately the only way to get it to punch through the track. We checked the sounds on all the other instruments and we were good to go, just in time, too. Barbra showed up promptly at 8:00 p.m. and we had figured everything out and were ready to proceed.

The first song and perhaps my favorite of all Harry Nilsson's compositions, was "Maybe." This was the first one I'd found for her and also the tune that initially got Clive's attention. I used to fantasize that one day I would produce this song with her and now it was happening right in front of me. It fit her like a glove, and she sang it magnificently. I always felt that if Barbra ever performed this in concert, it would bring the house down and leave the audience in tears.

Next, we did a Randy Newman number, "I'll Be Home." I brought Randy in to play piano on the track, which really thrilled Barbra. A number of other well-known musicians later participated on the album as well. Carole King sang background vocals on an immensely soulful ballad, "No Easy Way Down," which she'd written with her former lyricist and husband, Gerry Goffin. Richie Hayward, the drummer of the cutting-edge band, Little Feat, played on the gospel/rock rave up, "Free The People." And Zal Yanovsky, renowned guitarist of the highly acclaimed Lovin' Spoonful, played the tastiest licks along with Randy Newman's moody ragtime piano on what has come to be my favorite track on the entire record, Randy's little-known classic, "Let Me Go." Barbra sounds remarkably like Bessie Smith as she soulfully sings it.

To quote Barbra's liner notes again:

> *This was a new experience in more ways than one, when Richard introduced me to a whole new group of songwriters that included Laura Nyro, Joni Mitchell, and Randy Newman. During the sixties, I was always much younger than the musicians and producers I worked with. The first time I can remember being the same age as everyone else in the studio was during the Stoney End sessions.*

In fact, Barbra and I are almost exactly the same age—just two months apart. At the time, we were both twenty-eight.

"Stoney End" was the third song we recorded that night, and certainly the biggest stretch for her artistically. It was when faced with this challenge that Barbra showed me why she is the consummate pro—her homework was always done, and she showed up prepared to sing her heart out.

All of Barbra's first takes in the studio were pure magic—hearing that voice singing these songs—but the moment we ran down the first take of "Stoney End," it felt like a lightning bolt was going through me. I swear, my hair stood on end. It was one of the most amazing feelings I have ever had in the studio. We began with a blistering drum fill as Earl drove the track, and Carol Kaye played a funky Motown-like bass. But, above all, the thrill was in Barbra's performance. Her voice was doing things it had never done before. She was in the groove, feeling the pocket, and just hit the ball out of the park. Near the climactic ending, when she cried out, "MAMA…CRADLE ME AGAIN," we all just about lost it!

I immediately called everyone into the control room for a playback. We knew that we had discovered something that was totally unprecedented for her, and we were brimming with excitement. This completely validated the concept of the whole album. As we were listening to the playback, Barbra leaned over and whispered in my ear, "You were right, and I was wrong. But it's nice to be wrong." It was a moment I will remember for the rest of my life.

We recorded five songs that night—half the album! The session finished at five-thirty in the morning. Not one musician said a word about going home—not even the string players! We ended the evening with a haunting Joni Mitchell ballad, "I Don't Know Where I Stand," that Barbra especially loved. She delivered a breathtaking performance. The song featured a stunning arrangement by Gene Page for strings, oboe, acoustic guitar, and harp. As it was being recorded, I couldn't help but think, *What a perfect ending to a glorious recording session!*

Barbra and me in the studio.

That first session "broke the ice," and we started hanging out even more. When Barbra had to fulfill an old commitment to appear at the Riviera Hotel in Las Vegas, she invited me to come see the show. Watching her from the wings gave me a unique perspective. Only Barbra was visible to me, center stage, a diminutive, solitary figure in the spotlight, her body quivering with life, head tossed back as she sang. Though I could not see the audience, the adoration emanating from them was palpable as their energy combined with hers and made her appear to fill the stage. This was an intimate experience that I'll never forget.

After the show, Barbra and I were in her dressing room with her longtime manager, Marty Erlichman. As we were getting ready to order Chinese food, Marty asked, "What would you like to order, Dick?"

Barbra exploded, "What the fuck are you calling him Dick for? All you have to do is look at him to know that his name is Richard…not Dick!" Classic Barbra!

*   *   *

I prepared "Stoney End" for its single release and sent the final mix to her apartment in uptown New York. A few days later, she called me and said she was upset that there were no background vocals in the mix. I assured her that they were definitely on the record, but she insisted that she didn't hear any. I told her: "Look I'm coming to New York tomorrow anyway. I'll come over and we'll listen together and figure it out."

The day after I arrived, I went over to her apartment and we listened to the song. I told her, "You're right," I said, "we aren't hearing any background vocals. But that's because in this mix, I had all the background vocals coming from the left side, and your left speaker is out!" Now, here's the beauty of this story. One month later, I walked into the living room of her house back in LA and saw two gaping holes in the walls—several workmen were preparing to mount two giant studio monitors in the holes. They were also installing a professional tape deck and other state-of-the-art equipment. When Barbra does something, she does it all the way!

About a few weeks later, "Stoney End" was released as a single. It didn't catch on right away, so we were all a bit concerned. Then, suddenly, it broke big in San Francisco, and from there, it spread across the country like wildfire. It's always a special feeling to hear your record on the radio, but to hear it in your car when you're riding with the artist, well that's, as they say, as good as it gets! Barbra and I had a bet as to whether the single would be a hit. I said yes, she said no. The bet was settled as we were driving on Sunset Boulevard one evening, on our way to a dinner party. Humble Harve, the biggest DJ in LA, announced on the radio that the record had just hit No. 1!

What a thrill it was for us—like a fantasy come true! A few months later, the album was released and became my first Gold Record and first *Billboard* Top 10 album. It was also Barbra's first single since "People" to become a major radio hit. Particularly gratifying was the fact that several months earlier, Columbia had put out an album of her previous hits that had only sold three hundred fifty thousand copies—but the success of *Stoney End* carried that album to Gold status as well. With *Stoney End*, Barbra had broken through musically to a younger audience. This new group of fans was excited for her to continue to delve into this kind of music.

Six months later, Clive called me and said it was time to start thinking about a follow-up album. At our first meeting to go over material, we had an unexpected creative role reversal. This time, I decided that as a way to show my appreciation for Barbra's willingness to stretch and take chances on *Stoney End*, that I would propose, as our first selection for the new album, a real standard that would fall squarely in her comfort zone. "Since I Fell for You" had been written and was first a success in the '40s, then became a huge pop hit by Lenny Welch in the early '60s. It seemed like a no-brainer choice for Barbra, sort of like a quarterback delivering the ball right into the arms of his wide receiver without making him break stride!

I told her the next selection was hers to choose, and I was certain she would pick a song by Sondheim, Gershwin, or something comparable. Instead, she said there was a song on the new John Lennon album that I had given her that she liked. It must be "Love," I thought, but the one she liked was "Mother." I was so surprised. I turned to her and said, "'Mother!' You want to do 'Mother!' I can't believe that you want to do that song."

"Yeah," she said, "it has a nice melody to it."

Barbra and me listening to a playback in the studio.

I was stunned, but that's so typically Barbra—you never know what her next move is going to be. That's one of the things that makes her such a brilliant and creative artist.

The album was Lennon's first solo effort, and it reflected his intense involvement in primal scream therapy. "Mother" was the emotional centerpiece of it, born out of his own experience with his mother. John had never had much of a relationship with his mother because when he was five, she'd no longer wanted to raise a child and had handed him over to her sister Mimi. Around the age of fourteen, he'd started to reconcile with his mother, and by seventeen, they had become quite close. It was then that she was hit by a car and killed, prompting John to say that he lost his mother twice.

He spilled his guts out in the grooves of that track, creating a raw, guttural performance impossible for anyone else to cover…or so I thought. To my complete shock and amazement, Barbra said that was the song she wanted to record next. The song addresses both the mother and father, and Barbra lost her father when she was fifteen months old.

Mother, you had me but I never had you
I wanted you, but you didn't want me,
So I, I just gotta tell you,
Goodbye, goodbye

Father, you left me but I never left you
I needed you, you didn't need me,
So I, I just gotta tell you,
Goodbye, goodbye

Children, don't do
What I have done,
I couldn't walk,
And I tried to run

So, I just got to tell you,
Goodbye, goodbye

Mama don't go,
Daddy come home,
Mama don't go,
Daddy come home.

We cut both songs, "Mother" and "Since I Fell For You," in the same session—talk about a study in contrasts! Clive had the session filmed for the CBS Records annual international convention. On the Lennon song, Jim Keltner, one of the great studio drummers, and Larry Knechtel, the extraordinary piano and bass player who'd helped me on the Fats album, gave the groove a backbeat that was upright and proud, while Billy Preston played a gospel organ that brought it right to church. Then there was Barbra's performance. Whatever had inspired Lennon to make the song so profoundly anguished, Barbra found her own raw, moving way to pull the words from the depths of her soul—to make it her own. Once again, she showed me how artistically brave she was willing to be. There is no track we did together of which I am more proud. I remember being told that Chris Blackwell, the renowned founder and chairman of Island Records, gathered groups of friends and artists in his London flat to play them this track. The album, *Barbra Joan Streisand*, became our second Gold Record together.

* * *

In September of '72, Warren Beatty put together the first-ever-political fundraising concert for the Democratic presidential nominee, George McGovern. Held at the Los Angeles Forum, the evening featured Barbra, James Taylor, Carole King, and Quincy Jones' orchestra. Clive had asked me to record Barbra's performance for a live concert album. When I arrived at the venue Saturday afternoon for the dress rehearsal, I asked Barbra if she wanted to run through "Stoney End."

"Oh, I can't do 'Stoney End,'" she said very matter-of-factly. "It's been so long. I could never remember the lyrics."

"Barbra," I said, "you must do 'Stoney End!' No disrespect, but 'Stoney End' is why you're here tonight. I'll write the fucking lyrics on the floor of the stage, if need be."

I was serious. I had someone run out to get some chalk, and I got on my hands and knees and wrote the damn lyrics on the floor! I had forgotten how many verses there were in the song—they covered the entire floor of the Forum stage. Even then, she was reluctant, but she finally agreed to let the audience vote on which song they would prefer, between "Stoney End" and "Second Hand Rose." Fortunately—and not surprisingly—my efforts were not in vain.

Christmas party at Barbra's home, 1984.
Left to right: Neil Simon, Barbra, me, Marilyn Bergman, Burt Bacharach, Carole Bayer Sager.

There was some dispute as to who should close the show, but Marty Erlichman was steadfast in his negotiations that it would be Barbra and only Barbra. She proceeded to blow the roof off the Forum! One of the high points of her performance was a medley with her black background singers of "Where You Lead," a new Carole King song we had cut for the second album, combined with the soul classic, "Sweet Inspiration." Her performance was nominated for a Grammy Award and the album, *Live Concert at the Forum*, also went Gold. That made it three in a row!

I'm proud to say that even though more than forty-five years have passed since that first marathon recording session, Barbra remains a very dear friend to this day.

Chapter 14

The Stones at Nellcôte

I was in the process of finishing the *Barbra Joan Streisand* album and there was one track, "Space Captain," that I thought needed the gritty horns of Jim Price and Bobby Keys. There was one slight glitch—Jim and Bobby had left London and were now living in the south of France with The Stones, who had recently moved out of England to escape the U.K.'s stringent tax laws.

Although they all had separate residences, they were headquartered at Keith Richards' abode: Villa Nellcôte in Cap Ferrat. Jim and Bobby asked Keith if I could come down and overdub the horns after The Stones finished rehearsing, and he said it would be fine. So I hopped on a plane to Nice, grabbed a cab, and arrived at Nellcôte around four o'clock in the afternoon. As a token of my appreciation, I gave Keith two hits of mescaline, which he was very happy to receive.

His villa overlooked the Mediterranean, and everyone was hanging out on the back patio playing ping-pong. I wasn't exactly a stranger, given the memorable experience I'd had two years earlier when I'd watched the band mixing "Let It Bleed" at Olympic Studios while I was recording with Ella Fitzgerald there.

The album they were working on now was *Exile on Main Street.* There was a state-of-the-art remote truck parked in the circular driveway in front of the house, and they recorded everything, from rehearsals to master takes. All five members of the band were set up in a surprisingly small, dirt-floor room that had the feeling of an eighteenth-century dungeon. Only the horns, Jim and Bobby, were separate, in a smaller adjoining room.

No one was really sure who was going to show up on any given night because they didn't live near one another—especially Charlie and Bill, who had settled into plantation-like homes about two hours from Nellcôte. After dinner, as everyone started preparing for the rehearsal, there was a special buzz in the air as it had suddenly become apparent that, for the first time since they'd moved to France, all five members of the band were "in the house." Jim Price let me know that the rehearsal that night would begin at midnight and last until 6:00 a.m. Although there were no chairs, I was welcome to sit on the dirt floor. I couldn't think of a better place to be than sitting in the dirt and watching The Stones…for *six fucking hours*! Talk about feeling blessed!

The song they were working on that night, like most Stones songs, began with a Keith Richards classic guitar riff—this was the heart and soul of the band. The only exception might be "Sympathy for the Devil," which begins with congas and bongos, and features the funkiest bass I have ever heard Bill Wyman play. It also highlights Nicky Hopkins' understated, tension-filled gospel piano. For most of the others, it is Keith's infectious signature riffs that are as much a part of each song as the melody or lyrics. This one was no different. Keith kept driving the rhythm, much as Chuck Berry had done at those Brooklyn Paramount shows years earlier (see chapter two). The band jammed on this groove for what seemed like three hours without stopping. If, for instance, Bill had to go to the bathroom, Keith would pick up his bass and Jagger would grab a guitar. The key thing was that the music never stopped! Then there was Charlie, who had the most powerful backbeat in rock 'n' roll, which he so skillfully played just on the back end of the beat. Not to mention the lyrical, romantic guitar lines of Mick Taylor.

As the track reached fever pitch, Jagger took the mic. He began by making guttural sounds—not words but rather expressive, animal-like utterances—and continued like that for the next two hours, at which point the sounds started to morph into words. It was amazing to watch the band's creative process as the song emerged from the womb and, lo and behold, it ultimately became "Tumbling Dice"!

To top it off, I did get my horn overdub from Jim Price and Bobby Keys for the Streisand track. I will always be indebted to them for being the catalysts in affording me this once-in-a-lifetime experience.

Chapter 15

Making Magic with Harry Nilsson

I first met Harry Nilsson at a party that Phil Spector threw for Tiny Tim in June of 1968. He approached me, introduced himself, and told me how much he liked the *God Bless Tiny Tim* album. In return, I told him I was an admirer of his debut album, *Pandemonium Shadow Show*, both for his vocal prowess as well as his songwriting. We discovered that we were both from Brooklyn and were both Geminis—and felt an instant camaraderie. Harry typically looked like he had just woken up. His standard outfit was faded jeans, tennis sneakers, a rumpled white shirt in need of ironing, and his hair was generally unkempt.

In March of 1971, he paid a visit to my house on Wonderland Park Avenue in Laurel Canyon. Never one to mince words or hold back what was on his mind, he just came right out and asked me, "How'd you like to produce my next album?" I was thrilled because with Harry I finally had an artist to work with who would give me the chance to make a record with a sound that came closest to The Beatles. They were also great fans of Harry's, recognizing that they both operated in the same "rarified air." I immediately said yes, with two provisos: that we record the album in London, and that he trust me and let me call the shots. He agreed to both.

I knew that the London recording studios, particularly the engineers, were technically far more advanced than their American counterparts. This would enable us to take one giant step closer to a Beatles record. After doing my due diligence, I decided that the studio best suited to our needs was

Trident Sound, the hottest studio on the planet at the time. It was booked literally seven days a week, twenty-four hours a day. Among a few of the memorable records that came out of Trident were the first several Elton John albums and David Bowie's "Space Oddity," as well as his fourth album, "Hunky Dory." Trident, of course, had the great old recording console that bore its name. There were very few of these consoles in America, but one happened to be in Sunset Sound, Studio 2 in LA. Trident also had one of the best-sounding recording pianos in the world.

The next decision was the most critical one of all: the engineer. I needed someone who could take us into the future, so I consulted with my friend Glyn Johns. He had worked on most of the classic Rolling Stones albums, as well as with The Who, and numerous others. Glyn recommended a young twenty-one-year-old engineer, Robin Geoffrey Cable. He was on the staff at Trident and had done the early Elton John albums. Glyn said he was a brilliant engineer, and he was right. Robin helped give me the tools to paint the sounds on a canvas that I was envisioning in my head. In short, he was the perfect choice! Everything was coming back the way it was supposed to and beyond, especially the drums.

Although I was not technologically oriented, I learned more about sounds from working with Robin than from any other engineer at that time. Most importantly, I learned about *frequencies* and *equalization*, how to use different types of compressors, and choosing the proper microphone, which is the most significant decision you have to make in getting the right drum sound. Learning the technology was a very rewarding process and contributed immeasurably to my growth as a record producer. It allowed me to communicate with my engineer not just in terms of highs, mids, and lows, but in more specific detail; it was like being in a foreign country and finally being able to speak the language. The sounds that Robin Cable contributed mightily to *Nilsson Schmilsson*.

Harry and I arrived in London about ten days before the sessions were to begin. We had hoped this time would allow us to find some songs from British writers and publishers, since Harry didn't feel that he had any solid songs ready to record. I must say, I agreed—he had only bits and pieces, with hardly any lyrics. The one song that we felt very strongly about—"Without You"—was written and recorded by the British band Badfinger and released on The Beatles' Apple label. Both Harry and I felt confident that we could create some magic with this song and his voice.

We were still trudging up and down Oxford Street, meeting with publishers up until the very last minute—right up to the day before the first session—in hopes of miraculously finding another "Without You." Because Trident Studios booked so far in advance, I had to commit upfront to a full six weeks of studio time for cutting tracks. Normally, I would have postponed the sessions for at least two weeks, but here we were in London, ready to go, with studio, musicians—the works! All this and only one song! TALK ABOUT PRESSURE! Fortunately, I love a great challenge. The most important thing in helping me navigate through troubled waters has always been logic—my best friend.

I sat down with Harry the night before the first session and said, "You know those bits and pieces you didn't want to record? Well, they're about to become real songs."

Luckily, Harry trusted me and when we got to the session, he let me lead the way. The first song we did, "Gotta Get Up," wound up as the lead song on the album. I put my pragmatic hat on and structured the bits and pieces the way they would appear in their final song form, giving each its proper number of verses and choruses and adding the occasional bridge where it was appropriate. I also gave the musicians ideas to support the arrangements.

The stellar rhythm section included Jim Gordon, an American drummer then living in London, who later became a founding member of Derek and the Dominos and co-writer of their signature song, "Layla"; Klaus Voormann, the German bass player, who played on the solo albums of George Harrison, John Lennon, and Ringo Starr; Chris Spedding, the hottest session guitar player in London; and Nilsson on piano. Harry had a very percussive touch, and it was essential that he be on the piano, for it gave the track his signature and personality.

The first song went down like a dream. From the pounding of Nilsson's McCartney-esque opening piano, it dripped of Beatles magic. After two takes, the basic track for "Gotta Get Up" was in the win column.

As we moved on to the second song, "Driving Along," the results were exactly the same. We were taking unfinished fragments and turning them into something beautiful. This track featured acoustic guitars, a perfect electric guitar solo, and brilliant Nilsson vocals. It was as if everyone had set out to capture the same vibe, which is, after all, what you ultimately try to achieve in any recording session.

Then we moved on to "The Moonbeam Song," which was a psychedelic dream. If only people had a clue what it was about, it could have been a Nilsson classic. The track did have two outstanding components. First, I don't think that anyone has come so close to sounding like The Beach Boys—yet another indicator of Nilsson's vocal brilliance. The second special element was the introduction of the uniquely gifted British bass player, Herbie Flowers (but more about Herbie later).

The next song, "Down," can best be described as a combination of John Lennon and Paul McCartney's rawness. This was another example of some "bits and pieces" that led to a signature performance from Nilsson. On this track, I had the pleasure of working with one of the most creative horn tandems: Jim Price and Bobby Keys. They would lay down a track with Jim on trumpet and Bobby on tenor sax, then double it, and finally, they put down a track with Jim on trombone and Bobby on baritone sax.

Harry and me, feeling good.

Jim Price's outstanding arrangements resulted in the hottest horn sound you could imagine!

Before we knew it, we had half the album tracks done—no vocals yet, but the tracks were sounding so good that we had every reason to be optimistic. And our ace in the hole, "Without You," was still to be cut. One night, working late, Harry did a demo of "Without You," just him pounding the piano keys so hard you could feel his fingers bleeding, and singing as if his throat were being torn apart. By this point though, Harry had grown to hate the song. He said that it was just a piece of pop fluff—but he felt that this kind of over-the-top, angst-filled vocal performance might give it some sort of credibility. He wanted this demo to be the record! He said, "You never hear a performance like this on a record," he insisted and I told him there was a good reason why. I felt like I literally had to twist his arm to do a proper track with musicians.

It was midnight when we gathered to cut the track for "Without You." I made a few changes in the rhythm section with Jim Keltner, another one of my favorite drummers, Gary Wright of "Dream Weaver" fame on piano, John Uribe on acoustic guitar, and Klaus Voormann back on bass. I started to carefully mold the track into shape with the musicians, giving special emphasis to the dynamic contrasts that the song was based upon. But when I would ask the musicians to come in for a playback, Harry would say to them, "Does anybody know what this song is about? How could anyone like this song?"

I had to take him to a private room and implore him to stop sabotaging our efforts to make a proper track. He was playing dirty pool. Finally, I came up with a strategy to get him to stop: I told him that if he didn't like the new track better, we wouldn't use it. I was already totally convinced that we were on the verge of making a very special record. Much as I hated having to make that concession, the promise I made proved to be an effective way of silencing Harry. Without any further interference, in less than an hour, the basic track was done, other than some careful editing to select the best drum fills and insert them into the master.

The next day, I let Harry know that we were ready for his vocals, but he said he needed to have a meeting with me first. We met in the lounge of the Dorchester Hotel at four o'clock that afternoon for high tea, and I was eager to hear what Harry had on his mind. Not in my wildest dreams did I imagine he would tell me that he still liked the demo version better! After exhausting my considerable powers of persuasion, I reminded him of the commitment he made when he agreed to let me call the shots. He looked me dead in the eye and uttered a vintage Nilsson reply: "Well, I lied!"

Vexed, I looked at my watch and saw that it was six o'clock. "Holy shit, Harry," I said, "we're booked in the studio RIGHT NOW!" Without another word, we hustled out of the Dorchester, jumped into a taxi, and got to the studio where everything had been all set up for his vocals.

It was a once-in-a-lifetime performance! Harry was at his best. Not only did he deliver a Grammy Award–winning vocal, but we also never discussed the demo version again, nor did we have the slightest conflict for the duration of making the album. I never did understand the reason for Harry's fortunate about-face, but I figured it was best not to ask.

Me, Robin Cable, and Harry
(wearing the robe from the Nilsson Schmilsson album cover).

When it came time to do the vocals on "Gotta Get Up" and "Driving Along," he still didn't have a lyric. I looked at him and he looked at me, then he took a writing pad, went out to the studio, lay down on the floor with his head propped up on his elbow, and proceeded to finish the lyrics to both songs in less than an hour.

Harry had this little ditty of a song called "Coconut," which was pleasant and cute, that he sang in one voice. It dawned on me that it could be done with multiple voices playing different characters, as if it were an animated cartoon. The doctor, for example, would sing in a deep voice, with a little touch of doo-wop. I sang what I had in mind to Harry in a deep, R&B bass voice, "Now lemme get this straight…you put da lime in de coconut, you drink 'em bot'up."

Once we introduced the doctor's voice, the whole vocal arrangement opened up and Harry just ran with it, using his falsetto as the patient shrieking "Doctor, doctor," over and over, building to the climax with his trademark harmonies for the final verse. The record became a Top 10 hit, appeared in six movies, was featured prominently in *Reservoir Dogs*, and became the theme song for a lime-flavored Coca-Cola commercial. Although it was cut more than forty-five years ago, there is hardly a child born from that time to this day who doesn't know the song.

The third gem from the album, "Jump into the Fire," was very different from anything else on the record—a rock rave-up—and featured some off-the-chart bass playing by the aforementioned Herbie Flowers. He detuned his bass, which allowed him to play lower notes than the instrument is normally not capable of playing. This almost causes listeners' intestines to vibrate—it's like a musical colonoscopy. I had never heard a bass sound like that before. I had John Uribe play two completely separate blistering guitar solos, without listening to the first. Then I played them back together, one on the right and one on the left. Sometimes when you do crazy things like that, the results can be over the moon.

One evening, Jimmy Webb dropped by and put on a Little Richard–style piano part. I edited the track to create a thirty-two bar drum solo that featured Jim Keltner and Jim Gordon both playing "Lights Out." This was inspired by Ringo's solo on "Carry That Weight" from *Abbey Road.* Then Harry channeled Axl Rose with a vocal unlike anything he had ever done. I spiced it up with some vintage Trident tape delay, so that his vocal repeated each line in perfect timing with the track. It was a great effect.

"Jump into the Fire" has had considerable exposure in films and TV commercials; it was used to great effect in the Martin Scorsese film *Goodfellas,* in the scene with the helicopters hovering overhead and closing in on Ray Liotta. More recently, it was featured in a national commercial for IBM.

With the album nearly in the can, there were two major elements that had to be added: strings and horns on "Without You." There was only one person I wanted for this job—the brilliant British arranger Paul Buckmaster. His unique style and the way he wrote for strings were the outstanding elements of the classic early Elton John albums. I came to discover what made Paul's talent so unique: his strings, while providing a lush foundation, were also a part of the rhythm section, giving the track his inimitable signature. I was looking forward with great anticipation to meeting and working with him.

I asked Paul to meet me at my flat on Porchester Place near Marble Arch to go over the horn and string arrangements I heard in my head. I found him to be a striking, elegant, and soulful person who bore a slight resemblance to Errol Flynn. I'll never forget the first thing he said to me, in his dignified British accent: "Would you like to smoke some hash?" Right then I knew we were kindred spirits. After we had discussed the basic elements of the arrangement over a bottle of wine, my dear since-departed friend, Denny Cordell, stopped by to play me a record he had just finished that he was very excited about—and for good reason! The record was Joe Cocker's cover of The Beatles' "With a Little Help from My Friends." It left us mesmerized. Denny had previously produced the classic record by Procol Harum, *A Whiter Shade of Pale.*

Three nights later, the session with the strings and horns took place. The only time we could get the musicians together in the studio was at midnight, so although hard to believe, that was when the session began. Imagine—strings at midnight! Buckmaster wrote a stunning arrangement, and observing him take command of the musicians was truly like watching a master at work. When we finished the session at 2:00 a.m. and were able to listen to the record with all its components, Harry and I were thrilled beyond words, for we knew that we had just made a major record.

"Without You" was my first national No. 1 record, and it remained so for several weeks. It also became a huge international hit. Harry and I were both in Japan, basking in the glory of *Nilsson Schmilsson,* when the Grammy news came pouring in: The single and album had gone multi-Platinum and had received Grammy nominations for Record of the Year, Album of the Year, Best Contemporary Pop Vocal, and Best Engineered Record. (They did not have a separate Grammy for the producer until 1975.)

In the following years, I recorded two Nilsson songs with two wonderful female artists of all time: "Open Your Window" with Ella Fitzgerald and "Maybe" with Barbra Streisand.

From left to right: Me, Harry, and Rocco Laginestra (president of RCA Records) at a press conference in Tokyo, when we were welcomed to Japan for the first time.

What makes an artist so special is the way the sound of his or her music impacts on the ear and subsequently travels to the brain. The Beatles had it, The Stones had it, and Nilsson had it. Dreams do come true (sometimes).

Chapter 16

The Dream Is Over

When it came time to do the follow-up to *Nilsson Schmilsson*, Rocco Laginestra, then-president of RCA records, asked me if there was anything the company could do for me for the second album. I said, other than to increase my royalty, I couldn't think of a thing, but I asked them to let me marinate on it for a while. A few days later, I had a brainstorm. How about filming the making of the album?

When I presented the idea to Harry, he loved it. So as soon as we arrived back in London, we interviewed a few independent film crews, found one we liked, and started preparations to make our little documentary—always with the understanding that our first priority was to make a worthy follow-up to *Nilsson Schmilsson*.

Appropriately christened *Son of Schmilsson*, the prospects were exciting but the project proved to be a daunting task right away. Having a film crew in the studio every day, with lights blazing and two camera operators, was not always conducive to putting forth our best efforts. It required a great deal of discipline, which was not exactly Harry's strong suit. Despite this, everything appeared poised to create what would be potentially the most important album of his career…and mine as well.

Unfortunately, just when it seemed that all our dreams were coming true, everything gradually began to turn dark. It seemed that Harry had developed a death wish, for he would swallow any pill offered to him, then ask what it was that he had just consumed. The drinking, drugs, and incessant smoking were destroying his once brilliant, multifaceted voice, and it became obvious that Harry no longer cared about the quality of his songs. I had seen some signs of his addictions when we worked on the first album in London, but the success of that album was so great that I just wanted to continue forward. I had great expectations for the follow-up album, and I had no idea what was to come.

The first order of business should have been to work together and create great songs, hopefully written by Harry. Then, if needed, we would work on additional outside songs to remind people what a masterful interpreter he was. Let's not forget that "Without You" and "Everybody's Talkin'" were both written by other people and were hugely successful records. I was anticipating an entire album like that, but the best Harry could come up with for the critically important first single that would launch the album went like this: "You're breaking my heart, you're tearing it apart, so Fuck You! All I wanna do is have a good time, now I'm blue." Of all his songs for this album, this one had the most commercial potential, but when he insisted that the "Fuck You" lyric remain, it was as if he wanted to ensure that it would never be played on the radio.

Most of the other songs were satiric or didn't seem to make much sense, and there was no longer a mutual decision when it came to song selection. One day Harry showed up to do a vocal that could have become one of the more important tracks. But he had a half bottle of cognac in hand; the first half had been consumed earlier that day. He did two takes, but his voice sounded very raw and the vocals were alcohol-induced. Harry Nilsson, once the master singer, didn't care what his vocal sounded like now. The performance made me sad. After we listened back, he declared in a slurred voice, "Well, that's the vocal." I knew right then and there that our partnership was doomed.

I had looked forward to a lifetime of hits together, where every track would be a treasure. This album turned out to be the opposite. Sales went

Harry and me.

from five million for *Nilsson Schmilsson* to five hundred thousand, with his fan base shrinking fast.

Another crucial factor in the demise of *Son of Schmilsson* was that RCA Records released it six months prematurely. They needed the billing to make their quarterly profits, so they ignored the fact that "Coconut" went Top 10 on the *Billboard* Hot 100 the same week they decided to release *Son of Schmilsson*. This was sinful, for most record companies dream about having a Top 10 follow-up to a worldwide No. 1.

One afternoon a few months later, Harry and I regrouped as we tried to put the *Son of Schmilsson* debacle behind us. I asked Harry if he had given any serious thought to what he wanted to do for his next album. He said he'd already made his decision—he wanted to do an album of standards! It became clear that Harry was moving forward on this without me, and I was shocked—we were going through a break-up. The irony was that I have always loved standards, and some thirty years later, would produce standards albums with Carly Simon (*Moonlight Serenade*), Art Garfunkel (*Some Enchanted Evening*), The Temptations (*For Lovers Only*), and ultimately, four albums with Rod Stewart as part of *The Great American Songbook Collection*.

But timing is everything and, in my opinion, this was not the time for Harry Nilsson to come out with a goddamn standards album. He needed to straighten up, buckle down, and put forward his best creative genius as a singer and songwriter in order to deliver a worthy follow-up to *Nilsson Schmilsson*. I believed that he desperately needed to win back the millions of fans who'd been turned off by his last half-hearted effort.

To add insult to injury, Harry had decided to call the new standards album *A Little Touch of Schmilsson in the Night*. This made my blood turn cold, as I felt that Harry and I had created a Schmilsson *brand*—a vocal personality who was a little bit of a nut, a wild and wacky yet romantic dude. It just seemed totally wrong for him to use the Schmilsson name to promote a standards album considering the fact that the music had no relation to the title. I wanted to grab him by the lapels, shake him, and say, "Harry... what happened to you? We had such a creative chemistry! How about the acid trips we took in Hawaii and at the Children's Zoo in Kyoto on our trip to Japan? What about our documentary that we never even finished?" (We were definitely ahead of the curve on that one. MTV wouldn't come into being for another ten years.)

Harry had made seven albums prior to *Nilsson Schmilsson* and his quirky, whimsical lyrics and uniquely brilliant voice were more than evident on those. Yet with the exception of "Everybody's Talkin'" (written by Fred Neil), and "One (Is the Loneliest Number)," which Three Dog Night made into a hit, Harry never had a successful single or album before or after *Nilsson Schmilsson*. Instead, he continued his pursuit of deconstructing Harry. Even on his standards album, his voice was noticeably weak and lacked the verve and timbre that once represented his signature sound. It appeared that his plan to systematically destroy his voice was working.

It's still devastating to me to think about what Harry could have been. Harry was a complex guy. When I first met him, I felt that he was the nicest guy I'd ever met, but over time, he became somewhat of a Jekyll & Hyde. But, I came to cherish the friendship we had, and so it truly hurt me when I saw him continue to spiral downward without any regard for himself. I took comfort in knowing that at least he managed to find happiness in the end with his seven children and third wife, Una, with whom he was madly in love.

Harry died on January 15, 1994. He was only fifty-two.

Chapter 17

Carly Simon, No Secrets

From the moment I heard Carly Simon's first album, I was determined to work with her someday, some way. The reason for this was threefold. First, I fell in love with her voice—it sounded like a cross between a well-lubricated trumpet and a mellifluous bass clarinet; second, she had an ability to write unique, personal songs and melodies that captured the best qualities in her voice; and third, she had a unique look that personified beauty, heat, and sensuality.

In May of 1972, while I was finishing the *Son of Schmilsson* album in London, Abe Somer, my good friend and attorney, came to town. Before going to dinner one night, we met at the flat overlooking Hyde Park that I was renting from actor Richard Chamberlain. I felt the need to express to someone close to me just how much I wanted to produce Carly Simon's next album. Abe and I would share musical thoughts and ideas quite often, so I proceeded to play every track on her last album, going over in great detail how I would have produced her differently.

The following week I was back in LA working on another project, when I received a call from Jac Holzman, the founder and chairman of Elektra Records. He asked me, straight up, if I would like to produce one of his artists: CARLY SIMON. I almost flipped out and asked what made him call. He gave me a simple answer: He thought Carly and I would make a good fit. I told him that this was something I'd been dreaming of for some time.

Two weeks later, Carly and I had a "getting to know you" meeting at her apartment in New York. Everything went well, and we both agreed that we wanted to work together. There was just one stipulation. During the recording of her first two albums, Carly wound up having affairs with both of her producers, and that had ultimately interfered with the work. The most recent foray had had particularly disastrous consequences, as the producer involved had seriously contemplated leaving his wife. So, Arlyne Rothberg, Carly's trusted, long-time manager, had made Carly swear to what amounted to a blood oath that, come hell or high water, under no circumstances, would she and I *EVER* have an affair!

While I had always been inclined not to mix business and pleasure, I must say I felt that if Carly ever DID have an affair with a producer again, I would be the best candidate. But instead of having an affair, we became lifelong friends, a relationship that has now lasted over *forty-five years*!

Our next meeting took place in LA one month later, at my Wonderland Park house. She played me several songs she had written for the project and we started to discuss what the essence of the album should be. Carly had come from a folk music background, and prior to her career as a solo artist, she and her sister Lucy had performed in folk clubs as a duo called The Simon Sisters. One of the main things I wanted to bring to Carly's music was a bit more of a rock-influenced sound, with a particular emphasis on the drums. At one point she played me a song called "Ballad of a Vain Man." I instinctively started playing some conga drums I had nearby and added some fills in the places where it builds as she sang, *"I had some dreams they were clouds in my coffee..."*

She found my percussive accompaniment interesting but was leery about me changing her folk jewel into too much of a rock song. I assured her that when she heard the whole band play it, especially with tom-toms added to those particular sections, she would feel differently. I was convinced that those throbbing tom-tom fills would add something special.

After we went over several other songs, we decided to celebrate by smoking a little weed. Carly was never really a smoker, so after just a few hits, she started to feel a little dizzy. I suggested that she lie down on the couch and then I administered the surefire cure for too much pot—a pint of Häagen-Dazs vanilla ice cream. She recovered in a matter of minutes!

We both agreed to do the album in London, which had become a second home to me at that point. So, I booked Trident Studios with Robin Cable as the engineer. We arrived in London around the middle of September 1972. Carly had written some more wonderful, personal songs—notably, "The Right Thing to Do." She had written it for James Taylor, whom she was planning to marry as soon as we finished recording in London. It's a very tender, melodic love song with a moving lyric. This track turned out to be one of the best songs on the album, and I'm told it was a personal favorite of Michael Jackson's. I couldn't think of a better song to begin the album, and it later became a Top 10 single on the *Billboard* Hot 100.

We were all anxious to sink our teeth into "Ballad of a Vain Man." I knew that the choice of drummer was vitally important to this track. We tried it with Andy Newmark first, the drummer in Carly's band. Andy's a fine drummer, but he just wasn't right for the song. Then we cut the track with Barry Morgan—the hottest session drummer in London. This time it was almost on the money—meaning it was a perfectly good track, but I felt that something still wasn't quite right. It didn't have the magic I had envisioned for this exceptional song, and the most difficult part of my job was to figure out precisely how to mold it into its proper form. We included some instrumental overdubs, and Carly even added some vocals.

Everyone thought that we were getting close to the finished record, but it was too heavy-handed. Whenever we would play it back in the studio, my stomach tied up in knots and I found myself in a terrible dilemma. How could I have let this track progress so far, when deep in my gut I knew that the feel wasn't what it should be? It wasn't in the right pocket—the most important element in the making of any record. "Ballad of a Vain Man" is a unique song, like a musical play in three acts, and it required a drummer with a high level of musicianship and a special touch that combined finesse with a solid back beat. I was in a quandary as to who that person might be and where I might find him in London.

Then a miracle happened. From out of nowhere, the next afternoon, there was a phone call for me. The voice on the line said, "Hey, Richard, it's Jim Gordon, the drummer. Remember me?"

I had worked with Jim more than any other drummer over the previous four years. Most recently, he had contributed brilliantly to the *Nilsson Schmilsson* album. I knew instantly that he would provide the perfect solution for what I felt the track was lacking. But, was he in London? As luck would have it, he had just arrived to play a concert with Frank Zappa at Royal Albert Hall the following night. So I asked the most important question: "Can you be at Trident Studios tonight at seven?" When he said he could make it, I was ecstatic!

A few hours later, the drums were set up and I began to familiarize Jim with the song, first by playing the last version we had done. To show him how I wanted to improve the groove, I played "Let's Stay Together," the Al Green classic.

I felt such peace listening to him play so effortlessly on the first run-through. Before Jim had showed up, I had spent hours with other drummers who just couldn't get it right. Almost as soon as he sat down, Jim got the details and nuances. There was a special drum fill that was really important to me, as it set up the second, third, and fourth verses, but I didn't want just any old pedestrian fill. I wanted a Benny Benjamin "Motown" fill, which very few drummers can execute properly. Finally, there were those pulsating tom-tom fills that I had played on the congas that first time Carly played the song for me at my home in Los Angeles. Jim executed these fills to perfection and, in fact, they became two of the major hooks of the record.

Amidst all the excitement, I did something that was totally out of character for me. I realized as the session with Jim was getting underway that I had forgotten to call Carly to give her a heads-up as to what was happening. I tried to reach her, but she was already on her way to the studio. Then Jim asked if it would be okay for Frank Zappa to stop by. Since Frank was the one responsible for Jim being in London in the first place, I thought it was the least I could do. Frank was a veritable icon, widely regarded as the godfather of psychedelic rock by virtue of the groundbreaking 1966 album, *Freak Out*, by his group, The Mothers of Invention.

When Carly entered the studio, expecting just to add some finishing vocal touches on what we'd been working on over the previous week, she looked as if she had seen a ghost. Suddenly, she was greeted with a new track, a different drummer, and, just for a little extra color, FRANK ZAPPA!

She asked if we could speak in private in another room. The moment we were alone, she burst into tears and wanted to know why we were doing the track again when she felt that we had a perfectly good version. She had a right to be upset, but I explained to her that she should trust me: We finally had the perfect drummer who would help us to realize the record's ultimate potential. I was absolutely certain this was the moment we'd been waiting for.

Without another word, she wiped away her tears, gave me a hug, walked down to the studio, and took her place at the piano. But before we were done, there was still a bit of magic that would permeate the record.

While Klaus Voormann was warming up on the bass, he made a sound that I had never heard before—it sounded sort of like he'd run all his fingers along the strings at once. As soon as I heard it, I stopped him immediately, and asked him what he had just played. He replied, "What do you mean?" he replied (in his German accent), "I was just warming up my fingers."

"Klaus," I said, "do me a favor—play *exactly* what I just heard, even if it sounds like all the notes are muddled together!"

When Carly heard this, she leaned into the mic, and spontaneously whispered in a sensuous tone, "Son-of-a-Gun."

Thus, the most unique intro in pop music was born. After two bars, Jimmy Ryan, Carly's superb guitarist, entered with the sexiest acoustic rhythm guitar, and we were out of the starting gate—off and running! After two takes, I knew we had nailed it.

That weekend, Jimmy Ryan and I went into the studio to finish the guitars. First, we painstakingly went over the acoustic rhythm part until it was right in the pocket from top to bottom. Then, he doubled the acoustic and added an electric rhythm that gave the track a bit of a Stones feel. The solo came next—and the track required a very special solo. It had to be strong but not overplayed, with an explosive entrance, and reeking with melodic integrity—something like a George Harrison solo. We spent most of the weekend on that solo. It had to be just right!

Then came the biggest surprise in a record that was already full of surprises. I find it unfathomable that forty-four years after the record was released, most people, even educated music ears, are unaware that Mick Jagger is singing with Carly in the second, third, and fourth choruses. Here is the story behind that remarkable happening.

When we arrived in London, Carly said she had a great idea for the record. She suggested that we get Mick to sing on it! I looked at her in a state of disbelief. The Stones were at the peak of their career, which made it extremely unlikely that Mick would sing on anyone else's record—especially since he had never done it before. Besides, I genuinely felt that the song was an absolute hit with just Carly and background singers, and as great as it would be to have had Jagger sing on it, many people might then attribute its success, at least in part, to his presence on the record. I was concerned that it could potentially detract from the brilliant lyrics and stunningly constructed melody.

We were nearing completion of *No Secrets*, as the album came to be called, based on one of the best songs on the record, "We Have No Secrets."

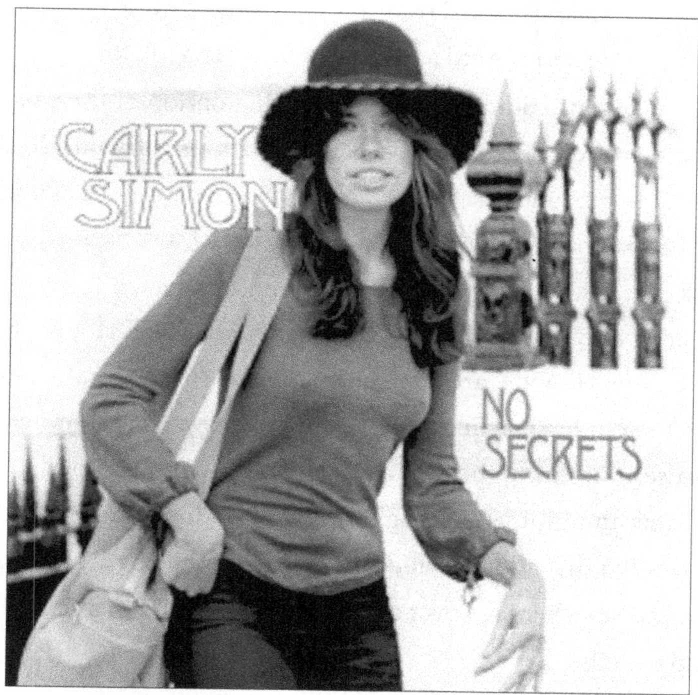

No Secrets *album cover.*

We changed our base of operations to AIR Studios owned by Sir George Martin. Its Studio A was a large room, suitable for an orchestra; Studio B, the rock 'n' roll room was located in the back; and Studio C, a state-of-the-art Neve mixing console, connected with an additional small and intimate room, which was excellent for vocals. I was exceptionally high on my way to the studio on this particular morning, and it was all I could do to not break into that fabulous song from the musical *Oklahoma!* about the feeling you have when everything goes your way!

I knew Carly and I had made a special album, and with "Ballad of a Vain Man" clearly becoming more infused with rock influences, it was obvious that the song should now be called, "You're So Vain." We had faced a number of challenges, and I was proud to have "scaled the mountain" and reached all my goals. The final record sounded exactly the way I had hoped it would—the greatest reward a record producer can ask for.

As I walked into Studio C that day, feeling on top of the world, who should be there but Mick Jagger! Carly and Mick were friends, so she had reached out to him and asked if he wanted to be a part of the album. I had no idea that was happening so you can imagine my surprise!

Mick greeted me warmly, and I told him how much it meant to me to have been a fly on the wall at the all-night rehearsal at Villa Nellcôte the year before. He and Carly eventually went out to the studio, took their places on their individual mics, and, as the track played back, started to sing the choruses. Watching those two large, plump, sensual mouths moving together was an unforgettable sight. It felt like a historic moment! Carly was so inspired that after she and Mick had done their part together, she went out and sang her lead over again—one take—and that's the vocal we ended up using!

When I mixed the record, I didn't want Mick's voice to dominate, yet I wanted it to be heard. The balance had to be perfect. So, for the second chorus, I mixed it in with Carly's and then made it gradually louder on each successive chorus. As I mentioned earlier, most people are unaware that Mick is on the record—but now that you know, play it for anyone and see how shocked they are. I must say that the sound of Mick's voice adds a unique edge to the sound of the record, especially when he and Carly sing, "Don't you, don't you, don't you!"

"You're So Vain" was finally finished. I consider this to be the closest I've come to making a perfect record and it is the one of which I am most proud. Both single and album debuted at No. 6 on the *Billboard* chart and almost immediately shot to No. 1—a rarity in those days!

Carly and me in the studio.

We moved over to Studio B, the rock 'n' roll room, which I had booked to finish a very special track. Carly had requested that we do one of James Taylor's songs on the album, but she wanted it to be one of his more thoughtful and penetrating compositions. I remembered that in the early part of his career he'd written a very bluesy song called "Night Owl." Carly decided to take a chance on the idea—and bingo! We cut a great track that rocked like crazy, featuring Nicky Hopkins on piano. It had a scorching sax solo by Bobby Keys, possibly the best I've ever heard him play: pure rock 'n' roll; background vocals by Doris Troy, who had a major hit in the early '60s with "Just One Look"; and Bonnie Bramlett of Delaney & Bonnie fame. And, of course, we had Carly, whose voice always added an essential ingredient to the background voices.

Carly really reached out and delivered a vocal performance that was unlike anything she'd ever done. I planned to put on the final overdubs that night. As if there weren't enough memorable moments to savor on that particular day, there were still more surprises waiting for us in the wings.

Paul and me.

Directly across the hall was Studio A, the biggest room there, and guess who should happen to be recording that night with a big orchestra—none other than Paul McCartney, with George Martin. They were doing the theme song for the upcoming James Bond movie, *Live and Let Die*, a McCartney masterpiece.

As we were putting on the final touches, the most fun of anything on the album, Paul and Linda McCartney entered the control room! They were done working on the "Live and Let Die" track and had come over to hang out at the "Night Owl" session. We had a bottle of tequila on hand to add some spice to the evening, and while the track was playing back, everyone was moving and grooving. It turned the session into a great party! The control room felt like it was spinning.

McCartney then pleasantly surprised me when he asked if he and Linda could join the background singers! Paul and I went into the studio together, sat down at the piano, and organized some background parts. This, as you can imagine, was an unexpected, incomparable thrill for me.

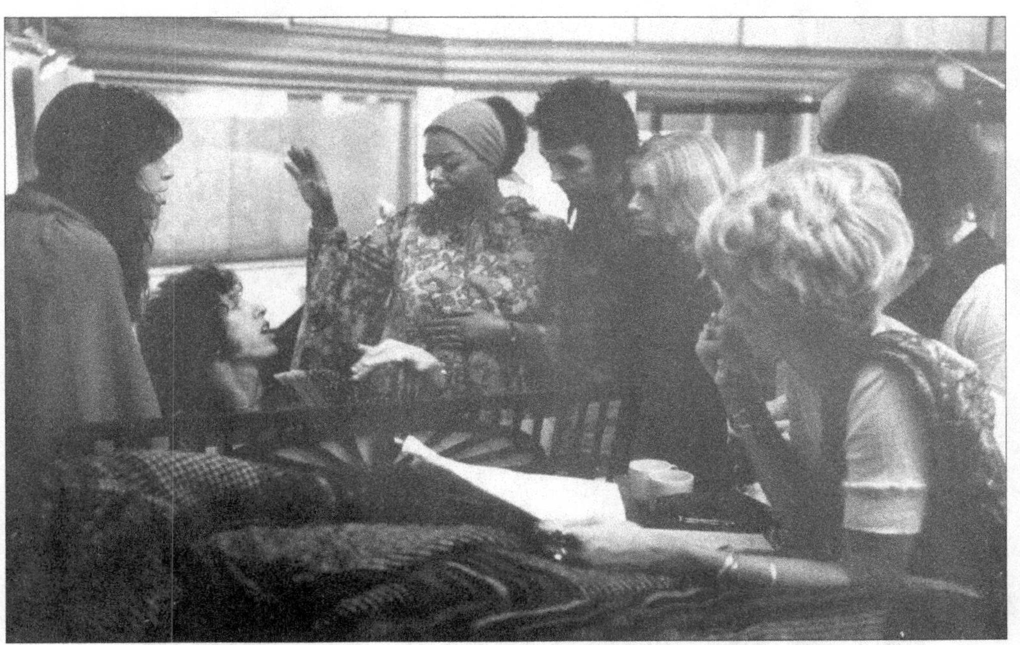

Left to right: Carly, me, Doris Troy, Paul, Linda, Jimmy Ryan, and Bonnie Bramlett rehearsing the background vocals for "Night Owl."

Incidentally, Paul McCartney was instrumental in getting James Taylor signed to Apple Records. Taylor released his self-titled debut album, *James Taylor*, on Apple, and it happened to be his only recording with that label. McCartney had been involved in the recording of Taylor's album, in which "Night Owl" was included.

After a couple of hours, the track was finished and so was Carly's album. All that remained was the mixing, which I did back in LA with Bill Schnee, who had become my ace-in-the-hole engineer.

The final chapter of the "You're So Vain" saga would not be complete without answering the question that continues to fascinate people forty-eight years later. I am still asked all the time who the song is about. Even when they are told the answer, it's as if they don't really want to know. They'd rather

Carly and Warren Beatty.

keep asking than put the matter to rest once and for all. It's more exciting! Since it's been revealed numerous times, I'll take this opportunity to give my insider's scoop: the person that the song is based on is really a composite of several men that Carly dated in the '60s and early '70s, but primarily, it's about my good friend, Warren Beatty.

* * *

A year later, Carly and I decided to see if we could make lightning strike twice, so we embarked on a follow-up record that would come to be called *Hotcakes*. Carly worked diligently to craft meaningful, personal songs for this album. Leading the pack was one of my favorite songs she ever wrote, "Haven't Got Time for the Pain." Her performance was exemplary! For an extra treat, we brought in the brilliant string arranger, Paul Buckmaster, from London, whom I hadn't worked with since the memorable "Without You" session a year earlier. Just when you think the record will fade, there is a sudden instrumental break—an inspired piece of neo-classical string writing by Buckmaster, influenced by Igor Stravinsky. The only other backing is by the brilliant percussionist Ralph MacDonald.

To complete the album, we needed a song that would come flying out of the box, ideally one that could work as a duet between Carly and James Taylor, who had just gotten married. I had a brainstorm. I remembered one of my favorite records that I felt would work well for James and Carly—Inez and Charlie Foxx's memorable "Mockingbird." The problem was that the song had only one verse—but James wisely got permission from the publisher to write some additional lyrics that were pure vintage James. The new verses gave the song some much-needed depth and relevance and put James' stamp all over it. Both artists went into orbit for their performance.

We cut most of the tracks, including "Mockingbird" and "Haven't Got Time for the Pain," at Producer's Workshop in LA with Bill Schnee engineering. The

"Mockingbird" track really smoked, featuring Dr. John on piano and organ, Robbie Robertson on guitar, Jim Keltner on drums and Klaus Voormann on bass, with a scorching tenor sax solo by Michael Brecker. The rhythm section for "Pain" was James Taylor and Jimmy Ryan on acoustic guitars, Jim and Klaus, once again, on drums and bass, and Carly on piano.

Both songs were obvious choices for singles. "Mockingbird" peaked at No. 5 on the *Billboard* chart, and "Haven't Got Time for the Pain," my favorite song on the album, reached No. 14. The album ascended to No. 2. It was a special treat having James play acoustic guitar on six of the tracks.

Carly and James Taylor performing "Mockingbird" at Madison Square Garden.

Hotcakes will always be a memorable experience because Carly was extremely pregnant when we began working on it. After two weeks in LA, we immediately traveled to New York and stayed for two months to finish the album at The Hit Factory.

Carly pregnant with her son Ben in the studio in 1973.

It was a bit challenging to get great vocal performances while eight months pregnant, but Carly, champ that she is, delivered with flying colors. Within a few weeks of completion, she gave birth to Sally, her first child, followed a few years later by Ben.

Chapter 18

Martha Reeves, Many Rivers to Cross

One day in January 1974, I got a call from an old friend, Artie Mogull, who had a long and colorful history in the record business and had recently been appointed executive vice president of A&R for MCA Records, the precursor to Universal Music. He told me he had just signed Martha Reeves and wanted me to produce her. I was intrigued because I had been a huge fan of her remarkable, soulful voice with its unmistakable cutting edge. I have always considered her versions of "Dancing in the Street" and "Nowhere to Run" two of the greatest records ever made.

What troubled me was that MCA Records didn't have much of an R&B department, especially when it came to promotion—which is the lifeblood of our industry. One of the most important criteria in deciding whether to commit to a project is to be sure that the record company is properly equipped *to deliver* that particular artist, both at the radio and retail level. That's where Artie Mogull loomed large! I knew that he wasn't afraid to push the pedal to the metal and do whatever was necessary to break an artist like Martha Reeves. He would unhesitatingly kick ass or bring in independent promotion, something this project would likely require.

I felt confident that I could make a great record with her, and Artie promised me that it would get every opportunity to be heard. That was all I needed to hear, and I signed on. Once I started working with Martha, I was amazed at how much she was capable of doing with her voice—how much depth there was and how much she could move in different directions and still be very comfortable. I gathered the best songs I could find, songs that would bring out the unique qualities of her voice. She, in turn, delivered ten sterling vocal performances.

The band I assembled was world-class. I was thrilled when I heard that the legendary Motown bass player James Jamerson was in LA. I immediately booked him for most of the sessions, and he was nothing short of amazing! On guitars, I had Melvin "Wah Wah Watson" Ragin and Dennis Coffey, who had a recent million-selling instrumental pop/R&B single, "Scorpio." On piano was the renowned Joe Sample, and on drums, good old "solid-as-a-rock" Jim Keltner and James Gadson. Horns were featured on several tracks and I had booked the best there were: Stevie Wonder's players, Trevor Lawrence and Steve Madaio. They played on all of Stevie's classic albums, most significantly on his landmark single, "Superstition."

This album was being produced at the same time that I was finishing up Carly's *Hotcakes* album. I asked James Taylor if he wanted to hear one of Martha's songs. After listening to "Power of Love," James was so inspired that he asked to do the horn arrangements for the song. I had a lot of respect for James and his talent, so even though I was surprised at his request, I trusted that he would know what to do. And he did not disappoint! He came to us with an incredible classic R&B horn arrangement and I was beyond impressed. This ended up being a huge score for Martha and me!

The tracks were all coming out superbly. To give you an idea of some of the other song selections I came up with: "Wild Night" (written by Van Morrison and featured in the movie *Thelma & Louise*); "I Got to Use My Imagination" (written by Gerry Goffin and Barry Goldberg); a completely unique big band arrangement of Marvin Gaye's "Ain't That Peculiar"; a little-known Carole King gem of a song called "Dixie Highway"; and the immortal song by Jimmy Cliff, "Many Rivers to Cross." The people I worked closely with on this album told me they thought it could be the best album

I'd ever produced. And, for the first time, my deal with MCA mandated the producer's credit be on the front cover of the album.

There was one critical problem: I wasn't the only one who recognized the value of Artie Mogull to their projects. Several new MCA artists wanted an "Artie Mogull clause" in their contracts stating that if Artie Mogull were to leave MCA for any reason, they would have the opportunity to leave as well. Needless to say, this did not go over too well. Once the corporate board found this out, Artie Mogull was promptly terminated. This left me on board a ship without a captain, but I was too deeply into the album to consider bailing out. All I could do was finish the work to the best of my ability and, I must say, I could not have been more proud of the final result.

A few months later, I found myself on a flight from LA to New York with Paul Drew, the most important radio consultant in the country at the time. We had just released "Wild Night" as Martha's new single, which, unfortunately, didn't connect with an audience.

"I'll bet you thought you had a big hit with that record," Paul said, and I admitted that I did. "So did I," he replied. It was just as I'd feared: MCA had had no idea how to launch this ship. Was it R&B, contemporary pop, or rock 'n' roll? Much to my chagrin, without anyone to chart a course, the album got lost at sea.

Chapter 19

Ringo Starr...Starring the Beatles

The Beatles were, by far, the biggest and most profound musical influence in my life and career. In 1966, they stopped performing live concerts because they could no longer hear themselves play over the incessant screaming of their fans—primarily teenage girls. They retired to the recording studio and wrapped themselves in a cocoon of creativity and artistic experimentation. A mix of genres, their music ranged wildly, from Paul's British music hall influences, to John's forays into electronic music and tape manipulation, to George's love of eastern musical culture. With all of this and the art of George Martin, who helped them incorporate cutting-edge string and horn arrangements, they redefined contemporary pop music with some of the finest songs of the second half of the twentieth century.

In the process, they were instrumental in turning the LP into a true art form, where the record had the potential to become not just a collection of brilliant songs, but also the soundtrack of our lives. Starting with *Rubber Soul* in 1965, the band made monumental leaps forward with *Revolver* later that year; and in May 1967, they released *Sgt. Pepper's Lonely Hearts Club Band.* This is arguably the greatest album of all time and contained some of their most interesting tracks, including "Strawberry Fields Forever," "Penny Lane," "Baby, You're a Rich Man," "Hello Goodbye," and "All You Need Is Love." Following *Sgt. Pepper* was *Magical Mystery Tour* in November 1967 and *The White Album* in 1968. That same year, they released "Hey Jude" under their own record label, Apple—this song became their first non-album single and was a No. 1 hit in many countries across the world, and many music critics still deem it one of the greatest songs of all time. They continued to produce albums and in 1969, they released *Abbey Road*, which included George's masterpiece, "Something," backed by Lennon's brilliant, acerbic, "Come Together." These iconic albums were all creative entities unto themselves and totally redefined the way people all over the world related to music—and then, in 1970, the band broke up.

Just before their breakup was reported in newspapers, Ringo Starr decided to record a solo album of standards. "I wondered, what shall I do with my life now that it's all over?" Ringo told an interviewer for the album's liner notes. "I was brought up with all of these songs, you know. My family used to sing them, my mother, my dad, my aunties and uncles. They were the first musical influences on me. I went to George Martin, The Beatles' longtime producer, and said, let's do an album of standards, and to make it interesting we'll have all the arrangements done by different people."

Ringo listed possible songs to record, figured out in what key they should be sung, and set about choosing arrangers. Paul McCartney, Maurice Gibb, and Quincy Jones were just a few of the people who participated. I was told that The Beatles were fans of the album I'd done with Tiny Tim and that, I would assume, was the reason I got a call from Ringo's representatives asking me if I would like to do a track. Naturally, I was delighted to be part of any Beatles project.

The song I was given was "Sentimental Journey," which became the title of the album. As an arranger, I never actually got to meet Ringo during the process. Instead, I cut the track in LA and sent it to him in London, where he did his vocals and finished the rest of the album.

One year later, in 1970, I was at Apple Studios in London producing an album with Fanny, the first all-girl rock band signed to a major label. (I'd signed them to Warner Brothers while I was a staff producer there. The band was composed of excellent musicians and counted David Bowie as one of its biggest fans.) We'd gone to London to record so that we could work with Geoff Emerick, the recording engineer for The Beatles' landmark albums.

Knowing I was in the building, Ringo came down one afternoon to thank me for contributing to his album. In addition to the Fanny project, I was also cutting a few tracks with Bobby Hatfield of The Righteous Brothers. I asked Ringo if he might be up for playing drums on the Hatfield session. I had always considered him one of the two best drummers in the history of rock—the other being Charlie Watts—so I was more than pleased when he happily complied. The session went great. Ringo was as delightful to work with in person as I had anticipated, and I liked him immediately. He was a true team player.

* * *

Two years later, I was back in London at Trident Studios, working on my second album with Harry Nilsson, *Son of Schmilsson*. I phoned Ringo to ask if he would consider playing on some Nilsson tracks. He agreed to do it, and enjoyed the session so much that he got in touch with George Harrison, who came down to the studio a few days later to put a guitar solo on one of the tracks! The dark days that came with that Nilsson album were certainly brightened by my new friendships and interactions with Ringo and George.

Now that we had worked together on more than one occasion, I felt that it wouldn't be inappropriate to begin my dream quest. For over a year, I tried to convince Ringo to make a different kind of solo album, one that would fully reflect the personality and charm of his voice. I envisioned it like a Beatles record but with Ringo singing lead on every track. I was insistent but he was resistant; he did not want to devote five months to making a record, and that's how long it had taken to make the last few Beatles albums.

The idea remained on the shelf for another year until, one day, I got a call from the producer of the upcoming Grammy Awards show asking me if I could persuade Harry Nilsson to be a presenter as our album, *Nilsson Schmilsson*, had been nominated in nearly every major category. Since Nilsson had never appeared live in his entire career, I told them I seriously doubted he would comply, but then a light bulb went off in my head! Knowing that Harry and Ringo had become very good friends, I told the Grammy people that if they could get Ringo to present it with him, I was sure Nilsson would agree. It meant the two artists would have to travel to Nashville, as that was where the awards were being held for the first and last time, but this surely would give the show a lot more spice!

My hunch was right on the money. A few days later, I got a call from Ringo. "Hey Rich, I'm not going to come all that way there just to present a Grammy Award. You know how you've been talking about doing an album? Well, why don't we go into the studio in Nashville and see what happens?"

"Great idea, Ring," I said (that was my nickname for him), "but I would strongly recommend that we go to LA and do the sessions there. All our friends that we would want to play on the album are already there. It's just a better environment for the record we want to make."

This made a lot of sense, and Ringo agreed. Little had I known that my idea of asking Ringo to co-present the Grammy with Nilsson would open the door to making my dream come true.

Two weeks later, we all arrived in Nashville and met in Ringo's hotel suite to play some song ideas for the proposed album. First, he played me a song he had written with George Harrison called "Photograph." It had a hauntingly romantic melody, very symbolic of George's best songs with a simple yet penetrating lyric:

Every time I see your face,
It reminds me of the places we used to go
But all I've got is a photograph,

And I realize you're not coming back anymore.

I thought I'd make it, the day you went away,
But I can't make it, till you come home again to stay.

I can't get used to living here
While my heart is broke, my tears I cry for you,
I want you here to have and hold,
As the years go by, and we grow old and gray

Now you're expecting me to live without you,
But that's not something that I'm looking forward to.

I can't get used to living here
While my heart is broke, my tears I cry for you,
I want you here to have and hold,
As the years go by, and we grow old and gray.

It was a perfect song for Ringo, although he had never done anything remotely like it before. It really expressed the emotion of longing for a lost love. I knew in an instant it would be a smash! This was an unexpected bonus since I thought I was going to have to come up with all the songs. But now it was my turn to show that I had a trump card to match "Photograph."

I proceeded to play a demo of a reworked, more contemporary arrangement of the rock 'n' roll classic "You're Sixteen (You're Beautiful, and You're Mine)." I got it from my old friend Artie Wayne at Warner/Chappell Music. Originally a hit by Johnny Burnette in the late '50s, I knew it had Ringo's imprint all over it. As it turned out, there was no song on the album more evocative of Ringo's spirit and charm than this one.

Knowing that we had two killer pieces of material to start with, we eagerly boarded the plane back to LA the next day. George was already there completing work on his second solo LP, *Living in the Material World,*

Klaus Voormann did a series of lithographs, one for each track on the album. This is the one for "Photograph."

and said that he was totally available to work on Ringo's project. This also marked the beginning of my very close friendship with George.

The following Monday, March 12, 1973, the recording began. Here was the stellar lineup for most of the sessions:

Also part of the session was drummer Jim Keltner. Ringo and Keltner loved to play together, and they complemented each other in a very special way.

Klaus was the closest thing to Paul McCartney on bass and had played on John's and George's solo albums. He had a special connection to The Beatles since he was the person who'd discovered them in 1962 when they were playing

Ringo on the drums.

Klaus Voormann on bass.

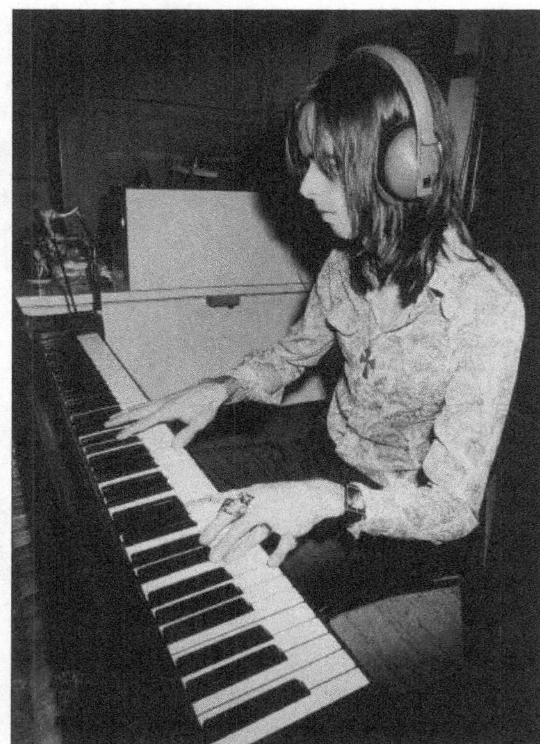

Nicky Hopkins on piano.

George Harrison on guitar.

at the Star-Club in Hamburg, Germany, a sleazy dive on Reeperbahn, a street lined with hookers. (Much later, in 1968, I'd have the opportunity to walk down that street with Tiny Tim.)

At the time, Klaus was attending art school in Hamburg. He went to the club to see this unknown group from Liverpool and was immediately intrigued. He then brought all his friends to see them and suddenly they were the toast of Hamburg! Four years later, Klaus created the cover art for The Beatles' *Revolver* album. I already had an auspicious musical history with Klaus, as he'd played on the Nilsson albums and Carly Simon's *No Secrets*.

Rounding out the rhythm section was my dear friend Nicky Hopkins, quite simply one of the all-time greatest rock 'n' roll piano players I've ever worked with.

The studio I chose was Sunset Sound, Studio 2. I had worked there extensively and felt it was just the right size to give everyone plenty of breathing room and still feel intimate. It also had a great-sounding Bechstein grand piano, a wonderful old Trident recording console, and a healthy supply of outboard equipment, i.e., a variety of compressors and API equalizers, among other things.

We started with "Photograph." I knew it would be the most demanding groove to nail just right, especially with two drummers, but I was eager to accept the challenge of producing my first track involving The Beatles. When we started to run it down, it instantly became clear that all of us were united in our love for Ringo!

Moreover, George's presence as a musician and co-writer cast a certain magic over the track; I soon realized that everyone involved also loved George. This enchanting song that they had written together motivated us to unite as a family, which helped to make it a very special record. But the real star (no pun intended), was Ringo's heartfelt vocal performance, highlighted by the soulful harmony vocal that George sang behind Ringo on the verses and the second half of the bridges, thus creating a unique Beatles vocal sound that expressed just how much affection George and Ringo had for each other.

The following night, we cut "You're Sixteen." The band was brimming with confidence knowing that we had nailed "Photograph" and were ready to rock and have a party—which is exactly what we did! Nicky Hopkins set the mood perfectly with a rolling piano intro, followed by Ringo and Klaus underpinning the track with a classic shuffle groove aided by Keltner's second drum/percussion part; he played only the hi-hat cymbals and the tastiest of snare fills, with a little drag roll attached. It was clearly evident that everyone was having a blast—it was pure rock 'n' roll! The song was a very charming lyric with a contemporary groove and it was of real musical merit, as each line rhymed perfectly with the line before it, with Ringo singing about "lips like strawberry wine," and "eyes that sparkle and shine." One particular lyric which says the love interest of the song stepped out of his dreams and into his car even inspired one of Klaus' lithographs.

A few nights later, Harry Nilsson, who had been eagerly waiting to make a contribution to the album, came in and put some vintage Nilsson backing vocals on "You're Sixteen." This added a special warmth and provided a bed that cradled Ringo's vocal. This recording will forever be associated with Ringo—in my opinion, it was the best performance of his career. The song can only be described as jubilant. Both tracks went on to become No. 1 Gold records and massive worldwide hits.

George came by the studio later that night all excited. He had written another song for the album, called "Sunshine Life For Me (Sail Away Raymond)." It was completely different from anything we had done—a sort of seafarer's hoedown and would require very special ethnic instrumentation: accordion, mandolin, banjo, and other things. George had just spoken with Robbie Robertson, the leader of the group called The Band. Not only did Robbie say he would play on the track, but he got the entire group to

Klaus' lithograph for "You're Sixteen."

participate. This was a very meaningful addition to the album since The Band was a most respected rock group and perfect casting for the song. The Band's fabled drummer, Levon Helm, left the drumming to Ringo and played mandolin on this unique track.

The last song we cut that first week was "Oh My My." A great friend of mine from New York, Vini Poncia, had recently moved to LA. Vini is a very gifted songwriter/producer with whom I had worked for years, so I put him together with Ringo and they came up with this song. It rocks more than any track on the album, as Ringo and Keltner came up with a monster rhythmic groove that sounded like thundering drums, while Klaus played this funky sliding bass part, and Billy Preston played probably some of the best gospel piano I'd ever heard. Martha Reeves, lead singer of "Dancing in the Street" and Merry Clayton of "Gimme Shelter" fame added the background vocals later. (Surprisingly, those two songs have a great deal in common with "Oh My My" as they truly fuse rock 'n' roll with R&B in a soulfully inspired way.)

"Oh My My" went on to become the third single from the album, and a Top 5 smash. It was the perfect way to conclude a memorable first week in the studio, and for the icing on the cake, it was captured brilliantly by my longtime recording and mixing engineer Bill Schnee. We had already worked together for the better part of ten years at this point. He deserved some special award for having put up with me for so long. Having Bill riding "shotgun" was a constant source of comfort and inspiration.

Just before we left for the weekend break, Ringo told me that he had heard from John, who had gotten the buzz on the album in New York and had written a song especially for it. He was coming to LA over the weekend and would be at the studio Monday night. Ringo was psyched and so was I.

John had a very electric presence. I played him the tracks we had cut, and he responded with the enthusiasm of a teenager. When "You're Sixteen" started playing, he thrust his fist in the air and started screaming. He predicted it would be a big hit.

Finally, it was time to hear John's song, which was called "I'm the Greatest," which he wrote as a chronology of Ringo's life and career with The Beatles. We all went out to the studio with a great deal of anticipation to hear it for the first time. John sat down at the piano and began to play the song in his uniquely percussive piano style. He rarely played piano on a Beatles record so this had a very fresh sound. He then sang for us,

When I was a little boy, way back home in Liverpool,
My mama told me, I was great.
Then when I was a teenager, I knew that I had got something going,
All my friends told me, I was great.

And now I'm a man, a woman took me by the hand,
And you know what she told me, I was great.

I was in the greatest show on earth, for what it was worth,
Now I'm only thirty-two, and all I wanna do, is boogaloo.
I looked in the mirror, I saw my wife and kids,
And you know what they told me, I was great.

Yes my name is Billy Shears,
You know it has been for so many years,
Now I'm only thirty-two,
And all I wanna do, is boogaloo.

I'M THE GREATEST, AND YOU BETTER BELIEVE IT BABY!

There is one line in the song that needs some explanation: "Yes, my name is Billy Shears, you know it has been for so many years." Billy Shears was the pseudonym that Ringo had been given as a member of The Lonely Hearts Club Band. When The Beatles set out to record that album, part of their fantasy in creating it was that they were not The Beatles performing, but rather, members of Pepper's band. As the opening title track of "Sgt. Pepper" starts to slow down at the end, there's a clever little musical interlude that serves as the intro to the next song, "With a Little Help from My Friends." In it, they introduce the featured singer on the next song—Ringo—by singing out in three-part harmony, "BIIIIILLY SHEEEEARRS."

As John was nearing the ending section of "I'm the Greatest," he pointed out that he hadn't quite finished the outro to his satisfaction. We were tossing around some ideas, when the assistant engineer called out that there was a phone call for me. I remember thinking, *Is he fucking crazy? I'm sitting here trying to help John Lennon finish his song and he's interrupting me with a phone call?!*

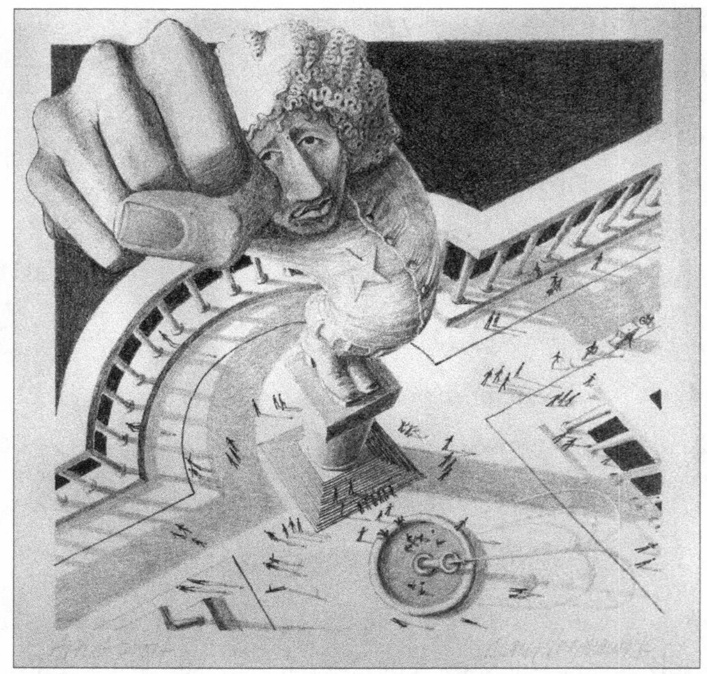

"I'm the Greatest" lithograph by Klaus Voormann.

Turned out that on the phone was Mal Evans, George's assistant. I figured that in all the excitement over John coming in to the studio, Ringo had probably forgotten to tell George what was going on.

"We hear there's a session going on," Mal said.

"Yes, Mal, there is."

"Well, is it OK if George comes down?"

"Would you hold on a minute, Mal?" I said as I started to walk from the control room back out to the studio. To myself, I was thinking, *You... Richard Perry...are about to ask JOHN LENNON...if it's okay for GEORGE HARRISON to come down, to play guitar on a record that you're producing with RINGO STARR...TAKE ME LORD!*

When I asked John, he replied, "Fucking hell, tell him to get down here and help us finish the song!"

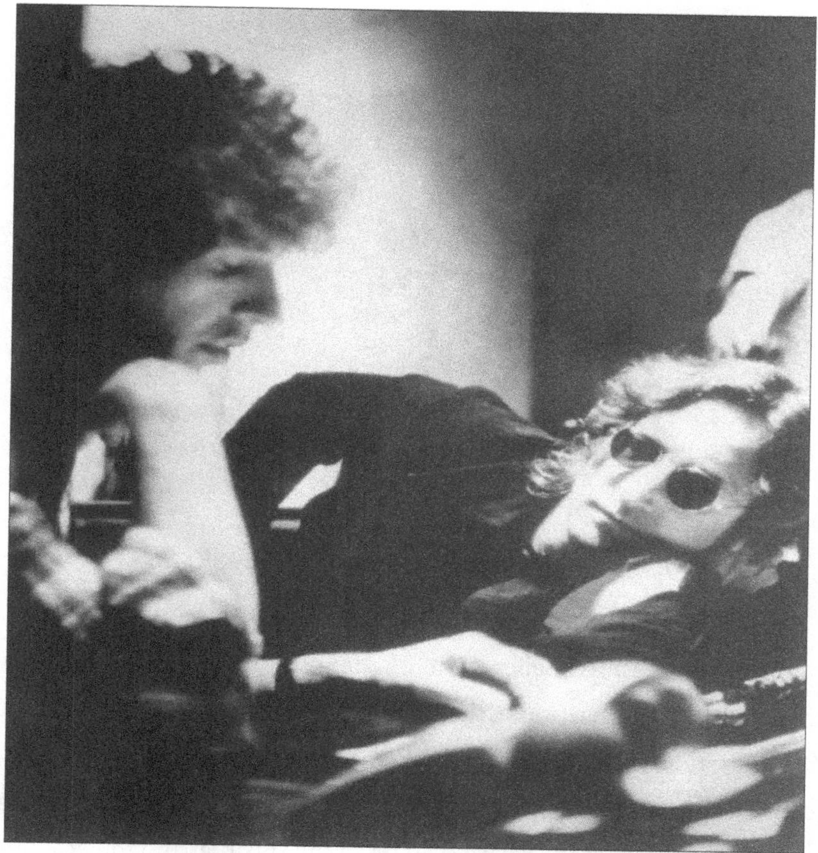

Sharing a special moment with John in the studio.

About twenty minutes later, we were running it down for the first time with the band—just Ringo on drums, John on piano, Klaus on bass, and Billy Preston on organ. George entered through the back door, with no fanfare. He didn't want to interrupt the run-through. He was carrying a small amp and his guitar, and he quietly plugged them in and started to play the quintessential Beatles guitar part—even though he had barely heard the song. His guitar not only added the final element to the track but took it to another level. Now it really sounded like a track that belonged on *Abbey Road*.

Clockwise from left to right: Peter Sellers, Jim Keltner, Ringo, Vini Poncia, George, Klaus (a little cut off), me, and Peter's date.

One of the reasons I believe that the chemistry was so effortless was that they all felt my appreciation of their talent. I had been through the gristmill with Barbra, Carly, and Nilsson, so I was very comfortable in my role as creative ringmaster (again, no pun intended). As I looked around the room, I realized that I was at the very epicenter of the spiritual and musical quest I had dreamed of for so many years. With three Beatles playing together, it was the closest to a Beatles reunion the world would ever see!

At this point, it seemed the entire planet knew that John and George were in the studio working on a Ringo album. Every night when we arrived at Sunset Sound, an avalanche of TV crews and photographers was waiting in the parking lot to greet us. By the end of each session, a small group of friends had gathered, standing silently along the back wall, just thrilled to be there. Peter Sellers was a frequent visitor.

When "I'm the Greatest" approached its climax, I wanted to hear the sound of a crowd cheering all the way through that section and continuing to build through the outro until the end. In my head, it couldn't be just any crowd. I wanted the crowd from *Sgt. Pepper*!

Normally, you'd have as much chance of getting something from a Beatles record as you would of getting into King Tut's tomb, but since the request was coming from The Beatles themselves, EMI Records was happy to comply. In fact, they sent me a four-track copy of the master of the opening Pepper track, leading into "With a Little Help from My Friends." Listening to the master tape made me really realize what a stunning achievement it was to have created that sound on only four tracks!

A few days later, I got a phone call from a well-respected Hollywood publicist whom I had known for a few years through Barbra Streisand. He told me there was a huge fundraising event that Saturday night at the palatial Bel-Air home of one of the major philanthropists in the community. They were tenting the backyard and Barbra was going to perform. He also mentioned that Burt Lancaster and Kirk Douglas would be there. Then came the payoff—he wanted to know if I could bring The Beatles! I told him, "I'd like to help you out, but to be completely candid, I don't give a flying fuck if the Pope will be there. I'm not about to jeopardize my relationship with these guys for one second by trying to get them to come to a frigging Hollywood fundraiser!" I did tell him that if I felt there was an opportunity to bring it up, I would try, but not to count on anything.

The next afternoon, I called Ringo. He was in a good mood, so I thought I'd give it a shot. I said, "Ring, forgive me for even bringing this up, but there's this Hollywood fundraising event tonight..." etc.

He didn't shoot me down. He even said he would mention it to John.

No more than five minutes later, he called back and said that John, ever the fan, not only would like to go, but he would be there with bells on, eager to meet Burt and Kirk. That evening, I picked up John and Ringo in my 1961 Bentley, which had once belonged to the famous film producer

Mervyn LeRoy. I even had his original license plates: MLR 400. They only made fifty of those cars.

As we were riding down Sunset toward Bel-Air, what song should come on the radio, but, "Walk on the Wild Side" by Lou Reed. Talk about the perfect song for the perfect moment! Totally surreal! When we arrived at the house, everyone was already seated for dinner in the tent. There were two women sitting at a desk in the entry hall to check people in as they arrived. John blew past them and bellowed out, "RICHARD PERRY AND FRIENDS HAVE ARRIVED!" As we entered the tent, you could hear a pin drop. The crème de la crème of Hollywood couldn't believe that The Beatles had just entered the room! What a fucking moment!

* * *

A week later, we headed back to London to finish work on the album. As fate would have it, I got a call from Paul McCartney, asking me if I would be the music supervisor for his first BBC television special. In the U.K., all musical numbers on TV had to be performed live. He wanted someone else in the sound booth besides the BBC engineer—someone who knew what his music should sound like. Naturally, I was extremely complimented by his request and couldn't help but think that it would also provide a golden opportunity to get him to contribute a song for Ringo.

An unexpected highlight for me, while working on the special, was when the producers announced that we would be doing one day on location in Liverpool. Paul took over a pub right on the riverfront dock, in the heart of the city, and filled it with his family and old mates. During the afternoon taping, I slipped away to see The Cavern, the club where The Beatles had first gained fame and which was about to be torn down. As I entered the place, I was overwhelmed by a sense of history. It was really like being in a cave—dark and dingy, with no ventilation at all. I imagined the place as we've seen it in documentary footage from the early '60s, packed with people and filled with cigarette smoke, with The Beatles' music blasting away. It gave me chills.

By the end of the week, we'd finished work on the BBC special. Paul Simon had just come to London to overdub some strings on a track for his new album, and we made plans to have dinner that night. I invited Harry Nilsson to join us and before leaving the BBC studios, I asked Paul and Linda as well. They said they would try to make it, but weren't sure. About ten minutes into dinner, they came striding in with beaming smiles.

After dinner we all went back to my suite at the Dorchester, where I had a full sound system set up, and we all played tracks from our albums. Last to play was Paul Simon, who had one "'little' song," as he put it, that he had just added strings to that afternoon. The song he played was "American Tune." It was a magnificent song that sounded like it could have been the follow-up to "Bridge Over Troubled Water." The British orchestrator, Del Newman, superbly arranged the strings.

The next day, I approached Paul McCartney about writing a song for Ringo's album. "Give me a deadline," he said. "I work best under pressure."

"Next Tuesday," I countered, to which he answered, "You're on!"

The following Monday night, Paul called and played the song for me over the phone. Entitled "Six O'Clock," it was a beautiful, heartfelt love song with a melody that had instant appeal.

The next night, we gathered at Apple studios to cut the track. The band was simple: Paul on piano, Ringo on drums, and Klaus on bass. We always think first of Paul's bass playing, but he is also an amazingly gifted, self-taught piano player—just listen to "Lady Madonna" or "Martha My Dear" for proof. He has a special touch and was able to give the track an instant Beatles quality. In fact, on two of the takes he spontaneously went into a jam on the fade that was very reminiscent of "Hey Jude." The track came out great! Afterward, Paul added a solo on "You're Sixteen," making a sound with his mouth like a kazoo. It was just what the track needed to put the finishing touch on it.

Before he left the studio, Ringo told me that he, John, and George planned to fire their business manager, Allen Klein, the following morning. He asked me to keep it in confidence until then. This was big news, since the hiring of Klein was one of the primary thorns in Paul's side, something that had exacerbated the break-up of The Beatles.

I met with Paul at his home in St. John's Wood the next morning to work up an arrangement for a string quartet that would play on the track we planned to complete that evening. An orchestrator sat in the meeting with us and wrote out the parts for the different instruments.

We decided to finish the track at the EMI recording studios on Abbey Road—the very same one The Beatles album had been named after—in Studio B, the hallowed ground of recording studios. The interesting thing about Studio B is that the control booth was one floor above the actual studio, so it allowed me to look down on the proceedings. This gave me a unique perspective, a feeling as if I were in a completely different world, far away from the performers. It was almost surreal, as if I were floating up above, watching these amazing artists perform down below.

EMI is where The Beatles made ALL of their records: the basic tracks, vocals, strings, and horns. As I sat with Paul McCartney in that studio, and we worked together on what would end up being a nine-hour session to finish all the remaining parts for the "Six O'Clock" track, I realized another longtime dream had come true. When we put on the string quartet, all I could think about was that I was in the very room where the strings had been recorded for "I Am the Walrus," "Yesterday," "Eleanor Rigby," and "She's Leaving Home," just to name a few.

After we finished the strings, Paul and Linda put on background vocals, giving it a bit of the "Wings" vocal sound, which fit the track perfectly. Lastly,

Paul played several synthesizer parts with a mini Moog, beginning with some backing lines to complement the vocals and strings, and then did a brilliant contrapuntal synthesizer solo that was actually composed of two interwoven lines. Synthesizer overdubs can be very time consuming as it takes several hours to get all the parts just right and even more time to find the perfect sound, given that there are endless options. As the clock passed 4:00 a.m., we had been working on the solo intensely for over five hours. I asked Paul if perhaps we had a good solo somewhere in the last several takes. Not wanting to settle—wanting to push through until we were both certain we'd nailed it—he smiled and said something that reflects Paul's perfectionism: "This is what it's all about, isn't it?"

"Absolutely," I replied.

Coincidently, we wrapped the recording of "Six O'Clock" at 6:00 a.m.

Paul offered to give me a ride back to my hotel. As we drove through Hyde Park in his Rolls Royce convertible and the sun burst through the morning clouds, we listened nonstop to Stevie Wonder's "Living for the City," from his newly released album, *Innervisions*. What a fitting way to say goodbye to my Gemini twin, Paul. (We share an exact birthday: June 18, 1942.)

* * *

You would think that I had been blessed enough just by that one recording experience. While I cherish all the ones that I've discussed so far, the blessing that still touches me the most was the friendship I developed with George Harrison. I offered to help George in any way I could as we spent more and more time in the studio together, and I'm proud to say that he thanked me on the album credits for *Living in the Material World*.

For a few months in 1973, George and his wife, Pattie Boyd, leased a beautiful house off Coldwater Canyon in Los Angeles as George recorded his album. She decorated it with Eastern artifacts—candles, incense, and shawls—making it feel like their home in London. It was always a hub of activity. Kumar Shankar, Ravi's son, and Mal Evans, were also staying there. I was a frequent guest for yoga and superb Indian food, as Kumar was an amazing cook.

On more than one occasion, I would come home from the studio to find George and Pattie waiting for me at the Beverly Hills home I was leasing for

One of my favorite photos is this one of George, Ringo, and me in April of 1973. It can be seen in the wonderful documentary that Marty Scorsese did about George in 2011. This is a film to be treasured, as it truly evokes George's spirit and humor.

the year. Ringo considered it his "home away from home," and it became a clubhouse for all of us. My assistant at the time, Tina Firestone, was always there to take care of everyone's needs, whether coffee, tea, wine, or weed.

One weekend, I decided to rent a house in Palm Springs and invited George, Ringo, Maureen, Pattie, and Linda to drive down. Since we'd all been working very hard, the desert sun was just what we needed.

After a splendid afternoon relaxing by the pool and goofing around, a glorious sunset emerged from behind the magnificent San Bernardino mountains. Everyone was suddenly feeling very sad that the day was winding down.

George expressed it as only he could. I'll never forget the sight of him, standing there in his bathing suit (a rarity already) with his hair in a ponytail,

Ringo, George, and me relaxing in Palm Springs.

pointing straight up as he proclaimed, "Why can't we just reach up and pull the sky back to twelve o'clock, and start the day all over again!"

*   *   *

The week after we returned from Palm Springs, I invited everyone to attend a very private screening of *Last Tango in Paris*. On another night, we all went to the Playboy Mansion—it was the first time any of us had ever been there. I brought Joni Mitchell as well, and as we entered the screening room, we were slightly taken aback by what we saw: the climactic scene from the movie *Behind the Green Door,* starring Marilyn Chambers and John Holmes—perhaps the most cutting edge pornographic film of all time. Quite a welcome to the mansion!

Just before we moved our base of operations back to London, George had one more little miracle to add to the Ringo album. We needed a special song to end the record, and he came up with a gem called "You and Me (Babe)." George's moving lyrics were the perfect way for Ringo to say goodbye to his audience. It was the last track we cut at Sunset Sound with only Ringo, George, Klaus, and Nicky Hopkins. I thought the song lent itself to a Memphis groove and should feel and sound like a Willie Mitchell track. Once I felt that we had successfully copped that groove, George played a funky acoustic rhythm guitar. This made the record entirely different from the normal Memphis sound and started to shape its own unique personality. I added some horns, trying to evoke the warmth and emotion of the Memphis Horns.

A few days later, George came in to put on the final touch—his signature slide guitar, both in the solo with two parts playing off each other, as well as throughout the track. At the end of a thrilling eight-hour session, he had done some of his sweetest and most inspiring guitar work. I wanted to give Ringo one last shot at a vocal on "You and Me (Babe)." With all the new elements added, I knew he would be inspired, and I wasn't wrong. He ended up giving a beautiful performance that took the track to yet another level.

From left to right: Me, Ringo, George, and Klaus cutting the track for "You and Me (Babe)."

For you and me babe, it's time that we part,
And between you babe, I gave you my heart,
For these few moments I wish we could start at the top again.

For you and me babe, it's the end of our date,
Me and the band, babe, all thought it was great,
To entertain you, but it's getting late and it's time to leave

Now I want to tell you that the pleasure really was mine,
Yeah I had a good time singing and drinking some wine,
And when the sun sets in the sky, and you close your sleepy eyes,
I'll be in some nightclub getting high, that's no lie.

Now you and me babe, we may meet again,
And in the meantime, stay out of the rain, but keep your nose dry,
And give us a smile if you like the show.

Now I want to tell you the pleasure really was mine,
Yeah I had a good time singing and drinking some wine,
Though I may not be in your town, you know that I can still be found,
Right here on this record spinning round, with the sounds.

For you and me Dave, they turned on the lights,
The violins stayed to wish you goodnight
Me and the band babe, are reaching the end
So it's off we go.

When he reached the outro section, Ringo knew that this would be the last time he would be singing on the album, so as the band was going off into the sunset, with George floating his guitar over the horns, Ringo

A lithograph by Klaus Voormann for the song, "You and Me (Babe)."

spontaneously began to thank everyone for being a part of the album—especially John, George, and Paul. It was a very warm, loving, and completely unexpected highlight for a record that had become special to everyone and reminded them why they were such kindred spirits and loved one other.

Once we finished "You and Me (Babe)" it was back on a plane to London, where the three of us planned to finish up the album together. The first order of business was to interview local artists and find one who could do the album artwork. As the album had taken on the aura of a Beatles project, I was determined that the cover, if not the entire package, should have that same distinctive Beatles look. We found Tim Bruckner, who was living in London. He understood the vision we had in mind and possessed the necessary talent to execute it. So, while we were mixing the album, we set Tim up in the studio next door where he created a painting.

The final album cover artwork depicts Ringo on the stage of a theater, with giant letters that spell out his name. Ringo himself forms the "I," leaning against the "R." The letters are lined with light bulbs and have a very theatrical look. Behind Ringo is a large balcony packed with people who, upon closer look, turn out to be caricatures of every person who had anything to do with the album—John, Paul, George, the members of The Band, Billy Preston, Nicky Hopkins, Peter Sellers, Harry Nilsson, the Blue Nun (logo for a German wine that we'd drunk while making the album), Marc Bolan, myself (with a phone in each ear), and a number of others. The whole process proved inspiring and unique, for as we were finishing the music, Tim was completing the painting—each one was feeding off the other. The cover ended up having a decidedly *Sgt. Pepper* look.

The crowning glory of the album was in Klaus' creation of ten pen-and-ink lithographs which depicted each song on the album—some of which I've included in this book. The first one hundred thousand were printed individually on parchment, signed and numbered.

In the 1973 year-end annual "Record World" poll acknowledging the best-selling artists of the year, Ringo *was No. 1.*

Before leaving London, George invited me to spend a weekend at Friar Park, his one-hundred-twenty-room castle-like estate that had originally been a monastery. It's a breathtaking place with tunnels, waterways, and caves, surrounded by beautiful gardens. That night, George screened what was probably his favorite movie of all time—*The Producers*. The key song in the movie, "Springtime for Hitler," made an impact on everyone in the room. For the rest of the evening no one could stop singing the song.

Back cover of the Ringo *album.*

The next day, George, Pattie, my friend Kelly, and I squeezed into George's Mini and headed for the Reading Jazz Festival where our dear friend, Derek Taylor, was promoting a unique singer, George Mele. Derek and his wife Joan, had eleven of the most beautiful children. He was a veritable Mr. Darling from *Peter Pan*. For any of our friends coming to London, an afternoon at Derek's charming home in Surrey was always a priority.

I had brought some mescaline with me to the festival. This was a hard-to-get psychedelic treat, so George and I happily indulged, tripping out as

Friar Park

we watched George Mele perform a few songs. After a while, the mescaline began to come on stronger and we knew that it was time to make our exit. George decided that we should visit Ringo, who had just bought John's estate in Ascot when John moved to New York. The estate was where John had recorded the *Imagine* album.

While we were buzzing along the English countryside back roads, we suddenly saw a police car come from out of nowhere, swinging around a turn and nearly hitting us. We all breathed a sigh of relief. Then George turned around, looked at me, his eyes bulging out of his head, and cried out: "THE BLUE MEANIES!!!!!!!!"

"Yellow Submarine" had come to life!

It was night by the time we arrived at Ascot. Ringo was happy to see us, and we started our hangout by drinking the first of several bottles of Dom Pérignon champagne. As I sat at the kitchen table eating beans and toast, Ringo looked at me and exclaimed, "I love beans and toast!"

Having consumed copious amounts of Dom (and beans and toast!), we knew that no one was in any condition to drive the back roads from Ascot to Henley. But, how in the hell were we going to find a car and driver at 11:00 p.m. in the English countryside!? After much persistence and a little luck, we miraculously found one. It was a joyful ride home, and as we pulled up to the gates of Friar Park, George was so thrilled we'd made it home safely that he practically hugged the gates.

As we walked into the house, we noticed that it seemed strangely quiet. Then, suddenly, everyone who had been waiting for us to return home, burst into a rendition of "Springtime for Hitler," at the top of their voices. They all had Hitler moustaches penciled on their faces. There was Derek Taylor with all eleven of his kids, Kumar Shankar, Ronnie Wood and his wife Jo, Mal Evans, and numerous other friends. We were blown away!

After that rousing welcome, George and I decided to mellow out by walking through the magnificent gardens of Friar Park with Derek. We must have walked for three hours, and the entire time Derek and George sang their favorite childhood nursery song, nonstop. I soon joined them.

Derek eventually bid us goodnight, and George and I, still in the twilight of our mescaline trip, continued to explore the seldom seen parts of Friar Park. We went into a basement room that looked like no one had been in it for years. In a dimly lit corner was a rickety old upright piano. Standing at the piano, George started playing some chords in a very basic, almost childlike style. Then, much to my amazement, he started singing "Something." I had no idea what could have motivated him to play his most famous song in that dark room, but it was the perfect, unexpected ending to a magical day and night.

Promotional photograph to used to debut Ringo's second album.

Left to right: John, me, Ringo, Bobby Keys, and Harry Nilsson.

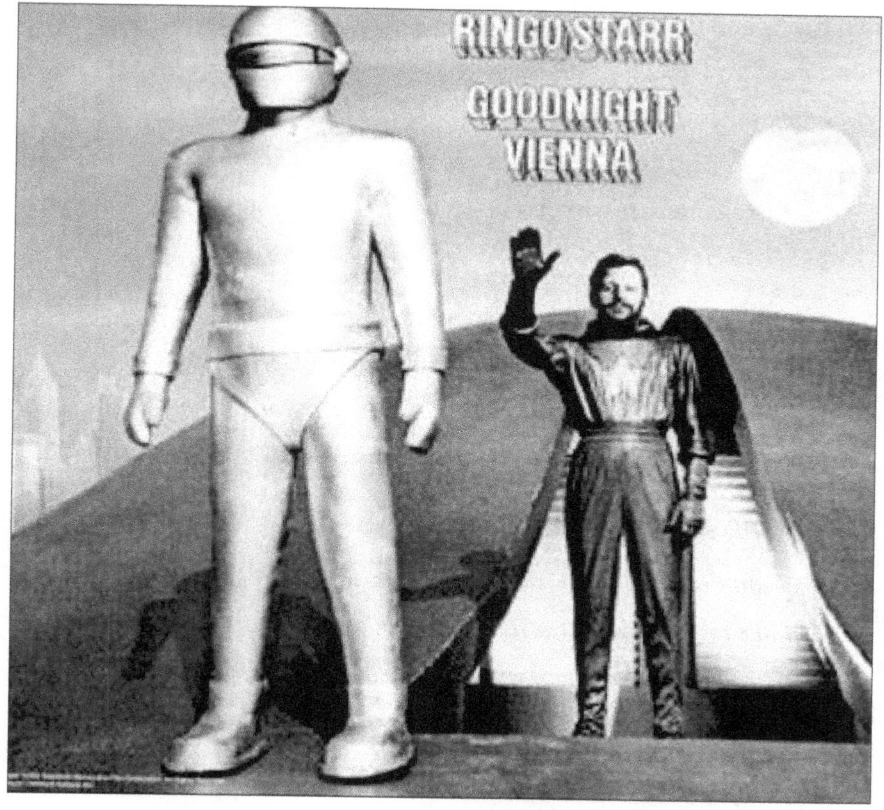

Goodnight Vienna *album cover.*

We finally said goodbye in the morning, as a car was going to pick me up and take me to Heathrow airport. I soon arrived back in LA to make final arrangements for the release of the *Ringo* album.

A year later, there was a follow-up Ringo album. John Lennon beckoned us back to the studio by writing a tripped out, super-funky rock 'n' roll song that instantly became the album's title, *Goodnight Vienna*. The song was a personal favorite of mine. It was aided tremendously by a spirited "garage-band"-sounding demo John had made that served as a marvelous template during the cutting of the track. I made sure that the band remained as close to John's demo as possible. John played acoustic rhythm guitar on two tracks and piano on "Goodnight Vienna." It was a special treat having him more involved.

I took my baby to a party last night, ah-hah-hah,
She was so beautiful, she made me uptight, ah-hah-hah,
Up came a butcher with her ju jus alight, ah-hah-hah,
It's all da-da-da-down to Goodnight Vienna.

Felt like a bohunk but I kept up my cool, ah-hah-hah,
Green as a frog, man, I was back into school, ah-hah-hah,
Zipped up my mouth 'cause I was starting to drool, ah-hah-hah,
It's all da-da-da-down to Goodnight Vienna.

Get it up, get it up, get it up, get it up,

She said she loved me but I knew she was lyin', ah-hah-hah,
Felt like an Arab who was dancing through Zion, ah-hah-hah,
Don't call no doctor when you just feel like cryin', ah-hah-hah,
It's all da-da-da down to Goodnight Vienna.

Get it up (Keep it up) Get it up (Keep it up) Get it up (Keep it up) Get it up (Keep it up)
I took my baby to a party last night, ah-hah-hah,
She was so beautiful, she made me uptight, ah-hah-hah,
Up came a butcher with his needles in sight, ah-hah-hah,
It's all down to Goodnight Vienna.

While the *Ringo* album was so uniquely special because it had all the Beatles participating, *Goodnight Vienna* had a few gems of its own and included a collection of songs, which also went Gold and beyond. For one thing, we managed to pick up another No. 1 record with a tour de force combo of Ringo and Harry Nilsson on the "No No Song." First released as a single in 1975, the "No No Song," shot to the top of the charts immediately—the lyrics describe a character who tries to sell everything from marijuana and cocaine to a recovering addict. Ringo sings the part of the recovering addict, belting out, "no, no, no, no," with Harry providing the perfect background vocals.

We also did a wonderful song by Allen Toussaint, "Occapella," featuring Dr. John on piano. Elton John and Bernie Taupin wrote a song for the album, "Snookeroo." Then John Lennon suggested that we do a cover of The Platters classic, "Only You (And You Alone)," which we produced as another Harry and Ringo collaboration; it ended up in the Top 30 on the *Billboard* chart.

The reason this picture kills me is because Ringo is doing his best Sinatra impression on "Only You (And You Alone)." He's totally into it, and the expression on John's face is bursting with joy, exuberance, and love as he cheers Ringo on.

This is one of my favorite photographs.

Chapter 20

The House on Cordell Drive

For years, I had wanted to become known as the best record producer in the world, so it meant a lot to me when, at a record industry function in 1973, Ahmet Ertegun, legendary chairman of Atlantic Records, introduced me to Bianca Jagger by saying:

Il est le meilleur producteur de musique au monde!
(He is the best music producer in the world!)

In order to achieve this, I had established very specific goals for myself. One of these was to have substantial success with three completely different artists. They turned out to be Barbra Streisand, Harry Nilsson, and Carly Simon. The albums I did with them were not only successful, but career-defining Gold or Platinum albums, with two of the three yielding Grammy-nominated Record-of-the-Year, No. 1 singles. These, of course, were followed by the *Ringo* album, and in my mind, I was just getting started.

Considering what I had accomplished during the previous eight years, I felt that it was finally time for me to stop and smell the roses. I wanted to enjoy some of what life had to offer. Since moving to California, I had been renting houses or apartments and felt that it was time for me to have my own home—it would be a monumental event. In 1974, at the ripe old age of thirty-two—and after looking for months—I finally found a house that had the potential to fulfill my dreams. The property was in the hills of West Hollywood, located in the area known as the Bird Streets. The house was a showstopper from day one, with a 320-degree view of Hollywood. Anybody who visited said that it was the best view in the city, and it really was incredible! During the day, you got a panoramic view of southern California blue skies and the hills of Los Angeles, where dreams begin for many aspiring artists. At night, you could see the lights of downtown sparkling like emeralds, rubies, and diamonds dancing in the distance.

The house had a great history—it was built by Ronald Reagan in 1941, when he was married to Jane Wyman. A picture of them lying on chaise lounges in bathing suits, circa 1944, hung in the entry hall. I bought the house from Marge and Gower Champion, a husband-and-wife dance team who'd appeared in several MGM musicals in the '40s and '50s. They lived there for eighteen years and raised three children. Gower Champion went on to become a very successful director-choreographer of Broadway musicals.

Living in this house was a little like falling in love. There is something so personal about creating your own space. With every wall that I knocked down and room I rebuilt, it was like leaving my own unique fingerprint on this property. I found that as I put more into the house, I received more and more pleasure from it. Some of the new additions I had built included a new master bedroom wing, his-and-hers master bathrooms, a new kitchen, an entry hall, two bars, a gym, a wine cellar, and a pool house.

The most significant addition, though, in my opinion, was my garage-turned-pub. The Champions had converted Ronald Reagan's garage into a dance studio. I turned it into a party room that became known as Perry's Pub. I decorated it in a "tropical deco" style, with white oak paneling on the walls, rattan furniture, palm trees, a curved bar in one corner of the room, and a vintage Seeburg Jukebox that filled the room with the sounds of my favorite 45-rpm singles. The Pub soon became a favorite place for friends to gather after dinner, and it was especially great for dancing.

It was impossible to enter this room and not feel a party vibe. Many friends would nudge me and say, "If these walls could talk." The Pub was a place where everyone could feel comfortable, relaxed, and have no trouble getting happy.

The parties in the Pub were legendary and have become permanently etched in the memory of those who were there, especially in the '80s and '90s. (In fact, I worked so hard through the '70s that I never even made it to Studio 54 before it shut down in 1980.) In the '90s, Mick Jagger and I, together with our great friend Steve Bing, would frequently get some friends together and have our own "rock 'n' roll dance parties," where we would dance to the tunes on my jukebox for hours. On one special night—my fiftieth birthday, in fact—I walked into the Pub to see what the vibe was like and was blown away by the sight of four girls dancing with Jagger and Wilt Chamberlain! I thought to myself, "Pretty cool casting for a great party!"

In later years, the Pub also became my recording studio, and I installed a state-of-the-art Pro Tools rig against the back wall. (Don't worry, I left plenty of room for dancing!) From 2005 to 2010, I produced a couple of albums there with Rod Stewart and Carly Simon. In fact, the studio credits on the albums proudly read, "recorded and mixed in Reagan's garage."

* * *

Shortly after moving into Cordell, I became obsessed with tennis. After a few years, I felt that I had to have my own court, so with the help of a fourteen-foot retaining wall, we leveled a mountain, doubled the lot space, and six months later, there was a beautiful court overlooking the city. Once that was in place, I became quite friendly with many of the tennis players I admired. They, in turn, were music junkies and were just as pleased to meet me, as I was to meet them. A few of my frequent visitors were John McEnroe, Andre Agassi, Vitas Gerulaitis, and Guillermo Vilas. Believe me, hitting with those guys was a unique thrill.

Perry's Pub

The tennis court I built.

Little did I know that I would have the joy of living in this home for *thirty-eight years*—it would be the longest relationship of my life!

The house on Cordell Drive.

Chapter 21

Sliced Steak

After fulfilling my longtime dream of working with members of The Beatles, I had finally fulfilled all my goals as a record producer, and I yearned to dive into a new challenge: I wanted to direct films. I knew that my first step would be to find a project worth developing into a film. It just so happened that there was a story I was passionate about, that I felt would be perfect: the birth of rock 'n' roll as it emerged through the lives of three men—George Goldner, Morris Levy, and Alan Freed.

I had it all thought out. The movie would begin in 1948 at the Palladium, George Goldner's stomping grounds and the birthplace of Latin music in New York, where it crossed over to the popular culture and came to be known as salsa. The story would then shift to Birdland, the Manhattan club owned by Morris Levy and named for Charlie "Bird" Parker that was the mecca of modern jazz. The third act would take place at the Brill Building and 1650 Broadway, where eighty percent of the independent record companies and publishers made their homes. So, here you had the emergence of the three most influential forms of music, all exploding simultaneously within five blocks of each other.

I didn't get to tell that intriguing story. But one day in 1973, I got a call from Linda, who shared with me some news about an annual fundraising banquet put on by the United Jewish Appeal. They would honor an executive from the music industry each year and Linda shared that the honoree that year would be Morris Levy. News of this honor came as a shock to me, as Morris was someone who had always been feared rather than admired.

Linda then told me that that Joe Smith, my great friend from the Warner Brothers days, was going to be the guest MC. After he graduated from Yale, Joe became one of the most important disc jockeys in the country. If you really wanted to get a record started, he was one of a handful of DJs you'd contact. Eventually, he was appointed head of regional promotion for Warner Brothers, and finally, its president. Joe had become known as the Don Rickles of our industry. Once Linda repeated a few of the jokes that Joe intended to tell that night, I knew that he would make this a night to remember!

I further discovered that the dais at Morris' banquet table would consist of the "pioneer panel" of the record industry, and Linda had been asked to sit on it in memory of her father, George, who had a love-hate relationship with Morris for years. While we were still together, Linda and I had always fantasized about working on a film project together that would focus on her father, but I realized this might be our only chance to produce something close to what we had always envisioned. This could be the last time all these pioneers were in the same room together.

After hearing all the details of the event, I became seriously intrigued. I told Linda that if we could film the evening, we had the potential to capture valuable material and create something special. By virtue of her friendship with Morris, Linda felt comfortable asking him if we could film the evening and he agreed!

The night itself turned out to be quite the event, thanks in large part to Joe's brilliant humor and the way he attacked everyone on the dais. As an example, his closing remarks were, "I want to thank Morris, a man I've known for many years, admired and enjoyed, and I just received word from two of his friends on the West Coast that my wife and two children have just been released, and now I'm free to conclude my part of the program."

Harry James' big band, Tito Puente, and Machito with his orchestra provided the music for the evening.

After months of judicious editing, the film had its premiere in New York at a Columbia Pictures screening room provided by Clive Davis. It was attended by the original cast of *Saturday Night Live*, Leiber and Stoller, and various other luminaries. Although it was never released to the public, within a matter of months, this little documentary became an "underground classic" in both the recording and film industries. Bob Dylan said it was one of the best films he had ever seen. I called it *Sliced Steak*.

Chapter 22

My First Real Vacation

In January of 1974, I got a call from Paul Simon asking if I wanted to go to the upcoming Grammy Awards with him. He was nominated for Album of the Year for *There Goes Rhymin' Simon*, and I was up for Record of the Year for "You're So Vain." I thought it would be a great idea for us to go together, and I told him so.

That year, the Grammys were held at the Hollywood Palladium and the nominees in the major categories were all seated together on folding chairs. They certainly have come a long way since then!

After the awards, Paul and I went out looking for some action. He was especially keen since he had recently separated from his first wife, Peggy. There were no festive late-night Grammy after parties in those days, so where could two cool, funny, talented guys go in a limo at 11:00 p.m.? Who could they call? Suddenly the answer came to both of us: CLIVE DAVIS.

If anyone could pull a rabbit out of a hat, it would be Clive. We called him and explained our plight. He told us that there was only one girl he felt he could call at that hour. Her name was Linda Marder. Miraculously, Linda said that two of her girlfriends, whom he also knew, had been visiting and were about to leave, but, if we came right over, they'd stay and have a drink with us. So, we picked Clive up at the Beverly Hills Hotel and headed to Linda's apartment.

While riding in the limo, Clive wisely gave us a little heads-up regarding the two girls we were about to meet. He told us that one of them, Edie Baskin, was five foot eleven, and the other, Gwen Welles, was about five foot five.

Obviously, it made sense for me to focus most of my attention on Edie, since I am six foot one, and Paul would set his sights on Gwen.

As we entered the apartment, Paul and I were delighted to see that both girls were extremely attractive! After spending a few minutes with them, we found them to be extremely interesting, and have fun personalities as well—the perfect combination! After some spirited conversation, we deftly launched into a roundtable discussion of teenage romance. We talked about our first kiss, then moved on to other topics: our first love, favorite make-out music, and finally, our first sexual encounters.

All in all, it turned out to be an enjoyable few hours of verbal intimacy. The only one who didn't seem to be having much fun was Gwen—who was in a cranky mood thanks to a painful stye in her eye. Her bad temper was exacerbated by the fact that she'd taken a shine to me and felt that I'd been ignoring her. Of course, she had no way of knowing that she had been designated as Paul's "date." I, in turn, had no way of knowing that in a mere four months, this girl with the stye would enter my life in a major way.

* * *

I soon forgot all about that evening, as I was about to leave for Europe on a well-earned vacation. My first stop would be London for a little bit of business mixed with pleasure. I had just engaged Rogers & Cowan, one of the largest PR firms in the world, to help me build my brand. Part of their strategy was to educate the entertainment industry about what exactly a record producer does. The fact is that the vast majority of people still don't know the answer to that question. To that end, and to welcome me to London, the firm threw a star-studded cocktail bash at a private club/restaurant called the White Elephant.

George and Ringo came with their wives. Also in attendance were Jack Nicholson with Anjelica Huston; David Hemmings, the star of the new

Michelangelo Antonioni film, *Blow Up*; Bianca Jagger; and Ann-Margret, who was in London to film a lead role in Ken Russell's version of The Who's *Tommy.*

That same night happened to be the premiere of the original theatrical production of *The Rocky Horror Show*, and to end the evening on a gala note, we all went to the wild after party thrown by the producer of the show, Michael White. He ended up becoming a close friend over the ensuing years.

I wasn't staying in London long—I was leaving for France to attend the Cannes Film Festival and start my vacation. So, the night before I left, I had dinner at with Paul and Linda McCartney at their home in St. John's Wood, then I paid a late night visit to Mick and Bianca Jagger at their home on Cheyne Walk in Chelsea. Mick asked me if I was going to be in London the next evening so we could have dinner. I told him that, unfortunately, I was leaving the next day, but I would try to come back before returning to LA. I think he felt that, since I had been so successful with *Ringo*, that perhaps I could perform a miracle with Charlie Watts.

The next morning, I met up with Abe Somer and we left for Cannes. Anyone arriving at the Cannes Film Festival for the first time is in for a special thrill. On our first night, the film making its world premiere was Robert Altman's *Thieves Like Us*. Thanks to our mutual friend, Carolyn Pfeiffer, an independent publicist living in London, Altman and I were introduced that night. We ended the evening by hanging out on the balcony of his suite at the Carlton Hotel, smoking some of the best weed in all of Europe. Altman was never without his perfectly rolled joints. We talked about music and film, especially the film that was to become his masterpiece, *Nashville*. That night marked the beginning of my twenty-five year friendship with Robert Altman.

A couple of nights later, the film *The Autobiography of Miss Jane Pittman* was being shown. It was the fictitious life story of an extraordinary woman, beginning when she was a young slave in the American South at the end of the

Civil War. The film starred Cicely Tyson, who was hailed for her performance of a character aged from twenty-three to one hundred and ten. Originally shown as a miniseries on CBS, it went on to win nine Emmy awards.

Cicely Tyson has enjoyed a stellar career in film, theater, and TV, and is known as one of the most talented and beautiful actresses in the industry. She was nominated for a Best Actress Academy Award for the film *Sounder*, and in 2013—at the age of eighty-nine—she won the Tony Award for Best Actress in the play *The Trip to Bountiful*. In 1981, she was married for the one and only time to Miles Davis.

Since Cicely was also a client of Rogers & Cowan, they made arrangements for me to accompany her to the screening. Her performance in the film was one of the greatest I had ever seen. Afterward, we went to Jimmy'z, the hottest club in Monte Carlo, owned and operated by Régine, the queen of nightlife in France. We danced until 4:00 a.m.

After quite the night in Cannes, Abe Somer and I were off again; we packed our bags and left the next day for Paris. Jerry Moss, president of A&M Records, and George Harrison were also meeting in Paris that same night to sign the final contracts for A&M to distribute George's new label, Dark Horse Records. We were all there to celebrate the launch of the first Beatle to have his own label!

Before we left Cannes, I had become quite friendly with Régine, who was entertaining the thought of becoming a pop singer in France. While I had no interest in producing her, I did find her *joie de vivre* quite attractive. We made plans to meet up in Paris while I was there, and she asked me if I would like to have dinner with anyone in particular.

"Anyone?" I questioned.

"Yes, anyone at all. It would be my pleasure," she replied.

After mulling over her offer, I came to the obvious choice: Brigitte Bardot. Régine called me back in fifteen minutes to tell me that Brigitte would meet us (me, Régine, and her husband), at eight-thirty for dinner at Régine's restaurant.

It turned out to be fortuitous that Régine and her husband were there, for Brigitte barely spoke a word of English, and I had only four years of high school French to get me by. But, even with the language barrier, I found Brigitte to be charming and very sweet. Later in the evening, George Harrison and his assistant, Terry Doran, stopped by to have a drink with us. Even George wanted to meet Brigitte!

Although I'd stopped in Paris for one night with Tiny Tim while he was on tour, I hadn't been in Paris long enough to enjoy it. Now that I was there for more time and could absorb every detail, I found myself amazed by the city—it was dazzling. From the entrances to the subway, to the beautiful Galeries Lafayette department store, no matter where you turn, you'll see the most beautiful Art Nouveau objets d'art.

On our last day in Paris, we wandered through the city and stumbled upon a local flea market. The street was shut down and all of the local shop owners had tables set up outside, displaying a variety of their available goods—from paintings to sculptures to other items of home décor. One vendor was selling silk-screen paintings by Alphonse Mucha, who was a well-known Art Nouveau artist. He'd lived in Paris in 1888 and created posters for a famous French stage actress. I was intrigued by the paintings and bought a couple, which I still have hanging in my office today.

Perhaps the greatest example of Art Nouveau is Maxim's. The restaurant is frequented by the crème de la crème of film, literature, art, and politics, and was featured in the Oscar-winning film *Gigi*. On our last night in Paris, Jerry, Abe, and I decided to go here for our final good-bye to the city.

Venturing out into a warm spring night and piling into our limo, we noted that the French elections had been held that day and Giscard d'Estaing was the new president of France. The French celebrate their elections as if they are New Year's Eve, and the city was going wild. After consuming countless bottles of Lafite Rothschild at Maxim's, we decided to join the celebration by standing on the seats of the limo with our heads sticking out of the sunroof and shouting, "Vive Giscard!"

I fulfilled Mick's request to make a final stop in London so we could get together. After a lovely dinner with him and Bianca, the three of us went to a private club for fun, and a little late night gambling, thus, bringing my event-filled, two-week holiday to a close.

Chapter 23

The Girl With the Stye In Her Eye

In May of 1974, a great friend of mine, the director Bob Rafelson, invited me to attend a screening of a new Robert Altman film, *California Split*. As I was watching the movie, I was struck by an actress in the film who seemed familiar to me, but for the life of me, I couldn't place her.

A month later, Bob invited me to a party that Bert Schneider was hosting at his home. This was a hot Hollywood party, and I was more than pleased to go. He and Bert had the most cutting-edge film production company in the business, having produced *Easy Rider*, *Five Easy Pieces* (Jack Nicholson's first starring vehicle and directed by Rafelson), and *The Last Picture Show* (directed by Peter Bogdanovich). They also created *The Monkees* TV show in 1966.

After socializing in the living room for about an hour, I made my way to the playroom at the back of the house. As I walked in, my eyes connected with a girl on the far side of the room. "Richard!" she called out. It was Gwen Welles, the actress from *California Split*!

"I *do* know her!" I said to myself, but I still couldn't put together HOW I knew her.

Seeing that I was confused, she said, "Remember the night with Clive?" and with that, it was like a bomb exploded in my brain! It was the girl with the stye in her eye! I was undeniably attracted to her. She had beautiful red hair, alabaster skin, a killer smile, a seductive laugh, and a perfect cleft in her chin. I wanted to just whisk her out of there, but unfortunately, she was accompanied by a date, so I knew I had to wait until some point in the future to see her.

I asked her to dinner on repeated occasions, but she always said she couldn't because she had a "meeting." It seemed that every night she had a goddamn meeting! I was wondering what the fuck was going on. Finally, I had enough and I told her if she didn't want to see me, we shouldn't waste each other's time.

I guess she realized it was time to come clean. The meetings she was referring to were Alcoholics Anonymous meetings! She told me that she was a recovering alcoholic and junkie and wanted to spare me the pain of entering into a relationship with someone so encumbered.

I, however, was a romantic to a fault and determined to consummate this relationship no matter how great the obstacles. Even knowing the facts, I was still driven by the force of her personality. I knew that Gwen was preparing to go to Nashville to appear in Robert Altman's film of the same name. She was playing a waitress who dreamt about being a singer, whose only problem was that she couldn't sing a lick! Her character was full of both humor and poignancy. The film was scheduled to start shooting in two weeks, so that didn't give me a lot of time to woo and pursue her. I simply wasn't prepared to settle for just a friendship.

The night after she told me the truth about her meetings, she came to my house and we fell in love fighting over a watermelon in the kitchen. We were both diehard foodies and Gwen was a sensational cook. Moreover, she turned me on to yoga, meditation, and nutrition. I became a vegetarian for five years and still don't eat red meat.

For our first real date, I got tickets to a production of *South Pacific* at the UCLA Amphitheater. I couldn't think of a more romantic musical. While driving home on Sunset, we discussed her sobriety. In those days, if I went out with a girl who didn't get high, I typically considered it two strikes against her in my book. In addition, I had a lot of confidence in my powers of persuasion. I felt that somehow there had to be a way to convince

Gwen to smoke an occasional joint or have a glass of wine with me. After all, these were my two greatest pleasures, and it was inconceivable to me that I wouldn't be able to share them with the person with whom I had just fallen in love. In the middle of our talk, Gwen abruptly addressed me: "Richard," she said, "you don't understand—I can never take a hit of a joint or have even a sip of wine for the rest of my life!"

I immediately burst into tears. I had seemingly everything I could want in my life, except the one thing I craved the most: a real romance, which I thought then would be extremely difficult to find. But my feelings for Gwen were greater than my desire to have a drinking and smoking partner. I just had to realign my priorities, despite the fact that collecting wines had become a passion of mine. One thing that did make it easier was that Gwen had this uncanny ability to absorb a contact high like no one I'd ever seen.

She was leaving for Nashville in ten days, and I immediately got her shooting schedule so I could plan my visits to the location. In addition, Altman graciously gave Gwen the green light to go to LA during two lengthy breaks in her schedule. The night that Altman and I had met in Cannes and hung out on the balcony of the Carlton Hotel must have had some resonance. Altman's locations, by the way, were a blast! Every day the shooting would end with a party!

On July 4, 1974, I traveled out to Nashville to spend time with Gwen. Leon Russell was appearing at the Nashville Speedway, and most of the cast planned to attend the show. Gwen and I were both starving so I went to get some food, but the only thing I could find was some ballpark hot dogs. Since I knew all too well that I couldn't show up with that as the only food, I meandered over to the backstage entrance and who should I run into but Mike Kelly, a record promotion man I knew from New York who I hadn't seen in five years. He greeted me with open arms and took me to the artists' buffet. Well, folks, when I showed up back at our seats with platters of watermelon, cantaloupe, and honeydew, any reservations that Gwen may have had about her feelings for me had quickly evaporated.

When we returned to LA from Nashville, I persuaded Gwen to live with me because, as I said before, I was romantic to a fault. We enjoyed five years of cohabitation. She was one of the most intelligent girls I've ever known, being well-versed in all forms of art, literature, film, and religion, and able to quote liberally from the Old and New Testaments. Moreover, she was a

With Gwen Welles, 1974.

seductress with a childlike, whimsical, and eccentric personality. I went to several AA meetings with her and developed a great respect for the program.

However, as time went on, the fragility of Gwen's health became too great an obstacle for us to continue to build a relationship. We parted in 1979, but remained extremely close until her death in 1993.

Gwen affected my life in many ways. For one thing, she introduced me to Daphna Kastner, a woman who, through the years, became one of my dearest friends. We became so close, in fact, that I am godfather to Roman Keitel, the son of Daphna and her husband, Harvey Keitel.

There were other unexpected ways Gwen affected my life. One day in the fall of 1975, out of the blue, she asked me if I wanted to visit Jane Fonda and Jane's then-husband, Tom Hayden. I learned that after Jane and her first husband, the French director Roger Vadim, had divorced, Vadim had begun a new relationship with none other than Gwen! They'd lived together in France for nearly two years, with Jane and Vadim's daughter, Vanessa, who'd stayed mainly with her father during this period. Jane was frequently on location at the time, as her career was exploding, so Gwen had helped raise Vanessa and, during Jane's visits, she and Gwen had become friends. They stayed friends even after Gwen and Roger called it quits—hence the connection between them. Were it not for this unusual series of events, I might never have met Jane!

In the course of our visit, it was revealed that Tom Hayden was running for the US Senate. I wanted to do something for Tom's campaign, so I offered to have a "meet and greet" cocktail party at my home and host some of the deepest political pockets in the music industry. Among the guests were Clarence Avant, Jerry Moss, Mo Ostin, Joe Smith, Jerry Weintraub, Quincy Jones, and many other notables. Impressing Jane was just an added bonus to this. (Like every other guy in the '70s, I had a crush on her!)

When Jane and Tom arrived, I was shocked to see that Tom was wearing a jean jacket. I took Jane aside and asked her if Tom was trying to remind the guests that he was a member of the Chicago Seven. Led by Abbie Hoffman, Jerry Rubin, and Tom Hayden, the Chicago Seven was a group of counter-culture leaders who organized protesters to go to the Democratic National Convention in 1968 to protest LBJ's pro-Vietnam War policies.

Members of The Manhattan Transfer—Tim Hauser, Janis Siegel, Laurel Masse, and Alan Paul—with Tom Hayden, Jane Fonda, their son, Troy Garity, and me.

Even though LBJ had declined to run for re-election, the country's nerves were raw-to-the-bone due to the recent assassinations of Bobby Kennedy and Martin Luther King Jr. Before he was assassinated, Bobby had won the California primary and was the presumed Democratic nominee. It seemed that Chicago Seven's purpose was to vent the anger that so many of us in the country were feeling, having had our last hope taken away from us as we handed Nixon a path to the White House.

So, you can imagine my surprise when Tom walked in wearing that jacket. Jane suggested that I tell Tom my feelings personally, though I hardly knew Tom. I was nervous as I approached him, but he took my comments like a real trooper and asked for my help.

The next day we met at Jerry Magnin's Polo Shop on Rodeo Drive, where Tom bought a dark suit and a brown tweed jacket. Jane later informed me that he wore those two items for the rest of the campaign.

A month later, I got The Manhattan Transfer, a group I was producing at the time, to do a benefit show for Tom. The following week, Jane and Tom came down to the studio to thank us for our help in his campaign.

Chapter 24

Studio 55

Anyone who sets out to pursue a career as a music producer will inevitably develop two supreme goals: one, to have his or her own recording studio, and two, to have his or her own label. I was fortunate enough to attain both.

By 1974, I was eager to have my own studio. I commissioned my longtime assistant, Larry Emerine, to look for the right building for sale, in the right location. After a few months, I was in serious negotiations with Tutti Camarata, the owner of Sunset Sound, a studio with a great history. I recorded both Ringo albums there in Studio 2. Furthermore, most of The Doors' records were done in Studio 1, reputed to have the best live echo chamber in the city. There were three studios in the complex, but therein lay the problem. Because of the size, the studio had to clear ten thousand dollars a month, which was too big a nut to take on, so I reluctantly had to pass.

We were continuing our search for the right home when Larry told me that he thought he had finally found the perfect place. It was located on a historic block on Melrose Avenue, right next door to Paramount Studios and KHJ Radio Station—the No. 1 pop station in LA for many years. Across the street was Lucy's El Adobe, a Mexican restaurant that had great food, killer margaritas, and was a famous hangout for the Democratic left wing. Pictures of Jerry Brown, Ted Kennedy, Tom Bradley, and many other leaders of the party covered the walls.

The facility was the site of the original Decca Recording Studios, operating in the '40s and '50s and had been used extensively by Bing Crosby,

The Andrews Sisters, and Ella Fitzgerald. Because of its close proximity to Paramount, Bing Crosby, who did many movies for the studio, found it very convenient to ride his bicycle from the Paramount lot next door to do many of his most famous recordings. In fact, it was in this Melrose Avenue studio that he made what is considered the biggest selling single of all time, "White Christmas." With that detail, I was convinced that this was the recording studio for me and I bought it that week.

The studio had two rooms—Studios A and Studio B. Studio A was in need of major reconstruction and, as part of that, we shifted the control room from the back to the front (which made a lot more sense). I worked solely out of Studio B for the first year but not before we installed a new Neve console. Studio B was a small room, but it could hold a rhythm section comfortably and had a nice punchy sound.

At the end of each day, Larry Emerine, who was now my studio manager, would show me the progress that had taken place in Studio A, for he knew how thrilled I was to see this dream of mine come closer to reality. One thing we preserved was the acoustical tiles from the original Decca days, the kind that are no longer used in modern studios.

Two days before my birthday, which is June 18, I was working in Studio B when Larry came in and, as he did each day, asked me if I would like to see the newest developments in Studio A. Unbeknownst to me, along with my two assistants, Kathleen Carey and Robin Rinehart, he had very secretly planned a surprise birthday party for me. Guests had been instructed to enter through the back alley where the musicians had their instruments delivered.

I had no way of knowing that about one hundred people had gathered in the back of Studio A until I entered the room and heard everyone cry out, SURPRISE! That was one of two times in my life I was caught with my "pants down." (The second time was nearly four decades later.) What really shocked me was that about one hour into the party, who should appear? Paul and Ringo! Paul was in town for the first tour with his new band, Wings.

We named the complex Studio 55. This was at least two years before Studio 54 became the rage of New York. I remember being pissed off that they chose a name so close to ours, but it was pure coincidence. Their name had been based on the fact that the club was located on West 54th Street.

Meanwhile, Studio 55 was rapidly becoming one of the premier recording facilities in Los Angeles. The Studio A remodel was complete and we'd installed a state-of-the-art Neve recording console. In Studio B, we had the first Neve computerized mixing board in LA. I'll never forget watching the faders moving on their own!

Our motto—"The Best Coffee in Town"—came about because most every other studio had coffee that tasted like it was made with dishwater. So, we really did set out to have the best coffee, as well as providing a great studio. (We also served the best popcorn—made with olive oil and Spike seasoning.)

David Dubow (a lovely man who used to work for me) standing in front of Studio 55.

Studio A control room.

Studio B control room.

Studio 55 became a home for many artists and producers. For example, Jimmy Iovine did the first two solo albums with Stevie Nicks there and one with Bob Seger. The musicians, who would later comprise the group Toto, became my "house band" and did most of their records there, as did Bette Midler, Cher, The Go-Go's, and numerous other artists. Most important, Studio 55 was the creative center for all of my recording work from 1975 to 1992.

Chapter 25

You Make Me Feel Like Dancing

One day out of the blue, I got a call from Adam Faith, Leo Sayer's manager, who had been a British pop star in the '60s. Adam was confident, with a swagger and charisma I found very appealing. He was calling me to see if I would be interested in producing Leo.

Leo Sayer was one of the most versatile and soulful singers that I had ever heard, and he was also a songwriter of considerable talent. His only fault was that he'd led a very provincial life—nothing like what you would expect from a pop star. Leo had made his Los Angeles debut at the Troubadour, where he'd appeared in clown costume and makeup and been the talk of the town for days. His career continued to sputter along, yielding just one legitimate hit, "Long Tall Glasses."

I knew that Leo had the potential to be one of the great singers, so I decided to give it a shot. Ultimately, our work together resulted in Leo having two of the most successful records of his career. In the studio, I surrounded Leo with some of the best musicians in Los Angeles, and we all gravitated toward the music we had in common: Motown. The first songs we recorded were "Tears of a Clown," "What Becomes of the Brokenhearted," and "Reflections," the last of which featured a stellar synthesizer arrangement by James Newton Howard.

When we had filled each reel of tape, the assistant engineer would have to rewind it before replacing it with a fresh one. This process would take approximately two minutes and during this brief respite, the musicians would frequently jam. During one such break, they started playing a very infectious rhythm, and Leo started to sing in this funky falsetto voice that I had never heard before. He was just making it up. I looked to see if the 24-track machine was recording. It wasn't. I called out to the engineers to make sure that *someone* was getting it down.

Leo then went on a six-month road trip. When he returned, he played me the songs he had written on the road, ostensibly for the album. I had the difficult task of telling him I didn't feel any of them were worthy of inclusion. In other words, we had to start over. I did, however, have one bit of good news. "Remember that little jam session we had with the musicians during a break? Well, I think that could be developed into a smash!"

Leo didn't remember it at all, and it still had to be converted into a song. I felt that Vini Poncia would be the perfect candidate to work with Leo. He'd had great success collaborating with Ringo and they'd written four songs together, including one Top 5 hit, "Oh My My." Moreover, I was convinced that Leo and Vini would have great working chemistry.

On the day Vini and Leo planned to finish the song, Vini had a terrible backache, and he began their writing session by telling Leo that he was in so much pain, he was only good for about twenty minutes. This may have turned out to be a blessing in disguise, as the pressure of the pain in his back forced them to move more quickly while maintaining a high level of creativity. It turned out to be the best twenty minutes of their careers, as they came up with a jewel of a song: "You Make Me Feel Like Dancing"!

We cut the track the next day with Steve Gadd on drums, Chuck Rainey on bass, John Barnes on clavinet, and Larry Carlton and Ray Parker Jr. on guitars. I had wanted to work with Steve Gadd ever since I heard him play on Paul Simon's classic record "50 Ways to Leave Your Lover." He has a unique talent for creating rhythms that always seem to serve the groove of the song in a special way, and this was no exception—the track was superb!

Then, it was time to put on the background vocals. I've always loved working with background singers, and this time we came up with a special arrangement for them. I borrowed some hooks from Lou Reed's "Walk on the Wild Side" and The Rolling Stones' "Sympathy for the Devil." Gene Page neatly wrapped this up in a brilliant string arrangement.

The song met all the requirements of what it takes to make a song truly great. It had non-stop hooks that never let up, complemented by a tour de force vocal performance from Leo. The record shot to No. 1 on the *Billboard* Hot 100, and sold over a million copies.

* * *

After this considerable run of success, one day I had an epiphany. I called Tom Draper, head of R&B Promotion for Warner Brothers at the time, and said, "Tom, I got this crazy idea that the Leo Sayer record could cross into the black market. Yes, Tom, I fully realize that black radio won't go near a white artist, especially a kid from the north of England. But…indulge me on this one, Tom, and try to get the record started *somewhere, anywhere*—I don't care if it's Topeka, Kansas, or Lubbock, Texas."

Tom reluctantly agreed, and two months later the record had reached No. 1 on the *Billboard* R&B chart and sold an additional *one million records!* For the pièce de résistance, "You Make Me Feel Like Dancing" won the Grammy Award for Best R&B Song of the Year!

Carole Bayer Sager, my good friend from the "Nobody Does It Better" saga, wrote Leo a truly outstanding song with Albert Hammond called "When I Need You." It couldn't have been more different from "You Make Me Feel Like Dancing," but once Leo sang it, we had abundant proof of the depth of his versatility. "When I Need You" is a heartfelt song that deals with the loneliness of being on the road.

These two records were particularly close to me because they featured two of the finest drummers I've ever had the pleasure to work with: Jeff Porcaro and Steve Gadd.

Proving that lightning can strike twice, this record also reached No. 1 again, on both the *Billboard* Hot 100 and R&B charts, and sold well over two million copies! Both records became massive worldwide hits. "When I Need You" was one of the biggest records of the year in England, and was reputed to be Princess Diana's favorite song. Leo was now firmly established as an international pop star and received a Grammy Award for best male vocal performance.

I became very close to Leo in the years we worked together. In fact, there were many times when I was tempted to suggest that we go out and do tequila shots together, but, suffice it to say, his lifestyle was in sharp contrast to the incredibly soulful quality of his voice. Overall, working with Leo Sayer was one of the most pleasant experiences I've ever had, and he was genuinely one of the nicest human beings I've ever known.

Chapter 26

The Beat Goes On

The following years were filled with a variety of music projects. To begin with, I did an album with Art Garfunkel called *Breakaway.* It contained an eclectic group of songs from writers as diverse as Stevie Wonder ("I Believe [When I Fall in Love It Will Be Forever]"), Antônio Carlos Jobim ("Waters of March"), Bruce Johnston ("Disney Girls"), Hal David ("99 Miles from LA"), the standard of all standards, "I Only Have Eyes for You," and the first songs ever recorded by a new writer, Stephen Bishop.

Art was a very complex individual. On the one hand, he could be totally charming, with an abundant sense of humor and a high degree of intelligence, much like your favorite college professor. But he also had a much darker side and a hair-trigger temper that could ignite without a moment's notice. Nevertheless, for many years, I felt of all the albums I had produced until the late '90s, *Breakaway* was the one that gave me the most personal listening pleasure. Art's serene, angelic voice performing this collection of songs made it one of his best-selling albums and was certified Gold.

* * *

The one artist I wanted to work with more than any other was Frank Sinatra. I felt that the album I'd done with Ella Fitzgerald was my "audition" piece, but no one could break through Frank's "iron curtain" and set up a meeting. That is, until my friend Jerry Weintraub got involved.

Jerry had been Frank's concert promoter for some time and had his respect. So, during the Christmas holiday of 1975, Weintraub arranged a meeting between Frank and me at Sinatra's Palm Springs estate. The first person I met there was his mother, Dolly. She had a heart as big as a house and a warm, welcoming disposition. When the Chairman entered the room, he greeted me with a firm handshake and asked me if I wanted a drink.

As the desert sun set behind the mountains, I told Frank that I wanted to make a classic Sinatra album, much like the ones he'd done for Capitol Records in the '50s—"Only the Lonely," "Come Fly with Me," and "In The Wee Small Hours"—when he pioneered the idea of the concept album. I brought a few song ideas to show him what I had in mind.

First and foremost was the classic Leon Russell composition "A Song for You." Denny Cordell, Leon's partner in Shelter Records and producer of his album, had called me as soon as he had finished the record, wanting me to hear it right away. While I loved the entire album, I was particularly taken with "A Song for You." It was then that Denny told me that Leon had written the song for Sinatra. I couldn't imagine any song more appropriate for Frank, and he sensed its potential as well.

Another song I presented to him was the George Harrison gem, "Isn't It a Pity," which he also thought he could sing. Ultimately, that one was covered beautifully by Nina Simone.

All in all, I thought the meeting was very successful, and Frank seemed eager to get together again. He liked the songs I'd brought him and the direction I wanted to take him in. The one fly in the ointment was that Frank was a creature of habit and was used to having all material forwarded to Sarge Weiss, an old emissary of his, who was playing the role of his A&R man. This effectively blocked my direct communication with Frank.

My interactions with Sinatra had their ups and downs, yet whenever I would see him, be it backstage at a concert, or at a party, he always seemed glad to see me. He once greeted me by saying, "Hey buddy, I've been thinking about you!" Unfortunately, that's as far as it went. But I just couldn't get the idea out of my head of him singing "A Song for You." It seemed like the perfect swan song, and a great way for him to close out his glorious career.

The song was covered by a wide variety of great artists over the years, including The Carpenters, The Temptations, and even Whitney Houston, but it still seems a shame that it was never recorded by the man it was written for. Although I never got to realize my dream of doing the song with Sinatra, seventeen years later I made what I felt was a perfect record with the only other artist qualified to sing this song: Ray Charles.

Chapter 27

The Beat Keeps Going

In 1977, Gwen and I had become good friends with Tony Curtis and his third wife, Leslie. Tony was a wild man—sort of a combination of his characters in *Sweet Smell of Success* and *Some Like It Hot*. One cool October night, the four of us happened to be in New York. Before we left, a friend of mine from LA suggested that I pay a visit to this quasi-doctor friend of his, who lived on the West Side. What made him unique was that he treated his patients' ailments with recreational drugs—which was right up Tony's and my alley!

When we entered his apartment, he spoke to us in a calm, soothing voice. His name was Elliot and he asked us what drug we would prefer for a cocktail. On this night he was featuring Colombian, Indica, and Thai Stick (all different types of weed). After we indulged in the last, Elliot introduced us to the star of the show, which, I must say, was a high like nothing I had ever experienced: an acid enema! The closest thing I could compare it to would be the best mushroom trip you've ever had, where your entire body felt buzzed.

* * *

About a month later, Tony and Leslie had a big Hollywood party, and among the guests was Elia Kazan. There was no director whom I admired more. Not only had he discovered Brando at a summer stock theater, he'd fought bitterly with the producer to let him cast Brando in the role of Stanley

Kowalski for the Broadway debut of *A Streetcar Named Desire*, a career-making role if ever there was one. He directed him in the film as well, and Brando earned his first Oscar. A few years later, Kazan directed Brando to his second Oscar for *On the Waterfront*, which also netted a second Oscar for Kazan. (His first had been for Best Director for *Gentleman's Agreement*.) Kazan later went on to direct *East of Eden*, which introduced James Dean to movie audiences; *A Face in the Crowd*, where he elicited the performance of a lifetime from Andy Griffith; and finally, *Splendor in the Grass*, the stunning film debut of Warren Beatty.

You can understand why I was so in awe of the man upon meeting him. We engaged in several minutes of spirited conversation, and then he said something I will never forget. His wife at the time, Barbara Loden, was standing with us; she was quite a bit younger than Kazan and clearly had an understanding of and familiarity with pop music. When Kazan asked me who I'd worked with, Barbara chimed in, "You mean you don't know?!" Kazan then looked me dead in the eye and said, "Why should I conceal my ignorance?"

For a genius the likes of Kazan to expose himself so openly showed how his curiosity fed his brilliant talent.

Kazan liked an occasional game of tennis, something we shared. We would play on the court of the famed director, William Wyler, who was too old to play, and so, was happy to let Kazan use it. One day after tennis, we went back to my house and—coincidentally—found Gwen watching *Splendor in the Grass*. Kazan and I joined her for a very powerful, emotional scene between Warren Beatty and Natalie Wood. At the end of it, Kazan was like a little kid as he exuded, "Oh, that was good, wasn't it?"

* * *

It was around this time that I embarked on a friendship with Carole Bayer Sager. A talented lyricist, she was relentless in her efforts to get me to record some of her songs. One song, in particular, that caught my attention was "Midnight Blue" which she wrote with Melissa Manchester. Since I was occupied with other projects, I arranged for Vini Poncia to produce the record for Clive Davis' new label, Arista, where it subsequently went Top 10.

Carole soon began a relationship with Marvin Hamlisch, the noted Broadway and film composer whose resume included *A Chorus Line, The Way We Were,* and *The Sting.* In 1976, Marvin was composing the score for the new James Bond movie, *The Spy Who Loved Me.* At the same time, he and Carole wrote a song together, which originally had nothing to do with the Bond film, called "Nobody Does It Better." They played me a demo they'd made of the song, and even though it didn't show well as a demo, there was something about it that intrigued me. I told Marvin and Carole how I felt, but that I didn't have an artist who would be a good fit.

Shortly afterward, Marvin had a meeting with Cubby Broccoli, who controlled The Bond franchise, and his production team. The main purpose of the meeting was for Marvin to play them the title song he had written for the film. As it turned out, nobody liked the song and Marvin started to panic—until he remembered that I'd liked the song "Nobody Does It Better." He had so much respect for my song sense that he figured he might as well give it a shot and play it for them.

Well, everyone loved it (even though it's the only song in over fifty years of Bond films that doesn't have the same title as the movie)! The producers felt strongly that the title of the movie had to appear *somewhere* in the song, so Carole came up with the perfect lyric to fulfill this request, writing "the spy who loved me, is keeping all my secrets safe tonight."

Now the only thing that remained was to find the perfect artist to record it. I hadn't been in the studio with Carly Simon in over two years, but I thought that this could be just the right vehicle for us to collaborate again. Marvin and Carole weren't as eager for Carly at first, but I knew in my gut that she would kill it, and apart from "You're So Vain," it would turn out to be her biggest hit.

I recorded the basic track at Studio 55, and when it came time to add the strings and horns, I contacted the noted British arranger Richard Hewson, known for his work with The Beatles on "The Long and Winding Road," "She's Leaving Home," "Across the Universe," and others. Since Marvin was in London recording the score for the film, I felt it made sense for us to overdub the orchestra there, which would give him the opportunity to be present for the recording session of the song he'd co-written. It would also give me the chance to work with Richard Hewson.

To make the experience even more special, I arranged for us to do the session at Abbey Road, Studio B, the very same Beatles studio where I'd worked with McCartney on his track for the *Ringo* album four years prior. Richard Hewson's arrangement was stellar in every respect, and "Nobody Does It Better" became one of the most popular Bond songs of all time, reaching No. 2 on the *Billboard* Hot 100, and remaining there for a month!

Chapter 28

Diana

In late 1977, Berry Gordy, founder of Motown Records, called me to say that he loved what I'd done with Martha Reeves and the vibe of her album. He wanted me to do the same for Diana Ross. I readily accepted.

Working with Diana was a joy. She always showed up with her A-game, so it was imperative that I show up with mine—meaning I had to come to the table with great songs, great musicians, and great arrangements. She has probably had more hits than any other female artist, if you include The Supremes' records as well as her solo recordings. When you hear Diana's voice on a record, you immediately recognize her unmistakably unique sound—so it was with a great deal of anticipation that I considered what I might do with her.

I was particularly proud of the first song on the album, "Gettin' Ready for Love." It was written by Tom Snow and Franne Golde, two very talented songwriters who just happened to be affiliated with Braintree Music, my publishing company. There is a special sense of satisfaction when your first single comes from within your own house. It's just a very cool song, embracing jazz, R&B, and contemporary pop influences—with a monster chorus that was perfect for Diana!

Another one of my favorites was "Too Shy to Say," Stevie Wonder's monumental ballad to which only an artist with Diana's penchant for romantic interpretation and phrasing could bring a fresh vulnerability. The most dramatic song on the album was a Bill Withers composition, "The Same

Love That Made Me Laugh." It begins with Diana singing at her sultry best and then explodes into the chorus. Gene Page significantly enhanced all the songs with stunning string arrangements.

I always think that if there is a song title that can work as the title of the album, it adds a little extra clout to the project. For that reason, it was fortuitous when I came across a wonderful R&B song called "Baby It's Me." It was pretty much a no-brainer that we use that as our album title. The album cover was truly a work of art in its own right, featuring a photo by the renowned fashion photographer Francesco Scavullo.

As soon as the final mix was completed on the first single, "Gettin' Ready for Love," I went up to Berry Gordy's house to play it for him. Little did I know that it was Smokey Robinson's birthday, and there was a hell of a party

Baby It's Me *album cover.*

going on! The moment the record began to play, everyone was inspired by Diana's performance and started to dance—led by Smokey.

The album achieved Gold status and much critical praise. One critic said, "It is a treasure trove of irresistible tracks that beckons the listener to the boudoir. Next to *Lady Sings the Blues*, *Baby It's Me* has to be one of the best albums in Ross' lexicon." Another critic wrote, "This is the perfect Diana Ross record. Richard Perry was at the height of his production powers."

Diana and me.

Around 1980, Diana and I both happened to be in Aspen and turned up at the same party. I was with my girlfriend of two years, Rae Dawn Chong, daughter of Tommy Chong. The party was very static and much in need of someone to inject some life into the proceedings. Suddenly, Stevie Wonder's track "Master Blaster (Jammin')" started playing, and Diana and Rae Dawn decided to take matters into their own hands. They pushed the couches and chairs up against the walls and started to dance. I joined them and within a matter of minutes, party fever had spread throughout the room. It was a kick to see the girls completely turn the party around. Diana happened to be staying in a house with an indoor pool and she invited us to come by the following day to go for a swim. It was a blast!

* * *

Three years later, I was in the middle of producing an album with Julio Iglesias. One of the outstanding tracks was called "All of You," which I thought would make a great duet for Julio and Diana. She loved the idea but thought that the lyrics were too weak. I told Julio that I would figure out a solution to the lyric problem and asked Cynthia Weil, one of my favorite lyricists, to write new lyrics that night. When Diana heard it, she loved it, and agreed to sing the track. With that, Julio and I planned to meet her in New York and record.

When I got to New York, I met Diana in the studio to lay down her vocal track. I presented her with yet another version of the lyric, but it didn't quite go as expected. Diana was not happy and wanted to sing only the Cynthia lyric. All of the Columbia label heads had come down to watch Diana record her part so I didn't want to delay anymore. I agreed to go back to Cynthia's lyric and asked Diana to please record.

Meanwhile, Julio's flight from Miami was delayed, and when I told Diana about the delay, she said jokingly, "Who needs Julio anyway?" When Julio finally arrived about an hour later, he was thrilled to see that I had turned the session into a triumph. To show his appreciation, he took off the large gold watch he was wearing, completely encrusted in diamonds, and gave it to me. Even more valuable, Diana delivered a superb vocal performance. The record went on to become a worldwide success.

The following day, Diana and I made plans to "hang out." First, I met her at her office where she was having a fitting, so I got my very own private fashion show. Then we went to a movie—*Eating Raoul*—a popular art film of the early '80s. Dinner followed at Elaine's, a celebrity hangout. We ended the evening by riding through Central Park in my limo for an hour, as we listened to a Billie Holiday tape that I'd brought with me. Diana donned a pair of sunglasses while we consumed a bottle of 1966 La Tache!

Diana and I have maintained a friendly connection throughout the years, and just a few months ago, while shopping at the Whole Foods Market in Beverly Hills, I suddenly heard a familiar voice say to me from behind, "Mr. Perry, is that you?" I turned around and there she was!

Chapter 29

Showtime

In 1978, I was ready to make my big move—to create my own label. I knew right away who I wanted to be my partner: Elektra Records. The other record companies that I would have considered worthwhile candidates (Warner Brothers, Atlantic, Columbia, or Arista) were already overloaded with custom label deals. While Elektra was part of Warner Brothers, they did not distribute as many labels as Warner did, which gave them more of a boutique record feel. I found that extremely appealing. Moreover, Joe Smith, the first person I met with when I interviewed for the Warner job and who later became the president of Warner Brothers Records, was then appointed to the same position for the newly merged Elektra and Asylum Records. Joe and I had known each other for over a decade, so I knew right away that he was the perfect person to work with on such a partnership.

Joe was probably the biggest Lakers fan in Los Angeles. He occupied four floor seats right under the basket and never missed a game. In 1979, Magic Johnson was drafted by the Lakers and the whole town went basketball crazy. One year later, the Lakers were deeply embroiled in the four-out-of-seven series. Kareem Abdul-Jabbar, the Lakers' legendary center, had sprained his ankle during game five and had been advised not to travel to Philadelphia for game six. It made sense for Kareem to rest his ankle for the inevitable game seven, as everyone assumed that there would be no way the Lakers could win game six without him.

It was then that Joe Smith called me and said he had secured the Warner plane to go to Philadelphia for game six. He wanted to know if I was interested in joining him. Even though it would probably be a slaughter, I figured it would be a unique experience, so I unhesitatingly accepted his invitation.

From the moment we arrived in Philadelphia, everyone considered us to be part of the Lakers' entourage. We stayed in the same hotel, rode with the team on the bus to the Philadelphia arena (while Magic performed his "E.J. the D.J." routine to help keep the team loose and relaxed), and watched them go through their pre-game warm-ups. Still, I could tell many people were wondering, *Who the hell are these guys?*

Back then, it was pretty rare to attend games outside of those in your own backyard, so people were surprised to see us sitting in the crowd. Even "Chick" Hearn, the Lakers' legendary play-by-play announcer, interviewed Joe during halftime, and Pat O'Brien interviewed me during the pre-game warm-ups, which appeared two nights later on *The CBS Sunday Sports Final.*

Magic, having just defeated Larry Bird's Indiana State team for the NCAA Championship a year earlier, was on the verge of winning his first NBA Championship—but he was now without Kareem, the team's leading scorer and rebounder! It would be a daunting task.

Magic played all five positions during the game and even jumped at center. At halftime, the score was tied. As the second half progressed, the momentum gradually built in favor of the Lakers, as Magic dazzled the 76ers with his no-look passes and distribution of the ball to all his teammates. By the time the fourth quarter began, the Lakers had established a commanding lead, and Joe and I were going nuts as we realized that we were witnessing a milestone event in NBA history!

We couldn't contain our excitement, much to the ire of the Philadelphia fans who surrounded us. Eventually, one of them turned around and shouted, "Shut up you Hollywood f*ggots!" At that point, I suggested to Joe that we get the fuck out of there. Since we were in the fifth row, we made our way down to the court and spent the last three minutes of the game with the team, in a state of jubilation.

As soon as the game ended, the team was rushed into the locker room, as were Joe and I. We were blown away to see that the first person to visit was Dr. J (Julius Erving), who came in to congratulate Magic. What a class act! It's no wonder that everyone has long held him in the highest esteem in professional basketball. Magic's final numbers were 42 points, 15 rebounds, 7 assists, and 3 steals. Henceforth, Lakers games were known as "Showtime."

The crowning touch to this glorious weekend came when the Lakers found out that they had to be back in LA at noon the following day for a hastily organized victory party in the parking lot of the Forum. Keep in mind that nobody had the slightest idea the Lakers could win that game, except maybe Magic. Lakers management discovered that they couldn't take the championship trophy on the plane because it was too big to fit in the overhead luggage compartment, and there was no time to have a crate built. (This was years before the NBA chartered planes for their teams to travel.) So, they asked Joe and me if we would take the trophy on our plane and bring it to the celebration. Naturally, we were thrilled.

When we got back to LA, we immediately headed out in our limo toward the Forum, but the traffic was practically at a standstill. We finally talked the driver into getting in the middle lane, which wasn't legal. As we approached an intersection, there was a cop directing traffic who looked like he wanted to arrest us. But once we explained where we had come from and showed him the trophy, he said, "Follow me." Our trip ended with a police motorcycle escort right up to the stage, where the team was standing in front of thousands of cheering fans. What a memorable weekend!

Chapter 30

Planet Records and The Pointer Sisters

After I picked a name for my label—Planet Records—came the most important decision I had to make: Who would be the first artist I would sign? I had just set up my offices on Sunset Boulevard (in a building once owned by Phil Spector that I had passed frequently, dreaming that I might make it my home one day). I got a call from Steve Wax, the executive vice president of Elektra Records. He wanted to know if I had any interest in signing The Pointer Sisters. I'd seen their first album cover with Blue Thumb Records—a picture of them wearing thrift shop dresses—and heard the cross-pollination of R&B and jazz in their song selection. My answer was a resounding yes! I was definitely interested in signing them as my first artist on Planet Records.

The only thing that concerned me was that two of the girls, June and Bonnie, had left the group to pursue solo careers and were being managed by their husbands. This is not often a recipe for success. When the remaining Pointer Sisters, Anita and Ruth, came to audition for me, I discovered that they had put a new girl in the group whose voice was decidedly weaker than theirs. I found this strange because typically, when choosing a new person, a group would make sure that he or she was a strong singer. To make matters worse, I could hear that Anita and Ruth were singing more softly, in an attempt to hide the blatant differences in vocal quality. The results were simply dreadful.

After they'd sung a few songs, I felt I should put everyone out of their misery and gave them the "Don't call me, I'll call you" line. The new girl had come alone in a cab, so she was the first to leave. Then as Anita and Ruth were on their way out the door and we were saying goodbye for the last time, something came over me—like a wave of empathy. I just couldn't let them go.

"There has to be a better ending to the story than this," I told them. As pitiful as their audition had been, there was something about the warmth of their personalities that appealed to me. "Come upstairs to my office and let's talk for another minute or two."

Once we were seated comfortably, I got right to it. "Okay...tell me what happened. How did you get to this point? Where are your sisters?" I was curious as to whether there was a chance of bringing June and/or Bonnie back into the group. Their response was negative across the board, but still...I found I was not prepared to give up on them. One thing seemed clear—they definitely needed a new strong lead vocal. Anita had more of a pop quality in her voice and Ruth's voice was exceptionally deep, so putting together the right vocals was my first order of business.

At the time the girls were managed by Forest Hamilton, who also managed a male instrumental group with a dynamic female lead singer named Sylvia St. James, whose forte was gospel music. After much negotiation, Sylvia became the latest Pointer Sister. Feeling that I had to play with the cards that were available, I started to cut a few tracks with Sylvia singing lead.

After a few weeks of experimenting, Anita and Ruth asked for a meeting at my house, at which point they informed me that they could not continue with this lineup. The chemistry with Sylvia just wasn't there. I had to admit that no matter how much potential they may have had, it still wasn't The Pointer Sisters. Here they were at a record company that was in a position to offer them almost anything a new artist could want or need, and all they could mount was a splintered, incomplete group.

"What's June doing?" I asked. "Where is she right now?"

"She's home," they said, "but if you want to talk to her, you'll have to go through her husband." Filled with frustration and desperation, I insisted that they give me June's phone number.

The voice at the other end was Bill Whitmore, June's husband, also known as "W." He greeted me with the most unpleasant "hello" one could imagine. I introduced myself and, not wanting to beat around the bush, I told him I had cut some tracks and had one in particular that I thought was perfect for the girls. Furthermore, I said that I was aware they had some major problems with their previous record company, and I assured him that, should June decide to come back to the group, those problems would be a thing of the past. Bill said he would talk it over with June. Shortly after our conversation, he finally agreed to give it a try.

The beauty of my timing in approaching June was that the song I had in mind was the Sly and the Family Stone classic "Everybody Is a Star." It had been written for the specific voices in the Family Stone, so it was difficult to imagine anyone else performing it, except for The Pointer Sisters, whose own voices fit the material, almost as well as Sly and company. Another reason the song was such a good fit for the girls was that they had frequent conflicts about who would sing lead, and here was a song that, in its very title, preached equality.

When I heard June sing it, I was thrilled beyond measure. Her voice not only had exactly the right edgy and vibrant quality but provided the missing link to their sound. With Ruth on the bottom, Anita in the middle, and June on top, I finally had the real Pointer Sisters!

Once we started recording in earnest, I had to decide in which direction I wanted to take them. I was cognizant of the fact that they were born and raised in Oakland, California, and had spent a great deal of time at the Fillmore West, singing backup for artists such as Tower of Power, Taj Mahal, and Dave Mason. I thought it would be unique for a black female group with their distinctive voices to sing soulful covers of songs written by established rock artists.

In November 1978, Planet Records released their first album of The Pointer Sisters. Titled *Energy*, the album featured songs by the likes of Fleetwood Mac, Steely Dan, and others. Bruce Springsteen was also involved—he wrote one of the tracks titled "Fire," which ended up becoming The Pointer Sisters' first Top 5 hit and signature song. Both the album and single were certified Gold.

My favorite track on *Energy* was a jewel of a song by Allen Toussaint, "Happiness." The Pointers had a history with Toussaint as their very first hit had been one of his songs, "Yes We Can Can." "Happiness" featured a searing lead vocal by June that offered abundant proof of why it was so vitally important to have her back in the group. The Pointers later told me that they dedicated this song to me, which really touched me because I'd always felt close with the lyric as it reminds the listener to love to live and live life freely and full of inspiration. It ends with a call to keep happiness forever: "Happiness, say you'll leave me never."

To this day, The Pointers open their shows with this song.

Their next album, *Priority*, was the final step in The Pointer Sisters' rock 'n' roll experiment. While it didn't connect with an audience, it got great critical praise and was a "balls out" rock album that featured Rick Marotta, Waddy Wachtel, Nicky Hopkins, and Bill Payne (of the highly respected band, Little Feat). Some of the songs on it were "Who Do You Love?" by Ian Hunter, "The Shape I'm In" by Robbie Robertson, "Blind Faith" by Gerry Rafferty and Joe Egan, "All Your Love" by Bob Seger, and "Happy" by Mick Jagger and Keith Richards. This is a record of which I am extremely proud, and I still listen to it all the time.

In the two years that followed, The Pointer Sisters made two additional major Top 5 singles—"Slow Hand" and "He's So Shy." Both sold a million records and were certified Gold, along with two more albums that also achieved Gold status.

From left to right: Anita, me, Ruth, and June.

Even though we'd made these three outstanding singles, it seemed that we were only selling albums on the strength of the singles' success. At the time, radio was very prejudiced, and the general feeling in the radio community was that The Pointer Sisters were too pop to be embraced by black radio—but I felt it was imperative for them to capture a black audience.

Then, in the fall of 1983, we released *Break Out,* the landmark album that became the biggest success of their recording careers. Ruth Pointer described the album in her book, *Still So Excited!: My Life as a Pointer*

Sister: "*Break Out* signaled the dawn of the techno age that followed in the 1980s and demonstrated that warmth, soul, and artistry could be compatible with the machine-based sounds."[1] The album was filled with the space-age dance grooves so typical of the techno sound, and I felt this brought a new dimension to The Pointer Sisters' sound. People seemed to agree as the album received four Top 10 hits that were spread between the pop and R&B charts, while the LP itself spent a year and a half on the *Billboard* Top 200.

The first single was "I Need You;" although it was far from being the best track on the album, it was a solid R&B record, peaking at No. 13 on the *Billboard* R&B chart. As a result, black radio was waiting for the group's next single, "Automatic," and was totally responsible for forcing its release as the second single from the album, while also sending a message to everyone in the radio world that The Pointer Sisters were no longer just a pop act. Because it featured Ruth's deep voice, some people even thought that Stevie Wonder was singing the lead vocal. This is a classic example of a well-crafted, finely written song about somebody hypnotized by their lover. It was completely different when compared to the standard love songs out there at the time. The unique, futuristic beats and Ruth's deep vocals complemented one another perfectly to make this a hit. As she sings each time, she can't control it and she can't speak—she feels totally automatic. It still remains one of my favorites of all The Pointers' tracks.

At this time, something happened to me that led me to what would be the biggest mistake of my career. I got a call from my friend, Freddy DeMann, a well-known, successful manager, who wanted to know if I would be interested in producing one of his artists: MADONNA.

I asked Freddie to send me some demos of the songs she had in mind to record. Coincidentally, I was working on a dance mix for "Automatic" with Madonna's boyfriend at the time, John "Jellybean" Benitez, one of the best dance/club mixers in the business. John said that his girlfriend wanted to meet me, so we arranged a meeting after our mix session the next day.

The get-together went great and Madonna told me that she loved "Automatic." I was so embroiled in the phenomenal success that The Pointer Sisters and I were having with *Break Out*, that when I received Madonna's demos and listened to them, I politely declined Freddy's offer. The material sounded strictly club-oriented, and that's not my favorite genre of music, but I had completely misread Madonna's potential.

Some months later, a song emerged that carried Madonna's album way up the charts. Billy Steinberg, who, ironically, was the lead singer of one of the bands I had signed to Planet Records under the name Billy Thermal, had written the song, "Like a Virgin."

Six months later, I was backstage at the American Music Awards. During a commercial break, I watched as a girl crossed the stage and headed straight toward me. Looking me dead in the eye, she said: "Congratulations on all your success." It was a very impressive gesture by Madonna.

In 1981, I changed our distribution partner from Elektra to RCA. We started inauspiciously with a Pointers album that was meant to feature a new song, "I'm So Excited." It had been written by my associate producer Trevor Lawrence, with Anita, June, and Ruth, and we all thought it was going to be a big, fat hit. However, the record unexpectedly failed to connect with an audience.

Around this same time, MTV was created. When it looked like it was going to revolutionize the record industry, I was more than ready to jump into the fray. We all wanted to be a part of the new music-video world, so we went ahead and made preparations to make a video for "I'm So Excited"—despite its disappointing chart performance. I co-directed it with Kenny Ortega, who has become one of the most in-demand video director-choreographers.

I must say, the video is a stunner. It begins with the girls primping and preparing to go out that night and do the town. They end up at what turns out to be a wild party, featuring the best dancers in LA, choreographed by my friend Toni Basil.

I sent a copy to my friend, Les Garland, who was then executive producer of MTV and responsible for all elements of programming. A few days later, I called him to get his reaction to the video and he said, "Great video, man." I asked him when he could play it and he said that unfortunately he couldn't, to which I replied, "Why the fuck not?" He told me the company was called MTV, not Les Garland Video.

Making the "I'm So Excited" video.

It became clear that he couldn't play it because The Pointer Sisters were a black act. It wasn't until 1983 that the color barrier at MTV was shattered, starting with Michael Jackson's "Billy Jean" video, closely followed by Prince's "1999" and "Little Red Corvette." Next came Tina Turner's "Better Be Good to Me," and finally, it was The Pointer Sisters' turn. These artists helped break down the walls of prejudice at MTV. A year later, MTV held its first annual Video Music Awards, and guess which was one of the videos they used to promote the show? "I'm So Excited." Now *that* was poetic justice.

That little victory notwithstanding, it was still a very down period for all of us. Making matters worse, RCA appointed a new executive vice president to run the record company. This meant that the man with whom I had a very close relationship and with whom I had made our new distribution deal was gone. This was even more disheartening since the new executive vice president was an industry outsider named José Menendez, recruited from RCA's Hertz Rent-a-Car division, no less. He refused to let us make a video for "Automatic," and the act he had just signed to be the flagship artists of his new regime at RCA was Menudo, a group of pre-teen Latino boys.

It's not unusual for a new executive coming in to try and diminish previous successes because they can't take any credit for them. It seemed quite clear to all of us that Menendez was hell-bent on destroying all the years of hard work we had put into The Pointer Sisters.

I grew to hate him and was tempted on more than one occasion to go to his office and throw a brick through his window. (Two years later, I heard on the news that Menendez's two teenage sons murdered him and their mother while they were watching TV and eating strawberries one evening in their Beverly Hills home.)

Even without a video, "Automatic" was a Top 5 record on the *Billboard* Hot 100 and R&B charts. We'd finally achieved our goal of having simultaneous success on both major charts. In 1984, The Pointer Sisters won a Grammy for Best Vocal Arrangement for Two or More Voices for "Automatic."

The third single really felt as if it should have been the first one. "Jump (For My Love)" had more obvious hit potential written all over it. Practically from the day the record was released, it burned its way up the charts, the R&B and pop numbers matching each other stride for stride and both peaking at No. 3. This was the culmination of all our efforts, and The Pointer Sisters won a Grammy for Best Pop Vocal Performance by a Duo or Group.

Once again, though, RCA let us know that they would stop at nothing to devalue The Pointers' continued success by not allowing us to make a video for "Jump (For My Love)" either. When I received this news, the telephone wires must have short circuited, for I was screaming! I told Menendez I refused to let them keep us out of the video business. Finally, they came back to me and reluctantly said they would approve a budget of $30,000, which, compared to other videos, was a paltry sum.

I meditated on it and I thought, *Fuck them, I'll find a way to make a great video for $30,000!* So I came up with an inspired idea, if I do say so myself. First, I got film clips of Olympic track and field athletes (high jumpers, hurdlers, broad jumpers, triple jumpers). Then I had a conversation with then-Commissioner of the NBA, David Stern, who agreed to let me use two clips of any NBA players of my choice (Magic Johnson and Dr. J). I carefully edited this footage together, intercut with The Pointers' very sensual performance. This was their breakthrough video that thrust them into heavy rotation on MTV.

Since "I'm So Excited" had never really seen the light of day, Gregg Geller, Senior VP of A&R for RCA at the time, came up with a unique idea: Why not add that song to the *Break Out* album? I did a remix of the track and released it as the fourth single from the album, and finally, "I'm So Excited" got the recognition it so richly deserved. It became an enormous success, playing at most major sporting events. When the Lakers were at the peak of their "Showtime" dynasty, the song was always played at the start of the fourth quarter and the crowd would go nuts. It could also be heard in numerous films. Today, it is a worldwide anthem and has become their signature song.

The fifth and last major single to emerge from *Break Out* was "Neutron Dance."

It had always been one of my favorite tracks, and I kept asking the promotion people if they'd gotten any feedback on it from radio. The response was always less than enthusiastic. Nevertheless, I loved that track and was determined to see it get a real shot.

Then I got a call from two friends of mine, Don Simpson and Jerry Bruckheimer. They were preparing their next movie, *Beverly Hills Cop,* which starred Eddie Murphy. I questioned them on the fact that on Eddie's first two movies, *48 Hrs.* and *Trading Places,* there was no word of mouth regarding a soundtrack, so what made them think that this would be different? They explained that in this movie, "Eddie is a Detroit cop who goes on a mission to Beverly Hills to avenge the murder of his best friend. Just picture Eddie driving down Rodeo Drive in his beat-up, old jalopy that he drove out from Detroit," they said. "Count me in," I replied without a moment's hesitation.

It seemed that the director of the movie, Marty Brest, had discovered "Neutron Dance" on the album and had put it on what is known as a "temp track"—a temporary track that evokes the tempo, mood, and flavor the director wants to impart for a particular scene. The chances are always slim that a director will use what's on the temp track in the actual film for fear that the songs might be too familiar.

Marty had put "Neutron Dance" under the groundbreaking scene of Eddie dangling from the back of a garbage truck, while being chased by the police all over the city. It set the tone for the entire movie, but Simpson and Bruckheimer felt they couldn't really use it since it came from a current hit album that had already sold over three million copies. Therefore, they wanted me to come up with a song that was similar to "Neutron Dance."

I explained to them that this was a special song and created a dynamic chemistry between Eddie, the garbage truck, and the music. I assured them that in spite of its presence on *Break Out*, nobody really knew the track. I was getting ready to release it as a single anyway, so why not help each other? It was a win-win situation and, sure enough, they couldn't come up with a song that came close to the magic of "Neutron Dance." So, Simpson and Bruckheimer bit the bullet and joined forces with us, using the entire song in that memorable scene, as well as over closing credits.

Our video contained ample footage from the movie, and helped to propel the soundtrack and *Break Out* to new heights. The soundtrack wound up selling three million copies and the song remained a stalwart track on *Break Out*. It sold an additional million units for total sales of nearly *five million*. It remained on the charts for eighteen months. Eddie Murphy grew so attached to the song that when he went on his RAW tour later in the year, he played "Neutron Dance" in its entirety before he took the stage.

Our goal of reaching a black audience was cemented with the sisters having received two American Music Awards for Best Black Video Group (Soul/R&B) in 1985 and again in 1986. In addition, I received a Grammy nomination for Best Video Director (Short Form).

The Pointers were also named the fourth most popular black female group of all time! One last thing that deserves mention; the girls wanted an equal number of lead vocals on each album, e.g., three songs for each girl and one where they all sang together. To make my job even more challenging, they wanted the songs to have equal single potential, as much as possible. All this with three completely different voices!

Over the years, Planet Records released other albums. Among them were records by Bill Medley and Bobby Hatfield (both formerly of The Righteous

Brothers); Billy Steinberg, recording under the name Billy Thermal (co-writer of "Like a Virgin," "True Colors," and "I Touch Myself"); power pop band The Plimsouls; and Greg Phillinganes (keyboard virtuoso who played with Michael Jackson, Stevie Wonder, and Lionel Richie). In 1985, I sold the rights to Planet Records to RCA so I could concentrate all my efforts on what I did best: producing records.

Chapter 31

Tina Turner

In 1977, Mike Stewart, then-president of United Artists Music, asked me if I would like to meet Tina Turner. Like almost everyone else on the planet, I was a longtime fan. After meeting her, I found her congenial, warm, and best of all, looking for a producer! Apart from Phil Spector's monumental production of "River Deep, Mountain High," her then-husband, Ike Turner, had produced all of her other records, and the artist had always been billed as Ike and Tina Turner.

Tina had just won a protracted court battle with Ike, who had claimed that since he'd given her his name, he owned it. When Tina won the case, Ike was bitter. I discussed my desire to sign Tina with my trusted friend and attorney, Abe Somer, who advised me to steer clear of the situation for fear that Ike would come after me with a gun. Anyone who would foster Tina's recording career would be considered an enemy of Ike's, he reasoned. Heeding Abe's advice, I decided not to pursue Tina any further but felt that our paths would cross again if the timing was right.

As the next few years passed, Tina and Ike separated, and Tina got her solo act together. In 1981, she assembled a great band, plus her own version of The Ikettes (the name Ike had given the backup singers who also danced behind Tina). The most exciting event of all was the announcement of Tina Turner's official opening at a new club in New York, The Ritz, which was owned by an old friend of mine, Jerry Brandt.

I happened to be in New York with Rod Stewart that same weekend and we were both eager to see Tina's debut. She had put together some inspired choices of material: Prince's "Let's Pretend We're Married," a completely unique interpretation of The Beatles' "Help" (done as a soulful ballad), which completely brought the house down, and an outstanding cover of Al Green's "Let's Stay Together" had become a big hit in the U.K. All in all, her show was off the charts!

After the show, I immediately went to her dressing room and I complimented her performance, for it truly was something special. "Maybe the time is right for us to finally get together and make some music," I told her—and that's exactly what we did!

I was beyond excited at the thought of signing Tina to Planet Records. So much so that we started recording even before we had a contract. Initially, we cut "Johnny and Mary" by Robert Palmer, which would be featured in the movie *Summer Lovers*; and her rendition of The Beatles' "Help," as it had been so successful in her solo debut. A crew from ABC's *20/20* came down to the studio to film us recording. If I'd needed any validation that it was all really happening, this was it!

There was, however, one bump in the road. Since Tina's cover of Al Green's "Let's Stay Together," had become a Top 10 record in the U.K., her previous label, EMI, was reluctant to release her in that territory. I knew that in order to make this happen, I would have to do it without getting the rights in the U.K., but without that as part of the deal, RCA was shuffling their feet in getting back to me promptly.

Two weeks went by without an answer and I decided that come hell or high water, I was going to make sure RCA didn't blow this deal. When I got back to Tina's manager, Roger Davies, I discovered that, much to my chagrin, he had already signed her to EMI Worldwide without even giving me the courtesy of a call. To say that I was disappointed would be a gross understatement and after that, Tina and I didn't speak for several months.

Then one Saturday night, I was at a hot new private club in West Hollywood called Tramp. They had a chic restaurant and a separate room for cocktails and dancing. Just as I entered the room, I heard someone call out my name, "RICHARD!" It was Tina, and as we walked toward each other, we started dancing together to Prince's "Baby I'm a Star," which was playing in the background. We hung out for the rest of the evening and before saying goodnight, made a date for dinner the following Monday. I took her to Morton's Steakhouse, a very popular place to be, especially on Monday night. During dinner, many people came over to our table to meet Tina and congratulate her on her debut album for Capitol (the flagship label for EMI in America).

After dinner we went back to my house for a nightcap and a dip in my hot tub. That marked the beginning of a very close friendship between us. And, even though we weren't working together, I was glad to see her career taking off. Her album was all over the radio. One night, after a wonderful dinner at her home, I got in my car around midnight, turned on the radio and what should be playing but "Private Dancer," one of my favorite tracks from her album. It was a special moment for me, where art and life were synergistically combined.

While spending time with Tina was a constant joy, there are two special highlights that resonate in my memory. The first was when we both wound up in London at the same time. She was doing concerts all over England to promote her hit of "Let's Stay Together," and I was there to do a video with The Pointer Sisters. One night, Tina played Wembley Arena, which has a capacity of around twelve thousand—it was a big gig for her. Tina didn't like people in her dressing room before she went on, and there were only two people she allowed in on that night—Roger Davies and myself. How ironic!

The second highlight was much more significant. It was when she asked if I would accompany her to the Grammy Awards in 1984. At first, I was reluctant because I was very pissed off at NARAS (the National Academy of Recording Arts and Sciences) for not giving me a Grammy nomination. I had just completed the most productive year of my career. I had produced six Top 10 records: four by The Pointer Sisters, plus the global smash "To All the Girls I've Loved Before" by Willie Nelson and Julio Iglesias, and "Rhythm of the Night" by DeBarge, which reached No. 1 on the *Billboard* R&B chart. To top it all off, *Billboard* had named me Producer of the Year. All of this, and no Grammy nod! I just thought it would be too painful to go.

Tina and me.

Then I thought it over and realized just how much Tina wanted me to be there with her. I told her that I would be happy and proud to be her date on that special night. By the end of the evening, she had won four Grammys, and when they announced her name for Record of the Year, I was the first person on my feet to lead the standing ovation.

After the awards show, we went straight to the airport so she could catch a flight to Paris to begin a European tour.

Chapter 32

Elizabeth Taylor

My relationship with Tina was special, but little did I know that another one was just around the corner.

As I mentioned in earlier chapters, I had developed a friendship with Carole Bayer Sager, and in the '70s, we had two memorable records together: "Nobody Does It Better" and "When I Need You." By the early '80s, Carole and Burt Bacharach were married, and Carole had become extremely close friends with Elizabeth Taylor. One day, Carole called to ask if I would like to have dinner with her, Burt, and Elizabeth. I was intrigued, to say the least. Elizabeth and I hit it off right away, and although she was a great kisser, she had one cardinal rule: no sex without marriage!

Quite simply put, Elizabeth Taylor was one of the kindest, most generous, and most fun-loving people I've ever known. We shared many memorable evenings together. She founded an organization known as amfAR and raised millions of dollars for AIDS research. I accompanied her to several AIDS fundraising banquets.

One day, Elizabeth called and said something that almost made me faint: "Sugar, have you ever heard of Erté?" Of course I had heard of Erté! Erté was a famous French artist, and I was (and still am) a huge fan of his work. I started collecting Erté pieces of art in the early '70s and continued for many years. Among other things, he was involved in French musical revues for which he created the costumes and set designs, always brilliant and often done in watercolors. These sketches have become highly collectible. The detail that he put into all his work was astonishing. He also could be known as the father of art deco.

There's no way Elizabeth knew how much I enjoyed Erté's work—funny how things happen like that. I tried to maintain my cool composure when I answered her, but could not help but reveal what a huge fan I was. "Well, Sugar, would you like to come with me to this black-tie event to celebrate his ninety-seventh birthday? We will be sitting with Erté."

Elizabeth, Erté, and me.

Apparently, Erté had recently delved into a new medium: bronze sculptures. They were all on display at a gallery before the dinner—all of them magnificent! Elizabeth came over to me and asked if I liked them. "Absolutely!" I replied. "Well," she said, "why don't you pick out the one you like best as a gift from me to you." The one I chose was titled *The Wedding*, and it depicted a bride and groom holding hands, looking as if they are about to take their sacred vows. That bronze statue has remained in the entry hall of my home for over thirty years and is one of my most prized possessions.

Elizabeth and me.

I still remember how open and approachable Elizabeth was about everything and how willing she was to answer any questions I asked about her life, notably the men she was close to, both friends and husbands. As a result, I was privy to intimate details about James Dean, Montgomery Clift, Mike Todd, and Richard Burton.

Perhaps my most personal Elizabeth story involved—of all things—my cat Raymond. Even though I had never thought of myself as a "cat person," I wound up having cats for thirty years, either Persian or Himalayan, and all of them real beauties. I took a great deal of pride in my cats, but my favorite was Raymond, a black-haired Persian. He used to take strolls around my property but would always come home—except for one night when he inexplicably failed to return. I was sure he would show up the following morning but still, no Raymond. By the third day, I had given up hope. I spoke to Elizabeth that morning, as we had plans to have dinner that night. I happened to mention that it looked like my favorite cat was gone. She was very sympathetic.

When I went to pick her up that evening and waited for her to come downstairs, as she slowly descended and got closer to me, I couldn't believe my eyes! Cradled in her arms was the most beautiful cat I had ever seen. He was a caramel-colored Persian with the cutest pushed-in face. She knew the breeder had planned to keep the cat, but Elizabeth Taylor is not to be denied. The breeder reluctantly agreed to let her purchase the animal.

It's always somewhat of a gamble when someone gives you a pet, but in this case, I couldn't help but fall instantly in love. I named the cat Todd, in honor of Mike Todd, Elizabeth's third husband, and one of the loves of her life (the other being Richard Burton). Mike had died tragically, many years earlier, in a plane crash.

When I took the cat home that night, we both fell asleep with his head resting on my stomach and his eyes looking up at me. I woke up the next morning, and he was in exactly the same position! I never had a closer relationship with any animal like the one I had with Todd.

As luck would have it, Raymond miraculously showed up a few days later, and he and Todd became brothers.

About a year after I got him, I decided to mate Todd—and since he was such an outstanding cat, I wanted to review prospective females. She had to have a warm, winning personality and be worthy of giving birth to what would surely be a special litter. After several "interviews," I found the perfect mate for him—named Cookie.

Usually, when people try to bring cats together to mate, they put them in a closet, or at most, in a small bedroom. I was thinking that this was their honeymoon, so I put them in my guest bedroom with its own bathroom.

As soon as I put them in there, they crawled under the bed. *No point in hanging around*, I figured, so I left for about an hour. When I came back, I stood at the entrance to the room and Todd emerged from under the bed, looking up at me as if to say, "Thank you, man!" Then Cookie came out and sat right next to Todd, who then put his right paw around Cookie's neck! As I stood there watching them in disbelief, I knew better than to call out to anyone or even move a muscle. This was a moment for me alone to witness.

Todd

Chapter 33

Julio and Willie

Dick Asher was president of Columbia Records in 1983. He was very eager to have me produce Julio Iglesias, whom he swore was one of the biggest selling artists on Columbia Records, if not the world. Although I had hardly heard of Julio, I soon discovered that he was indeed an international icon, especially loved in every Spanish-speaking country on the planet. When I first met him, he said I reminded him of a playboy, not a record producer!

My goal was to break Julio into the English-speaking markets. The only problem was that his English was often hard to interpret unless I was talking with him on a social basis. When it came to the details of the work, such as discussing arrangements and other elements of the recording process, we often had difficulty communicating. The only time his English improved was when he enlisted the aid of a vocal coach, who was usually a beautiful woman.

Nevertheless, we began our work together. We started out by cutting several interesting tracks, including "The Air That I Breathe," originally made famous by The Hollies, with background vocals by The Beach Boys (featuring Brian Wilson); "All of You," a beautiful Latinesque ballad done as a duet with Diana Ross, with a melody by Julio's compadre, Tony Renis, and a lyric by Cynthia Weil; and "To Be with You," a classic song made famous by Joe Cuba in the '50s, featuring the great Stan Getz on tenor sax solo.

Then came the pièce de rèsistance. Albert Hammond came into my office one day and said he had a great idea for Julio. Albert was a very talented songwriter who, along with Carole Bayer Sager, had written the melody of "When I Need You" for Leo Sayer. He'd also collaborated with Hal David on a haunting ballad, "99 Miles from LA," which I had recorded with Art Garfunkel eight years earlier. Albert presented me with a song titled, "To All the Girls I've Loved Before." He had originally written it for Art but after listening to it, decided it just didn't feel right for him. When Albert suggested this song, I remembered it right away and knew in an instant that it was destined to be a home run.

Meanwhile, Willie Nelson's wife, Connie, was a big Julio fan and had let Willie know that she thought it would be wonderful for the two of them to do a duet. We were all pretty excited about the idea, but we needed the right song. I knew that "To All the Girls I've Loved Before" was it—the perfect fit for these two very different artists.

We sent the song to Willie and once he heard it, he agreed. I cut the track two days later, and then had Julio add a rough vocal on it. Even then, it sounded immediately like it had the potential to be an important record.

A few days later, Julio, Albert, and I flew to Austin to put Willie's vocal and guitar on the track. Working with Willie was a sheer delight; he had a knack for doing everything right on the first take. When he was done, we were all convinced that we had a major hit, as Willie's voice served as a perfect complement to Julio's. After we finished the session, Connie prepared us a sumptuous Texas barbeque.

There was a strong buzz surrounding the record, and a lot of anticipation before it was even ready to come out. Hugh Hefner adopted it as his theme song, and with Willie's major participation, it opened up the country market so wide that the Academy of Country Music named it Record of the Year. It went to No. 1 on *Billboard's* Country Music chart, hit the Top 5 on the Hot 100, was awarded a Gold record for one million units sold, and became an international hit.

Julio, me, and Willie

It was decided that the debut performance of the song would take place at the Grand Ole Opry, the temple of country music in Nashville. Willie asked me to conduct the orchestra to make sure that it sounded exactly as it did on the record. I hadn't been a conductor since my Tiny Tim days! Feeling a little nervous, yet very excited knowing I would be up there at the request of the great Willie Nelson, I was only too happy to oblige. When the time came for us to perform the song, I took my place at the conductor's podium. The audience immediately connected with the song. I couldn't help but think, *Here I am, conducting the orchestra at the Grand Ole Opry!*

After the performance, I saw Willie in the lobby of the Jack Tar Hotel, where we were both staying. "Do you want to go upstairs and smoke a fatty?" he asked.

Within ten minutes, a group of some of the most revered names in country music had gathered in Willie's suite: Kris Kristofferson, Roger Miller,

Mickey Newbury, and a guy who looked like a Hell's Angel, wearing a jean jacket with the sleeves cut off, and his body covered with tattoos. "Look at all the talent in this room and not a guitar in sight," Willie bellowed out. He summoned one of his aides to go out and get a guitar from his bus.

As the guitar was passed around, it became clear to me that each person was playing a new song that no one had ever heard before. The person who got the greatest response—and looks of disbelief—was Roger Miller, who played a song about a farmer who has an affair with his cow!

After a magical evening, we all said goodnight. I had to turn in anyway, as I had to be in New York the following evening to go to Radio City Music Hall, where The Pointer Sisters were opening for Lionel Richie.

Chapter 34

A Musical Whirlwind

One day in 1983, Suzanne de Passe—one of my dearest friends, and Berry Gordy's right arm at Motown for many years—called me to express concern that we hadn't done any business together since I'd produced Diana Ross' album *Baby It's Me* in 1977. "I'm sending you a demo of a song by a new writer," she said. "Her name is Diane Warren, and the song is 'Rhythm of the Night.' I think it's a hit for DeBarge."

I had already been following DeBarge's career for a while and was particularly fond of two of their hits: "All This Love" and "Time Will Reveal." They were both beautiful ballads featuring their romantic lead singer, El DeBarge. The rest of the group was made up of the DeBarge family, not unlike The Jackson Five.

"Rhythm of the Night" was different from anything they had done before. It was an infectious, up-tempo, dance-oriented number. I liked it immediately and it was the first time that a record company handed me a hit on a silver platter. It turned out to be Diane Warren's first big success, and as an extra bonus, was featured in Berry Gordy's movie *The Last Dragon.* The record eventually reached No. 1 on the *Billboard* R&B and Adult Contemporary charts and No. 3 on the *Billboard* Hot 100. It also became a huge international hit and is still a staple in dance clubs all over the world.

Diane Warren has become a good friend through the years, sometimes asking for my opinion on songs she has written and whether she should finish them. I would ask her to show me the lyrics, then make notes in the margin in red ink, as if I'm grading a student's college term paper. On one occasion I wrote, "Shows continued improvement—keep up the good work…B+." As a result, over our thirty-five years of our friendship, not once has she ever called me Richard. She always refers to me as *Professor*.

* * *

In 1987, I helped establish a new theater at the prep school I'd attended for eight years, Poly Prep. I was deeply honored that this state-of-the-art facility not only bore my name, but that it became an important cultural resource for the community.

Years later, Meryl Streep's daughters attended the school and it came about that Meryl was asked to direct two one-act plays there. So, once when I was talking with the actress at a *Vanity Fair* annual Oscar party, she told me that she made her directorial debut at the Richard Perry Theatre. I thought that was a pretty cool piece of information!

* * *

My next project was a "labor of love" inspired by the Alan Freed rock 'n' roll shows I'd attended in the '50s. As these shows had had a lasting impact on me, I decided to ask contemporary artists of the '80s to perform classic oldies of the '50s on an album that would come to be called *Rock, Rhythm & Blues*.

The first person to commit to the project was Elton John, to whom I will be eternally grateful. He did Fats Domino's "I'm Ready" in a medley with Wanda Jackson's "Let's Have a Party," with Elton playing his best Little Richard piano solo. Other showstoppers included Michael McDonald's killer performance on Jerry Butler & the Impressions' "For Your Precious Love," followed by Rick James' memorable interpretation of The Drifters' "This Magic Moment," in a medley with their "Dance With Me."

Back to school

A favorite song of mine, "Roll With Me Henry," originally made famous by Etta James, was sung on this album with gusto by Christine McVie, with backing by Fleetwood Mac. The remaining artists were Chaka Khan doing Little Willie John's "Fever," Manhattan Transfer performing Frankie Lymon's "I Wanna Be Your Girl," The Pointer Sisters singing The Bobbettes' "Mr. Lee," and Howard Hewett's soulful rendering of the Moonglows' beloved classic, "The Ten Commandments of Love." To end the album, "Goodnight My Love" was sung beautifully by El DeBarge.

The sleeper track on the record was by Randy Travis, who at that time was the hottest country artist on the map. We did a moving ballad originally made famous by Brook Benton, "It's Just a Matter of Time," which took advantage of Randy's extraordinary low register. We cut the track in Nashville, where I loved to record, and the whole session took three hours. The record went to No. 1 on the *Billboard* Country chart, but unfortunately, like with most country records, it failed to cross over to a pop audience.

Rick James performing "This Magic Moment" for the Rock, Rhythm & Blues *video.*

My dream for this labor-of-love project was to make a long-form video of the entire thing, but Warner Brothers, the label that had financed the album, would give me only enough money for three videos. Once again drawing blood from a stone, I directed these videos myself and, as with The Pointers' "Jump," got great results. In this case, I managed to capture the excitement of the Brooklyn Paramount shows and elicited some wonderful performances from Rick James, Randy Travis, and El DeBarge.

Rock, Rhythm & Blues *album cover.*

Chapter 35

An Evening with Bob Dylan

There was a girl who lived in New York in the '70s, whose name was Carole Childs. I met her through Carole Bayer Sager as they were best friends. I learned a lot about Carole: She was a diehard New Yorker, who loved to go to dance clubs, and she had a surprisingly good ear for music. Her dream was to move to LA and get a job in the record business. As our friendship grew, she would constantly ask me, "Rich, when are you gonna give me a job?" I would reply, "Carole, you must be patient and wait until the time is right."

The moment finally came where I felt that I could use an A&R person with a fresh ear. On my next trip to New York, I met with Carole and asked her whether or not she was ready to have her dreams come true. I moved Carole and her son to LA shortly thereafter and gave her an A&R position at Planet Records. After two years, she moved on to Geffen Records in a similar capacity. A few years earlier, Geffen had signed Bob Dylan and put out his album *Planet Waves*. It was Dylan's only break from Columbia Records. I knew that Carole and Bob's paths would cross and they eventually did—at the Bar Mitzvah of Bob's eldest son, Jakob Dylan. Bob had long been divorced from his first wife, Sara, and before long, Bob and Carole were living together. Their relationship lasted throughout the '80s and '90s, and they still remain close.

One day Carole said to me, "Rich, Bob wants to meet with you." When I asked her why, she said that he wanted to make a more produced album, and to quote Bob, "not one that was done in a week or two."

Needless to say, I was thrilled. I asked Carole what he liked to drink. "Just coffee," she answered. Bob arrived that night, right on time. I found one thing a little strange—he drove up in a Cadillac convertible with the top down. He'd driven all the way from Malibu, yet all he was wearing was a short sleeve Hawaiian shirt. One thing I neglected to mention was that it was a bitter cold December night, but he didn't seem to mind the cold at all.

Bob started our meeting by reiterating what Carole had told me—that he wanted to make a more produced album. Then, he asked if he could play some songs for me. He sat at the piano and began to play. After a few songs, he turned and asked me how I would produce each one. I asked him if he wanted me to tell him what I would actually have each instrument play and he said that was *exactly* what he wanted to know.

Starting with the drums, I gave him a detailed explanation of what I thought the music should sound like. What happened next can only be described as surreal—Bob Dylan asked me, "Rich, would you mind if I took some notes?" I was stunned!

Though we never worked together, Bob and Carole came over several times after that. One time in particular, he was especially eager for me to hear his new album—mainly because he didn't write any of the songs and was looking forward to the critics not overanalyzing what he was trying to say. Instead, he'd recorded songs by people like Woody Guthrie and others who had inspired him through the years.

I was supposed to go to a birthday dinner for a close friend that night, but Bob kept wanting to play me "just one more song." I explained that I had this dinner followed by a listening party that Mick Jagger was having for his new solo album, at which point Bob said, "Rich, I'll tell you what. If you'll listen to the rest of my album, then I'll go to Jagger's party with you." It was an offer I couldn't refuse.

When we arrived at the party, Mick was delighted to see the surprise guest I'd brought with me. Coincidently, Dylan, Jagger, and I had each recently completed an album that was meaningful to us. Bob's and Mick's were solo efforts, while mine was with Ray Charles. So there we were, the three of us huddled together swapping stories about our adventures in the studio. I felt blessed.

One of my last encounters with Bob came a few years later, in about 1994, when Carole called to tell me that Bob wanted to get together again—that he had something to play for me.

When they came over, Bob told me he was thinking of making a standards album. To that end, he'd made a demo of "I'm In the Mood for Love" that he wanted me to hear. It definitely had possibility, but Bob, for reasons only he knows, decided to wait until 2015 to release his standards collection. Entitled *Shadows in the Night*, it consists primarily of songs made famous by Sinatra, but with a country feel. Although I never got the chance to produce that album with him, I have remained a fan of Bob's music throughout the years. Overall, I am just grateful that I was able to get to know him on a personal level.

Chapter 36

Ray Charles

In 1990, Mo Ostin signed Ray Charles to Warner Brothers. It was an important signing for Mo and for the label. As soon as I heard the news, I charged into Mo's office to tell him how much it would mean to me to produce this album, which I knew was a once-in-a-lifetime opportunity.

Ray Charles had always been one of my favorite artists, but there was one major stumbling block. For many years Ray had produced himself and, as part of his deal, he insisted on taking on the same role. He had his own studio and was used to knocking off his albums quickly and, just as quickly, collecting his advance. In fact, he had already finished his first album for Warner Brothers prior to joining the label.

To no one's surprise, the record fell short and never found an audience. Finally, Mo agreed that it was time for me to step in and take the reins. First, I had to gain his trust—I don't think he was too pleased at the thought of some white Jewish guy producing the great Ray Charles. The first song I brought to him was the Leon Russell classic "A Song For You." Outside of Frank Sinatra, I felt that Ray was the only other artist who could do justice to the song, and I told him that he was meant to sing it. After the song's release, "A Song for You" became Ray's first Top 10 single in over twenty-five years and earned him the Grammy Award for Best R&B Male Vocal Performance.

As I continued to bring outstanding material to Ray, his confidence in me kept growing. He realized that we were making a special album together, which came to be called *My World*. When the album came out, Stephen Holden of *Rolling Stone* called it:

> *An album that brings the sixty-two-year-old father of modern soul back.... Produced by Richard Perry, who twenty years ago masterminded the entries of Barbra Streisand, Carly Simon, Ringo Starr, and Harry Nilsson into the pop mainstream, MY WORLD takes the sound of Charles' best sixties records and discreetly updates it by underlining the swelling gospel choruses with crisp, techno-improved beats.*[1]

Another noteworthy review came from *Billboard* magazine:

> *The Genius of Soul returns to peak incendiary form with an album that will come to be regarded as one of the best of his incomparable career. The visionary who first rocked the roadhouse with gospel fervor re-emerges with a vengeance on this righteous outpouring of hellfire and funky sanctity. Pass the word—there's hit potential galore here with the sexy-euphoric sounds of "Let Me Take Over," "One Drop of Love," and "I'll Be There," as well as the savvy sermonizing of "My World." Other instant classics on this astounding release include the spine-tingling "So Help Me God," the poignant "If I Could," and Ray's definitive rendering of Paul Simon's "Still Crazy After All These Years." The capper is the anthemic "None of Us Are Free," a soul rocker (featuring fierce guitar from Eric Clapton) for all seasons and all formats. Brother Ray is back, and he's taking no prisoners.*[2]

The song "None of Us Are Free," written by three of my favorite writers, Barry Mann, Cynthia Weil, and Brenda Russell, was an extremely well-crafted song, except for the bridge section, which I felt had almost a pop cabaret feel. I called Barry and asked if he and the other writers would consider reworking the bridge. When Barry got back to me, he said that they all agreed to change it under one condition: I had to be there during the rewrite so that they could be sure they were giving me what I wanted. We convened at Barry's office the following Saturday afternoon, and around twenty minutes later, the rewrite was done! It turned out to be my favorite section of the song.

When Eric Clapton agreed to add a guitar solo on this track, I was ecstatic. It was exactly what the track needed, and not to mention, I viewed this as a rare opportunity to work with him. Just imagine, Eric Clapton playing on a Ray Charles record! That combination alone got me high.

We met at a studio in New York where Eric had an entourage hanging out—which interfered with my recording process. Eric did a couple of takes, but they didn't have the magic I knew he was capable of. Finally, I asked everyone to please clear the room so I could have some time alone with Eric. When they were gone, I then told him that I wanted him to play a solo comparable to the one he did on "Layla." As we began to really get serious, I literally started screaming while he was playing to help inspire him. He proceeded to deliver a piercing solo full of emotion—vintage Clapton!

Ray and me in the studio.

When I encountered Eric several months later at the Warner Brothers Grammy Awards party after he'd won Record of the Year for "Tears in Heaven," he said to me, "Richard, you brought that solo out of me." A compliment like that, coming from arguably the greatest guitar player on Earth, is something that will stay with me forever.

During the making of the Ray Charles album, I also had the opportunity to work with one of my favorite singers: Mavis Staples. Those of us who love great singers can't easily forget her guttural, soulful voice on The Staple Singers' classics, "Respect Yourself" and "I'll Take You There." She sang the backgrounds on several of Ray's tracks, and her unique sound combined with Ray's vocals brought a distinct flavor to the project.

It would be remiss of me to end this chapter without making special mention of the vocals of "Brother Ray." Perhaps aided by the fact that all day long he drank gin and coffee, the skillful way he combined R&B, gospel, jazz, hip hop, and country was extraordinary. I believe that this album demonstrates why he will always be known as the "Genius of Soul."

Chapter 37

Rod Stewart

Rod Stewart and I met for the first time in 1980 while waiting in line to use the bathroom at a Beverly Hills wedding. After some pleasant conversation, Rod asked me, "How much do you get to produce an artist?" I was reluctant to start negotiating, but Rod pressed on, "How about for a biggie like me?"

Out of that double dose of Stewart humor, an enduring friendship was born—and it is now approaching forty years. In 1990, I was asked to produce a record with him called "The Motown Song" and, as a bonus, I brought in The Temptations to sing backing vocals. It became a Top 10 single, and for a while, Rod opened his show with it.

After close to ten years of marriage to his second wife—and two children—Rod got the shock of his life when Rachel Hunter said she wanted to get a divorce. He hadn't seen it coming, and it felt like someone tapping you on the shoulder and then whacking you across the side of your head with a baseball bat.

Rod's longtime manager and a personal friend of mine, Arnold Stiefel, broke the news to me and suggested I give Rod a call. Instead, Rod gave me a call the next day and, naturally, I told him how sorry I was to hear the news. I let him know that if there was anything I could do, I was there for him. "It's times like this that a man needs his friends the most," he replied. We made plans to have dinner a few nights later, and it was then that we started to become very close.

We began talking about the possibility of doing a standards album, since we were both very familiar with the repertoire. We were at a back table in our favorite restaurant as we exchanged song ideas and wrote them down on a napkin. As a means of "auditioning" the songs to see whether they would work or not, Rod sang them softly at our table. As I sat there and listened to him sing, it was clear that we both sensed we were on to something.

If a song turned us on, it made the napkin list. The following songs are a few that qualified in the early rounds: "You Go to My Head," "The Way You Look Tonight," "The Very Thought of You," "Angel Eyes," and "Where or When." Our process yielded quite an impressive list.

Rod and me toasting our new musical venture.

For our next move, we decided to bite the bullet and go in to the studio with five songs and some of the best jazz/pop musicians in the city. Rod offered to finance the session costs, which was a very rare thing for an artist to do.

After we listened to what we recorded, he said he didn't like it. When I asked him why, he said that so many people had done jazz-oriented standards albums and he wanted to do something different. I must admit, he made a very salient point. So I found a little demo studio in the Valley, and we started working on tracks that would allow for contemporary pop influences. We cut a number of songs and started to feel really good about the different direction we had taken.

As much as Rod and I believed in what we were doing, it proved a daunting task to find a record company willing to take a chance and come on board. The first two companies we approached passed, both saying something to the effect of, "How are we going to go with this to radio? It's a very tough sell."

At the time, Rod was signed to Atlantic Records (one of the two labels that had passed). I had another idea, though. I was certain that Clive Davis would not ask, "How are we going to take this to radio?" like the other labels had. So I subtly suggested that Arnold pursue a conversation with Clive. Well, Arnold worked his magic. I knew Clive would figure something out, and guess what? He did...television!

For many years there was no question that the music industry was ruled by radio. It was extremely rare to see an album advertised on television, mainly because of the cost factor. It also required a big pair of balls and an unquenchable belief in your artist for a company to go on TV to promote an album. There was no record company president who met those requirements more than Clive. He shared our vision and was prepared to let the world know that the best rock singer of our generation was just as effective at doing standards.

There was just one problem: Clive didn't like the modern influences in the tracks. Instead, he wanted the album to be filled with the spirit, as he called it, of "Fred [Astaire] and Ginger [Rogers]." With that, Rod and I were back to the drawing board. We recorded several tracks with a more classic sound, for example—lush with strings.

Clive's instincts must have been right on the money. At a meeting at his bungalow at the Beverly Hills Hotel with Rod, Arnold, and myself, he proceeded to play all of the new tracks we had cut, and, as a way of punctuating his point, started to sway to the music and dance around the room! The rest of us must have gotten caught up in the fervor, and within a matter of seconds we'd joined him as he kept bellowing out, "It's Fred and Ginger!" Just imagine, four grown men floating around the room to music of the '30s and '40s. Clive couldn't wait to get the album out. It seemed destined to be a hit!

In October 2002, the album was released and it took off instantly! An arrangement was made for Rod, backed by orchestra, to perform the entire album as part of the *A&E in Concert Series*. But right away there was a problem. We could not find someone to conduct. First, we asked the woman who played violin in Rod's band, but that ultimately didn't work out. Then, we decided the orchestra could fake it—do the equivalent of lip-syncing. Finally, I made Rod aware of my considerable experience in conducting and offered to step in and take over. After all, I knew the arrangements like the back of my hand.

Arnold called me to ask if I could be in New York the next day. I packed my tuxedo and caught the first plane in the morning. In just a day and a half, I had the musicians totally rehearsed and ready to go.

The concert was a triumph—so much so that when the car dropped Rod off at his hotel, he asked if I wanted to join him on a private yacht that he planned to charter in a few months. It remains the best holiday I've ever had. We still have vivid memories of the gentle waves lapping on the shore just covering our legs as we lay on the beach in St. Bart's, exchanging song ideas for Volume 2.

The Great American Songbook Volume 1 reached No. 4 on the *Billboard* chart, Volume 2 went to No. 2, and Volume 3 hit No. 1. Clive actually created a new method of TV promotion. Just imagine...your artist is the special music guest on *The View*, *Good Morning America*, or *Today*. Then, as the show breaks for a commercial, who should appear in the TV spot but your artist—in this case, Rod Stewart. The spots were usually thirty to sixty seconds and were sleek, sophisticated promotion videos, which made them very effective in reaching the artist's fan base. They were definitely a boon to sales.

It seemed that the public couldn't get enough of Rockin' Rod singing the greatest hits of Cole Porter, George Gershwin, Rodgers and Hart, and other giants of the *American Songbook*. He clearly appeared to have a great feel for this material. Oprah Winfrey was one of the many celebrities who fell in love with the first album, telling her audience that the only gift they needed for Christmas that year was the Rod Stewart album, *It Had to Be You: The Great American Songbook*. The record went Platinum almost immediately, eventually reached sales of five million and became a huge hit all over the world.

Rod and Elton.

Around this time, Elton John had a fiftieth birthday party for which he took over a very popular restaurant in LA called Le Dome. The guest list was relatively small, about fifty people who were close to Elton, including Rod. The afternoon of the party, I got a call from Ahmet Ertegun, chairman and founder of Atlantic Records and a veritable legend in the music business. Ahmet and I had been good friends for decades. He had heard about the party and I invited him to come with me. After a lavish, joyful dinner, I wanted to do something special for Elton, to show my appreciation for the fact that he'd been the first artist to participate in my *Rock, Rhythm & Blues* "labor of love" project. So, I spontaneously offered to move the entire group to my house for an after-party.

Once everyone had arrived, Elton and Rod sat down next to each other at my art deco piano. Together, they sang oldies for two hours. Our minds were blown! There wasn't an inch of space in my living room as it was wall-to-wall with people, all with their jaws dropped. When Ahmet called me the following day, he said, "Could you believe Rod and Elton singing all those great songs together? What a night!"

Meanwhile, Rod and I were still diligently at work on Volume 2. As a little something extra, Rod and Cher did a fun-filled duet on "Bewitched, Bothered, and Bewildered," which features the following suggestive lines: "I'll sing to him, each spring to him, and worship the trousers that cling to him." Queen Latifah stepped in to do a duet on "As Time Goes By." On that number, Rod sang his part in LA, while Latifah did hers simultaneously in New York. Ahh, the miracle of technology!

Once it was clear that Volume 2 would match the popularity of Volume 1, Clive was now eager to have an entire collection of Rod singing the *Great American Songbook*. Volumes 3 and 4 (the latter of which I didn't produce), followed in the next two years.

Despite winning the Grammy for Best Traditional Vocal Performance, after four albums of standards, Rod felt it was time for a break. Another two years went by as we both pursued different projects.

Rod and I remained in close contact and were having dinner one night when out of the blue he said to me, “Let’s make the album we’ve always wanted to do, with just one proviso: Nobody, but *nobody*, can know about this—not Clive, not even Arnold. It’s our little secret, until it’s finished.” And once again, he offered to cover the recording costs!

The thought of making a secret album gave us both a rush. There were several differences between this collection and any of its predecessors. For one thing, many of the tracks had horn arrangements, something Rod had never had on any previous albums, to my knowledge. Second, there was more emphasis on the rhythm section, particularly the drums. To tie it all together, there was a variety of harmony vocals, many by my right-arm associate producer, Lauren Wild, along with Anita Pointer and a number

Rod, Clive, and me.

of the best background singers in LA. The harmony parts were very subtle, and Rod seemed to appreciate the added touches they contributed.

One song that I particularly liked was a gorgeous ballad, "My Foolish Heart," delivered in a heartfelt performance by Rod. But the primary difference between Volume 5 and the others was the inclusion of several up-tempo numbers on this album that beckoned the listener to dance—such songs as "That Old Black Magic," "I Get a Kick Out of You," "Beyond the Sea," "Cheek to Cheek," "Love Me Or Leave Me," and "Bye, Bye Blackbird" (done with a New Orleans feel).

When we presented the finished album to Clive and Arnold, they were both very surprised, to say the least. Naturally, they had suggestions for other songs, which we tried to accommodate. The important thing was that the team (Rod, Clive, Arnold, and myself) was working together again. The songs we chose were all classics, and this remains my favorite of all the songbook albums.

What I will cherish most about Volume 5 is that it solidified a creative bond and continued friendship with Clive. And although we've had some differences along the way, as all friends do, we have enjoyed a more than fifty-year friendship, and I truly consider Clive one of my closest friends.

The Great American Songbook series has enjoyed unprecedented success as the biggest selling ongoing series of new music recordings in history, with over eighteen million copies sold worldwide.

Chapter 38

Moonlight Serenade

Still bitten by the standards bug, I approached Carly Simon. I asked her if she would like to work together again and revisit this genre. She had released three standards albums over the previous twenty years, but the material had been very esoteric. I wanted her to record songs that might appeal to a wider audience. To seal the deal, I offered to finance the recording costs. I believed in the project so much that it seemed like a worthwhile gamble to take.

She agreed! We started with five tracks: "In the Still of the Night," "Where or When," "Moonglow," and "My One and Only Love." The fifth song we selected was "Moonlight Serenade"—the most popular song of the World War II era. It had been a favorite of mine since my high school days when I'd first gotten turned on to the music of Glenn Miller. My father had owned an EP of Glenn Miller that was the size of a 45rpm single, with two songs on each side. I could stack it with my other singles and have it play during my make-out parties. I cannot emphasize enough the impact that this record had on me, and I was so glad that Carly agreed to sing it.

Up until this point, this song had rarely been recorded with vocals, so with Carly on deck, I knew our version would stand out. I subsequently realized that it also provided the perfect title for the album.

The first label to show immediate interest in the project was Columbia Records, followed by Blue Note and then Concord Records. At the eleventh hour, Warner Brothers Records jumped into the fray and made a very generous offer, which showed us just how much they really wanted this album. We ended up going into a veritable bidding war—something I had always dreamed about but had never experienced. In the end, we made our deal with Columbia.

With the help of my associate producer Lauren Wild, we got quite a bit of film footage documenting our recording process, from doing the basic tracks in LA to recording Carly's vocals in New York. Columbia released two versions of the album: first a vinyl LP and then a deluxe version on DualDisc (which was a double-sided disc—CD on one side and DVD on the other). The latter allowed us to take our studio footage and interviews with Carly and myself and make a sweet, personal documentary. We had a story to tell about our forty-eight-year friendship. Additional footage was taken at Martha's Vineyard, where Carly has lived for fifty years, to capture her home and the surrounding environment.

In 2005, *Moonlight Serenade* debuted at No. 7 on the *Billboard* Top 200 chart and, with that, Carly gained her first Top 10 chart entry in twenty-seven years.

The following year, Carly was offered a deal she couldn't refuse: passage on the Queen Mary II for her, the band, and the rest of her entourage. In return, she would perform the entire *Moonlight Serenade* album, with orchestral accompaniment (conducted by me), along with about eight songs that were past hits including "You're So Vain," "Nobody Does It Better," "Let The River Run," and "Coming Around Again." We also brought about a dozen elegant dancers with us, to accentuate the feeling of a 1940s ballroom—except it was the ballroom of the Queen Mary II. What a perfect setting!

The crowning touch was that the entire event was filmed with multi-track recording as a documentary for PBS, making it the first time a concert was filmed on the high seas! Carly's fear of performing live is well known. In order to get her on stage, I had to ply her with vodka—which seemed to work wonders, as she gave one of her finest shows. When we did "Nobody Does It Better," she came over to me on the podium while I was conducting and threw her arms around me. It was great to see her having such a good time while performing live. I will always have fond memories of this concert.

Carly performing while I conduct "Nobody Does It Better."

Carly and me celebrating after the concert.

Chapter 39

Some Enchanted Evening

One year after making *Moonlight Serenade,* a friend said he'd heard Art Garfunkel being interviewed on radio and that Art had mentioned he'd like to work with me again. I found this to be interesting news as it had been close to thirty years since we did the *Breakaway* album (1975), a longtime favorite of mine.

In 1992, we'd tried to work together and had actually started production on a new record, but, due to our creative differences, the work relationship kind of fell apart. It bothered me to see all of our efforts go down the tubes however, Art just wasn't ready to be a team player. We'd been halfway through the album and even had a great title for it: *Committed to Love* (the name came from a beautiful song by Walter Afanasieff). Regrettably, it was the end of that project. That was the last time we'd spoken about working together, so it was certainly a surprise to hear that Art had publicly declared his desire to work together again!

In 2007, Art and I got together once *again* to discuss the feasibility of doing an album of—guess what?—standards! This would make my fifth standards album in five years! While I remain proud of all my song selections in this genre, this group contains some of my all-time favorites—many of which are not heard as often as they should be. A few of these nearly forgotten gems are "I'm Glad There Is You," "I Remember You," "Quiet Nights of Quiet Stars" (a masterpiece by Antônio Carlos Jobim), "Easy Living" (made famous by Billie Holiday), and "What'll I Do?" (by the great Irving Berlin). What's more, some of the songs are from the greatest musicals in history, such as "I've Grown Accustomed to Her Face" from *My Fair Lady*, "Some Enchanted Evening" from *South Pacific*, and "If I Loved You" from *Carousel*. This album was aided by the extraordinary musicianship of Steve Gadd and Dean Parks.

Art felt that his voice didn't have the same resonance it had once had but I felt otherwise. To me, the sound of his voice will always be incomparable.

Once we'd completed the record, I sent Johnny Mathis a copy, as it had a dedication to him from Art. Johnny responded with a note that said:

> *Your latest effort with Art G. is a treasure for me. So many little vocal and musical surprises along the way make it such a listening delight. I get so much pleasure and inspiration when listening to two people at the top of their musical craft. Bless you both!*
> *Love, John*

I often start out my day by listening to many of the tracks on this album and I am always reminded of how much I love it.

Chapter 40

Jane

My life had been blessed, except for the greatest blessing of all—to find the love of my life and watch that love grow.

When I first cast my eyes on Jane Fonda, I developed a mad crush on her. I had a penchant for dating actresses, but if there was one actress I continued to fantasize about, it was Jane. She truly had the whole package: striking beauty, a warm personality, an extremely creative mind, and a highly cultivated intellect. All of this was accompanied by an infectious sense of humor, a smile to match, and a love for singing.

Earlier in the book, I described how Jane and I first met in 1975. I was producing The Manhattan Transfer at the time and got them to do a benefit for Tom Hayden's campaign for U.S. Senate (Tom was Jane's husband at the time). The following week, Jane and Tom came to the studio to thank us for doing the benefit, and my assistant took a picture of the entire group of us. To quote the title of the Rod Stewart song, "Every Picture Tells a Story," and to me, that picture reveals the beginning of my friendship with Jane Fonda.

While the group was rehearsing in the studio, I told her of my desire to direct films. After she watched me work with The Manhattan Transfer, she said, "I don't know what a record producer does, but you're a director!" Naturally, I was very flattered by this compliment, and we would stay in touch through the years.

In the early 1980s, a friend of mine said that he had to make a stop at Jane's workout studio on Robertson Boulevard. He asked if I wanted to take a ride with him, and I agreed immediately.

As we entered the studio, a class that Jane was leading had just ended. As she emerged from the group, sweating profusely, she gave me a big hug, which I thoroughly enjoyed despite the sweat.

On another occasion, The Pointer Sisters were headlining at the Universal Amphitheatre, and I invited Jane to the show. She was a fan of the girls and was happy to attend with a group of her friends.

We met again in Aspen during Christmas of 1985. My friends Don Simpson and Jerry Bruckheimer held a major Christmas party every year. This year, it was in the ballroom of the Hotel Jerome, an Aspen landmark. The music was by Jimmy Buffett and his band, and the joint was rocking! Much to my surprise, who should I see arriving but Jane. She was unescorted but with another couple, so I said, "Hi, Jane. Where's Tom?"

"He's staying home taking care of our son," she replied. "Why don't you be my date tonight, Richard?"

With that, we started to consume screwdrivers and dance the night away! I was trying to be a gentleman, but as we were dancing cheek to cheek, I somehow found my lips on her neck. That's as far as it went! I knew my boundaries!

Several months later, Jane and Tom announced they were getting a divorce. Shortly after that, I was skiing in Sun Valley, Idaho, when a friend of mine mentioned that Jane was in town. I asked him if there was any way he could find out exactly where she was. A few hours later, my friend told me that at that very moment, Jane could be found at the Sun Valley Health Spa.

I paged her at the spa, and we had a brief reunion on the telephone. Much to my surprise, she asked if I needed a ride back to LA. She had a plane leaving the next day.

When I called her back to make the arrangements, she said that, after thinking it over, she realized it wouldn't be such a great idea for her to walk off the plane with me because her divorce had just been announced. I understood at that moment that she needed some time to recover and heal before she could start dating again.

Then I met Rebecca Broussard, and, within five months of our first date, we were married. At the same time, Jane met Ted Turner, founder of CNN and one of the wealthiest men in America. He courted her for two years. Their marriage was announced just as mine was falling apart.

When I heard about Jane and Ted, any fantasy I may have harbored about Jane was permanently eradicated. I couldn't help but think that she and Ted made a perfect couple: flying all over the world in his private plane, dining with Gorbachev, Castro, and other world leaders. Ted also created the Goodwill Games, Russia's answer to the Olympic games, and they subsequently made several trips there.

Jane had quit acting at that point and moved to Atlanta, Ted's home base. But after ten years, their marriage ended. Jane decided to remain in Atlanta, which had now become her home.

On several occasions, I asked various people if they knew what Jane was up to or if she was coming to LA anytime soon. In 2000, I heard she was going to be a presenter at the Academy Awards, and my romantic fantasy was revived. Perhaps our paths would cross again, and what better setting than *Vanity Fair's* annual Oscar party? I was convinced I would see her there. I spent many hours looking for her, to no avail. Sadly, I concluded that she'd either left the party early or hadn't come at all—but at least my fantasy was reborn.

Ten years went by since Jane and Ted's divorce, and Jane wrote an extraordinary memoir that went to No. 1 on the *New York Times* Best Seller list. She is a remarkable writer!

It was now the beginning of June 2009, and I happened to ask my dear friend of thirty-four years, Carrie Fisher, if she knew Jane. Carrie then uttered the magic words: "Jane and I email all the time." She went on to tell me that

Jane had just finished doing a play on Broadway, *33 Variations*, and was now in Paris shooting a commercial for L'Oréal. Then Carrie said more magic words that would change my life, "Jane is coming to LA for knee replacement surgery and will remain here for a month of rehabilitation."

This was the opening I had been waiting for. I urged Carrie to email Jane and tell her that an old mutual friend, Richard Perry, wanted to reconnect with her, despite the fact we hadn't seen each other in thirty-two years—since that memorable Christmas party in Aspen.

I found out later that when Jane received Carrie's email, she told her longtime hair stylist, "Matthew, do you see the name on this email, Richard Perry? This could be fun!" Jane told Carrie, "If Richard wants to reconnect with me, then why don't you give him my email?"

Jane flew to LA the next day for her surgery, and thus began a weeklong courtship via email that, I must say, was a completely unique experience. While she was recovering in the hospital, I sent her a dusty-rose-colored orchid plant. She said she had never seen one quite like it.

Our relationship evolved considerably during her week of recovery. When it came time for her to leave the hospital, I still didn't have her phone number, so I sought Carrie's advice: "She's coming back from the hospital today—now can I call her?" Carrie, who had been quarterbacking our progress, replied, "No…wait one more day!"

I took Carrie's advice and on the morning of the next day, I emailed Jane and said: "It's time to throw caution to the wind…and exchange phone numbers." I included mine.

I'd barely gone three steps away from my computer when my bedroom phone rang. I couldn't believe when I heard Jane's unmistakable voice. The first thing she said to me was, "You sound the same."

We proceeded to talk for an hour and a half. Even though we were planning to have dinner with Carrie two nights hence, I persuaded Jane to come over and have lunch with me that afternoon, assuring her that it would make things more comfortable when the three of us got together.

When she showed up an hour later with her dog, she was still on crutches. She told me that I could be one of her crutches by putting my arm around her waist, which thrilled me beyond belief!

As we watched our dogs get to know each other, we ate our first lunch together. After I gave her a tour of the house, we went out to the pool house where I played a track from a musical I had been working on for quite some time called *Baby It's You*, featuring some of the greatest songs of the early '60s. The song I played was "Dedicated to the One I Love." As soon as it started playing, Jane stood up, dropped her crutches and said, "Dance with me." It was a moment I'll never forget.

In the spirit of being completely candid about my health, I felt it essential to reveal my two major disorders: Parkinson's disease and polio. She accepted the information gracefully and lovingly.

Dinner with Carrie two nights later was a celebration for the three of us. Jane and I were starting to fall in love, thanks primarily to our dear friend Carrie Fisher, to whom we will be eternally grateful—especially since she had to leave right after dinner, which gave Jane and me some much needed make-out time! Jane then pulled a surprise out of her hat. She invited me on a double date with her son Troy and his wife, Simone, on the following Monday night.

This was a clear indication that we were getting into something serious. It was very important to her to receive Troy's blessing on a new man in her life. She had gotten tickets to a concert at the Dorothy Chandler Pavilion, featuring Patti LuPone and Mandy Patinkin, two of the most venerated stars in musical theater. Both had won Tony Awards for their starring roles in *Evita*. Patti and her husband joined us for dinner after the concert.

I told Jane how moved I was by her invitation to spend time with Troy, but I thought we should have a date prior to my meeting him. I suggested we get together the preceding Saturday, but with two stipulations—that we make it a twenty-four-hour date with no limitation as to how high we wanted to get, especially when it came to smoking weed. She readily agreed.

As Jane's assistant drove her up my driveway, I felt my heart was about to leap out of my chest. When Jane got out of the car, however, she had a very worried look on her face. I asked her what was wrong, afraid that she was having a case of cold feet.

"You know how one of your stipulations was that there was no limit to our getting high?" she began. "Well, sometimes, when you get a little too high, it's easy to get caught up in endless conversation, and I don't want that to happen to us, so I want you to promise me that at some point during our twenty-four-hour date, *we will definitely make love.*"

That was a promise I was eager to fulfill.

The following Monday, while on our way to dinner, Jane and I burst into song together, something we would do frequently. We chose "It's a Grand Night for Singing." What made this night so meaningful was that Jane was particularly close to her son, so for her to ask me to accompany her on a night like this, spoke volumes, and I knew it.

As word got out about our relationship, Jane was liberally quoted as saying, "I came to LA to get a new knee and found a new lover." And when a friend asked her, "Are you doing your therapy?" she replied, "Of course, I'm in a new relationship—I have to be able to kneel."

I must admit it was quite heartwarming to see the outpouring of love and happiness that everyone bestowed on us. I would constantly hear about people saying, "Isn't it great how Jane and Richard found each other?" Once the flame had touched the kindling, an incendiary reaction had taken place. It seemed that everyone was on the sidelines cheering us on. One of many items that appeared on the Internet:

FONDA MOVES IN WITH PERRY. Actress Jane Fonda has taken her relationship with music producer Richard Perry to the next level—the pair has moved in together, according to U.S. Reports. Rumors surfaced last week alleging the duo was romantically involved after Fonda and Perry were reportedly seen "all over each other all night."

According to the *New York Post's* column, Page Six, "*the pair has been inseparable since, and are now sharing a home.*"

The next few months were filled with well-wishers who offered congratulations or invitations to dinner, etc. The first person to invite us to dinner was Barbra Streisand. Afterward, we went upstairs to Barbra's favorite place to listen to music: her bathroom floor! We started talking about her recording of John Lennon's "Mother," which we had worked on together in 1971. Barbra hadn't heard it in years, but miraculously, her husband, James Brolin, knew where there was a copy of the record. So, there we were, the four of us, sitting on Barbra's bathroom floor, listening to "Mother." The song, and Barbra's performance, are very emotional. Everyone was just as moved then as I had been when we first recorded it.

We then proceeded downstairs, and I introduced Rod Stewart's new album, Volume 5, which I had just completed. Since Barbra and I are both from Brooklyn, we started to swing dance, doing what was originally known as the Lindy. Barbra reminded me of a key move in the dance I had forgotten for years. From that time on, Jane and I incorporated that move whenever we danced together. Speaking of dancing, Jane and I frequently derived a great deal of pleasure by dancing together to the jukebox in Perry's Pub.

A few nights after our dinner at Barbra's, we went to Troy and Simone's for a barbeque. Jane explained it was very important to her that I establish a connection with her son, so I told her I would do my best to make that happen. About an hour later, Troy and I found a quiet spot to have a chat. I

The 57th Annual Grammy Awards

told him about *Jersey Boys*, a musical I thought that he and Simone would enjoy. It was playing in Las Vegas at the time, as was The Beatles' musical, *Love*. I invited them to join Jane and me in Vegas for two nights to see the shows. As I predicted, they loved them both, as did Jane.

As the summer progressed, Jane asked me to come to her ranch in New Mexico—it was her spiritual sanctuary. She had spent about seven months alone there while she wrote her memoir. There was a magnificent river that flowed through the back of the property. We spent several summer days there, and eventually five Thanksgiving and Christmas holidays there with her entire family: Troy, Simone, her daughter Vanessa, Vanessa's husband, Paul, Jane's grandchildren, Malcolm and Viva Vadim, and her stepdaughters, Nathalie Vadim and Mary Williams, both of whom have become and remain part of Jane's family. On occasion, my brother Roger and his girlfriend, Carolyne, would join us. I must say that these family gatherings were something special.

My relationship with Jane was the most wonderful one of my life. We were like two children discovering each other. Before we met, Jane had said she would never fall in love again. I told her I was very sorry to have messed up her plans.

In some ways we have little in common, yet we continue to enrich each other's lives. We remain the closest of friends even though we are no longer living together. In the eight years that we were in a relationship, I have enjoyed some of my best times. She is an extraordinary person, and I consider myself lucky to know her. She's ageless, with the spirit of a young girl and the wisdom of an old soul.

Chapter 41

The Windup

When I sat down to write this book, I asked myself, what message do I want the reader to walk away with after reading it? Is it simply about a kid from Brooklyn who was lucky enough to see his dreams come true? That's part of it, but it is more about sharing my passion and love for music, combined with expressing the kind of ambition, drive, and commitment it takes to not settle for anything less than the best. I also wanted to share the idea that life isn't just about work; it's about connections, friendships, and relationships. Remember that at the end of the day, it's not just about the work you did but the friends you've made along the way. I am blessed with an innate spirituality that has always made me look forward to each day with the power of positive thinking.

However, life is not without its challenges. Even as I write this, I am battling my two biggest physical impairments: Parkinson's disease and the residual effects of polio, known as post-polio syndrome. I continue to discover the unexpected, perplexing manner in which Parkinson's rears its ugly head and attacks the most vulnerable areas. In my case, it is my speech and my gait. My stuttering has gotten noticeably worse in the last five years, and while I have always managed the effects of polio, the Parkinson's devil recognizes it as an area of weakness in my musculature, notably impairing my movement, including walking, especially in crowds of people.

I used to love to dance. When The Pointer Sisters' recording of "Jump (For My Love)" was all over the radio, my friends would form a circle and urge me to dance to it, particularly with my favorite dance partners of the '80s: Michelle Phillips and Farrah Fawcett. While I was a student at Michigan, I even won the campus Twist contest.

In recent years, old man Parkinson's clearly felt that I was having too much fun, so he decided to intervene. Sadly, Jane's and my famous dance parties were affected as my legs began to feel as if they were disconnected from the rest of my body. I still love to dance, but I know now that I will never be able to experience the same pleasure and joy of moving to the music that I once did. Dancing is actually great therapy for Parkinson's, so I do try to get a session in once in a while. In addition, I'm extremely careful about what I eat, and I make sure to do some form of physical activity every day.

Looking back on my life and career, I have much for which I can be grateful. There have been numerous times when people have told me how much of an impact the music I produced has had on their lives.

I made music for almost fifty years. It was a long and winding road filled with joy, excitement, and the occasional disappointment, which I used as a learning experience. The credo upon which I built my career was to make each record the best that it could be—starting with the song, then the basic track, and finally and most important, the vocal performance. There is no greater turn-on than to hear a stellar track played back in the control room after you've been working on it for hours and to have it sound just the way you heard it in your dreams.

One of the main functions of a music producer is to guide and inspire the artists and musicians, helping them to reach their creative potential. I would carefully select the musicians who I felt had the best feel for the material and the ability to create and enhance the artist's particular style, hoping that the result would sound effortless. In that respect, a music producer is like the director of a movie, but in this case the record *is* the movie. Some of the most satisfying moments I ever experienced were when musicians would take me aside after a session and say, "Richard, working with you has made me a better musician!"

Throughout my career, I have always been attracted to a wide variety of music. I'm proud to say that I am one of the very few producers who has had a No. 1 record on all four major *Billboard* charts: pop, R&B, country, and dance. Moreover, many of the recordings for some of the artists I worked with, including The Pointer Sisters, Rod Stewart, Carly Simon, Ringo Starr, and Harry Nilsson, have been the most successful of their respective careers.

Another source of great satisfaction is that much of the music I produced continues to endure. With the emergence of the Internet and ongoing advancements in technology, music has become more accessible than ever. I, myself, continue to enjoy listening to many of the recordings I produced as they transport me back to that particular time and place.

As I bring my memoirs to a close, I reflect back on a life and career that has been truly blessed. The people I've met along the way, and the relationships that resulted, reaffirm to me what I have always felt: I am indeed a lucky man.

Discography

1967—CAPTAIN BEEFHEART AND HIS MAGIC BAND...*Safe As Milk*, Buddah

1968—TINY TIM...*God Bless Tiny Tim*, Reprise

1968—FATS DOMINO...*Fats Is Back*, featuring "Lady Madonna," Reprise

1968—THE HOLY MACKEREL (PAUL WILLIAMS)...*Holy Mackerel*, Reprise

1968—TINY TIM...*Tiny Tim's 2nd Album*, Reprise

1969—ANDERS & PONCIA...*The Anders & Poncia album*, Warner Brothers

1969—THEO BIKEL...*A New Day*, Reprise

1969—ELLA FITZGERALD...*Ella*, Reprise

196—TINY TIM...*For All My Little Friends*, Reprise

1970—FANNY...*Fanny*, Reprise

1970—RINGO STARR...*Sentimental Journey* (Title Track), Apple

1971—BARBRA STREISAND...*Stoney End*, featuring the single "Stoney End," Columbia

1971—FANNY...*Charity Ball*, Reprise

1971—NILSSON...*Nilsson Schmilsson*, featuring the singles "Without You," "Coconut" & "Jump Into The Fire," RCA

1971—BARBRA STREISAND...*Barbra Joan Streisand*, Columbia

1971—JOHNNY MATHIS...*You've Got A Friend*, Columbia

1971—PERCY FAITH...*Black Magic Woman*, Columbia

1971—SANDY POSEY... "Happy Happy Birthday," "Don't," Columbia

1972—NILSSON...*Son Of Schmilsson*, RCA

1972—BARBRA STREISAND...*Live Concert At The Forum*, Columbia

1972—CARLY SIMON...*No Secrets*, featuring the singles "You're So Vain," & "The Right Thing to Do," Elektra

1972—FANNY...*Fanny Hill*, Reprise

1972—BONES...*Bones* featuring "Roberta," Signpost

1972—BOBBY HATFIELD... "Stay With me," "OoWee Baby I Love You," & "In the Still Of The Night," Warner Brothers

1973—ANDY WILLIAMS...*Solitaire*, Columbia

1973—RINGO STARR...*Ringo*, featuring the singles "Photograph," "You're Sixteen," & "Oh My My," Apple

1974—MARTHA REEVES...*Martha Reeves*, Universal

1974—CARLY SIMON...*Hotcakes*, featuring the singles "Haven't Got Time For The Pain," & "Mockingbird," Elektra

1974—RINGO STARR...*Goodnight Vienna*, featuring the singles "No No Song" & "Only You," Apple

1975—LON & DERREK VAN EATON...*Who Do You Out Do*, A&M

1975—ART GARFUNKEL...*Breakaway*, featuring the single "I Only Have Eyes For You," Columbia

1975—CARLY SIMON...*Playing Possum*, Elektra

1975—MELISSA MANCHESTER (Executive Producer "Midnight Blue")... *Melissa*, Arista

1976—LEO SAYER...*Endless Flight*, featuring the singles "You Make Me Feel Like Dancing," & "When I Need You," Warner Brothers.

1976—MANHATTAN TRANSFER...*Coming Out*, Atlantic

1976—BURTON CUMMINGS...*Burton Cummings*, featuring the single "Stand Tall," Portrait

1977—CARLY SIMON..."Nobody Does It Better" (for the James Bond film, *The Spy Who Loved Me*), Elektra

1977—LEO SAYER...*Thunder In My Heart*, Warner Brothers

1977—DIANA ROSS...*Baby It's Me*, Motown

1977—BURTON CUMMINGS...*My Own Way To Rock*, Portrait

1978—LEO SAYER...*Leo Sayer*, Warner Brothers

1979—POINTER SISTERS...*Energy*, featuring the single "Fire," Planet

1979—NIGHT...*Night*, Planet

1979—CHRIS THOMPSON..."If You Remember Me" (From The MGM film, *The Champ*), Planet

1979—POINTER SISTERS...*Priority*, Planet

1980—SUE SAAD & THE NEXT...*Sue Saad & The Next*, Planet

1980—POINTER SISTERS...*Special Things*, featuring the single "He's So Shy," Planet

1981—MARK SAFFAN & THE KEEPERS...*Mark Saffan & The Keepers*, Planet

1981—MARVA KING...*Feels Right*, Planet

1981—POINTER SISTERS...*Black & White*, Planet

1982—POINTER SISTERS...*So Excited*, Planet

1982—FULL SWING...*The Good Times Are Back*, Planet

1982—BILL MEDLEY...*Right Here & Now*, Planet

1983—JUNE POINTER...*Baby Sister*, Planet

1983—POINTER SISTERS...*Break Out*, featuring the singles "Automatic," "Jump (For My Love)," " I'm So Excited," & "Neutron Dance," Planet

1983—TINA TURNER..."Help" "Johnny & Mary" & "Go Now" (from the film, *Summer Lovers*), Warner Brothers

1983—CARLY SIMON..."Someone Waits For You" (from the film, *Swing Shift*), Planet

1984—NEIL DIAMOND...*Primitive,* featuring the singles "Sleep With Me Tonight" & "Crazy," Columbia

1984—JULIO IGLESIAS...*1100 Bel Air Place*, featuring "To All The Girls I've Loved Before" (duet with Willie Nelson) "All Of You" (duet with Diana Ross) & "The Air That I Breathe" (featuring The Beach Boys), Columbia

1984—POINTER SISTERS... "Neutron Dance," from *Beverly Hills Cop,* Universal

1984—BARBRA STREISAND...*Emotion* (Title Track), Columbia

1984—DeBARGE...*Rhythm Of The Night*, Motown

1985—POINTER SISTERS...*Contact,* featuring the single "Dare Me," RCA

1985—GREG PHILLINGANES...*Pulse*, Planet

1986—PATTI LABELLE...*Winner in You*, featuring,"Oh, People" "Twisted" "Beat My Heart Like A Drum" & "You're Mine Tonight," MCA

1986—JEFFREY OSBORNE...*Emotional*, featuring "You Should Be Mine" (The Woo Woo Song), A&M

1986—POINTER SISTERS...*Hot Together*, Planet

1987—DONNA SUMMER..."Dinner With Gershwin" from *All Systems Go*, Geffen

1987—CARLY SIMON..."Hold On To What You've Got," Arista

1987—POINTER SISTERS...*Serious Slammin*, RCA

1989—THELMA HOUSTON & THE WINANS... *Lean On Me* (Soundtrack), Warner Brothers

1989—VARIOUS ARTISTS...*Rock Rhythm & Blues* Featuring: ELTON JOHN—I'm Ready," CHRISTINE MCVIE—"Roll With Me Henry," CHAKA KHAN—"Fever," MICHAEL MCDONALD—"For Your Precious Love," RANDY TRAVIS—"It's Just A Matter Of Time" EL DEBARGE—"Goodnight My Love," RICK JAMES—"This Magic Moment"/"Dance With Me," POINTER SISTERS—"Mr. Lee," HOWARD HEWITT—"The Ten Commandments of Love," MANHATTAN TRANSFER—"I Wanna Be Your Girl"

1990—LUTHER VANDROSS..."Michelle" from the unreleased film *Strawberry Fields*, Epic

1990—LAURA BRANIGAN...from Laura Branigan "Moonlight On Water" "Bad Attitude" & "Smoke Screen," Atlantic

1990—THELMA HOUSTON...*Throw You Down*, Reprise

1991—ROD STEWART... *Vagabond Heart*, featuring the single "The Motown Song," Warner Brothers

1991—BARBRA STREISAND...*Just For The Record* (Box Set), Columbia

1992—RANDY TRAVIS..."Jingle Bell Rock" from *A Very Special Christmas 2*, A&M

1992—VONDA SHEPARD...The Radical Light, featuring "Searchin' My Soul" (theme song for *Ally McBeal*) "Dreamin'" & "Love Will Come And Go," Warner Brothers.

1993—PEABO BRYSON..."I Never Saw A Miracle" from *Through The Fire*, Sony

1993—RAY CHARLES...*My World*, featuring "A Song For You," Warner Brothers.

1994—TOM JONES..."I Wanna Get Back With You" & "I Don't Think So" from *The Lead & How To Swing It*, Interscope

1994—TINA TURNER...Collected Recordings Sixties To Nineties, Capitol

1995—CARLY SIMON...*Clouds In My Coffee* 1965-1996, Arista

1995—THE TEMPTATIONS...*For Lovers Only*, featuring "Night and Day" from the film *What Women Want*, Motown

1995—HARRY NILSSON...*Personal Best: The Harry Nilsson Anthology*, RCA

1998—JULIO IGLESIAS...*My Life: The Greatest Hits* (#1), Sony

2000—TINY TIM...*Live! At The Royal Albert Hall*, Rhino

2001—DIANA ROSS...*Best of Diana Ross*, Motown

2001—POINTER SISTERS...*Legendary* (3 CD Set), BMG

2001—SYREETA...*Essential Syreeta*, Spectrum

2002—PERCY FAITH...*The Complete Percy Faith, Vol. 1*, Collectables

2002—FANNY...*First Time in a Long Time: The Reprise Recordings*, Reprise

2002—ROD STEWART..."It Had To Be You," *The Great American Songbook*, J

2002—RANDY TRAVIS...*Trail Of Memories: The Randy Travis Anthology*, Rhino

2003—PATTI LABELLE...*20th Century Masters: The Millennium Collection*, MCA

2003—POINTER SISTERS..."Jump (For My Love)," from the movie *Love Actually*, J

2003—ROD STEWART..."As Time Goes By," *The Great American Songbook Vol II*, J

2004—ROD STEWART...."Stardust," *The Great American Songbook Vol. III*, J

2004—FATS DOMINO...*Sweet Patootie: The Complete Reprise Recordings*, Rhino

2005—CARLY SIMON...*Moonlight Serenade*, Columbia

2006—THE MANHATTAN TRANSFER...*The Definitive Pop Collection*, Rhino

2007—RINGO STARR..."Photograph" from *The Very Best of Ringo Starr*, Capitol

2007—ART GARFUNKEL...*Some Enchanted Evening*, Rhino

2010—ROD STEWART..."Fly Me To The Moon," *The Great American Songbook Vol. V*, J

2011—*BABY IT'S YOU!*.... Original Broadway Cast Album, Verve

Awards

1973 **Producer Of The Year** (*Rolling Stone Magazine*)

1975 **Outstanding Achievement Award** (*University of Michigan*)

1977 **Producer of The Year** (*Billboard Magazine*)

1984 **Producer of The Year** (*Billboard Magazine*)

1984 **Academy of Country Music Record of the Year**

"To All The Girls I've Loved Before" Willie Nelson and Julio Iglesias

2015 **Grammy Trustees Award** *(A Special Merit Award voted by the Recording Academy's National Trustees, given to individuals who have made significant contributions, other than performance, during their careers in music. Presented at the Grammy Awards.)*

Acknowledgments

Clive Davis: Thank you for all your inspiration and support throughout this process.

Jane Fonda: My live-in editor. Your contributions continued to breathe life into this book.

Kenny Vance: Without you there never would have been a Cloud Nine.

Fred Perry: You got me on the right track, bro.

Lee Blackman: Thank you for your all your insight and assistance.

Roger Perry: You gave me an alternative way of looking at the book.

Michael Gruskoff: You were there from the very beginning of the book—thanks for the continued support.

Abe Somer: In addition to being a brilliant attorney, your dynamic personality and advise enriched my life and career.

Claudia McGinnis: You're the glue that held it all together.

Sara Stratton: Thank you for your expertise. You made this process seamless. I appreciate all you have done.

Ivania Ellis: Thank you for your editorial guidance.

Andrew Perry: Thank you for keeping the family together.

Mo Ostin & Joe Smith: You both played vitally important roles in my career and gave me the opportunity to show what I was capable of. Thank you for over fifty years of friendship.

Jamie Leffler: You were there by my side when I first started this book.

Valerie Gomez: I want to thank you for your loyalty and help with assisting me with clearances.

Linda Goldner Perry: From the time we met in 1965 to today, your friendship has been invaluable. I love that you have my back, and I greatly appreciate you for always being in my corner.

Endnotes

Chapter 4:

1. Ravan, Genya. "Chapter 3: Music Music Music." *Lollipop Lounge: Memoirs of a Rock and Roll Refugee.* New York: Billboard Books, 2004.

Chapter 9:

1. Aronowitz, Alfred G. "It's High Time Fame Came to Tiny Tim." *Life* Magazine. June 14, 1968. Page 10.

Chapter 30:

1. Pointer, Ruth. "Chapter 13: Breaking Out and Breaking Down." *Still So Excited!: My Life as a Pointer Sister*, 168. Chicago: Triumph Books, 2016.

Chapter 36:

1. Holden, Stephen. "My World." *Rolling Stone*. Rolling Stone, May 13, 1993. https://www.rollingstone.com/music/music-album-reviews/my-world-2-250172/.
2. *Billboard* magazine. March 20, 1993. Album Reviews, Edited by Paul Verna, Chris Morris, and Edward Morris. Page 64.

Photography Credits

Photos as listed below are covered under the copyrights mentioned on the Copyright Page. If the photo is not part of the personal Richard Perry collection, the appropriate credits were obtained by the author from the respective parties and are listed below:

Barry Feinstein Photography: 200; Bettmann/Getty Images: 35; Carly Simon and the Peter Simon Photo Archives: 167, 172; Chuck Blair/ The Watsonville Register-Pajaronian: 83; David Dubow: 242; Estate of Alan Freed (© Photo by Popsie. Used with permission of Alan Freed): 19; Francis Specker: 42; David Goddard/Getty Images: 208; George Rose/Hulton Archive/Getty Images: 20; *Hello!* Magazine/Photographer: Caesar Villona: 218-219; Herman Leonard Photography LLC: 116; Klaus Voormann: 184, 189, 192, 194, 204; Larry Emerine: 186, 193, 194, 203, 210, 213, 236 242; Lou Adler: 83; Mark Davis/Getty Images: 332; Michael Ochs Archives/Getty Images: 23, 24, 32, 84; Nancy S. Bishop (Nancybishopjournal.com): 60; Poly Prep Country Day School: 7, 8; Richard Perry personal collection: 3, 18, 21, 22, 44, 47, 48-49 (courtesy of Roger Perry), 50, 52, 66, 91, 92, 98, 99, 102, 105, 119 (courtesy of Linda Goldner Perry), 129, 132, 135 (included with permission from Barbra), 145, 147, 150, 168, 169, 170, 173, 201 (courtesy of Linda Goldner Perry), 234, 241, 259 (courtesy of Moshe Brakha), 271, 274, 284, 288-289 (courtesy of Elizabeth Taylor), 291, 295, 299, 300, 309, 312, 315, 317,

321, 332, 333, 338, 339; Robert W. Kelley/Getty Images: 34; Tanith Nyx (tanithnyx.wordpress.com): 77; The Maglieri Family: 78; Tim Bruckner: 206, 207; U-M News & Information Photographs Collection (Series E/ Eck Stanger/Bentley Historical Library, University of Michigan): 29, 32, 36, 55; Una Nilsson: 155; UniversalImagesGroup/Getty Images: 35; Walter Sanders/LIFE Picture Collection/Getty Images: 25; Wikipedia: 31 (unknown), 100-101 (David Iliff).

Album artwork reprinted as is: 123 (front cover photograph by Barry Feinstein); 33, 210, 211 (Capitol Records); 258 (front cover photograph by Francesco Scavullo); 94, 106, 165 (Rhino Entertainment Company); 301

Lyric Credits

The Author is grateful for permission to quote lyrics from the following songs:

Chapter 11

"Open Your Window." © 1968. Written by Harry Nilsson (Renewed); Golden Syrup Music (BMI). All Rights Reserved. Used by permission.

Chapter 13

"Mother." Written by John Lennon; Lennon Music/ATV Music Publishing. Lyrics reprinted with permission from Yoko Ono.

Chapter 19

"Photograph." Written by Richard Starkey & George Harrison, BMG Platinum Songs U.S. Lyrics reprinted with permission from Olivia Harrison.

"I'm The Greatest." Written by John Lennon; Lennon Music/ATV Music Publishing. Lyrics reprinted with permission from Yoko Ono.

"You and Me Babe." Written by George Harrison & Mal Evans. Lyrics reprinted with permission from Olivia Harrison.

"Goodnight Vienna." Written by John Lennon; Lennon Music/ATV Music Publishing. Lyrics reprinted with permission from Yoko Ono.

Index

CPSIA information can be obtained
at www.ICGtesting.com
Printed in the USA
LVHW030915080221
678693LV00001B/34